MW00560187

CONCRETE
HELL

CONCRETE HELL

URBAN WARFARE
FROM STALINGRAD TO IRAQ

LOUIS A. DIMARCO

First published in Great Britain in 2012 by Osprey Publishing
PO Box 883, Oxford, OX1 9PL, UK
1385 Broadway, 5th Floor, New York, NY 10018, USA
Email: info@ospreypublishing.com

Osprey Publishing is part of Bloomsbury Publishing Plc

© 2012 Louis A. DiMarco
This digital print on demand paperback edition first published in 2017 by
Osprey Publishing

All rights reserved. Apart from any fair dealing for the purpose of private study, research, criticism or review, as permitted under the Copyright, Designs and Patents Act, 1988, no part of this publication may be reproduced, stored in a retrieval system, or transmitted in any form or by any means, electronic, electrical, chemical, mechanical, optical, photocopying, recording or otherwise, without the prior written permission of the copyright owner. Enquiries should be addressed to the Publishers.

Every attempt has been made by the Publisher to secure the appropriate permissions for material reproduced in this book. If there has been any oversight we will be happy to rectify the situation and written submission should be made to the Publishers.

A CIP catalogue record for this book is available from the British Library.

ISBN: 978 1 4728 3338 9
ePub ISBN: 978 1 78200 313 7
PDF ISBN: 978 1 78200 314 4

Index by Zoe Ross
Typeset in Palatino and Helvetica
Originated by PDQ Digital Media Solutions, Suffolk, UK

The Woodland Trust
Osprey Publishing is supporting the Woodland Trust, the UK's leading woodland conservation charity, by funding the dedication of trees.

www.ospreypublishing.com

Front cover: US Army soldier in Iraq, 2003. (Corbis)

DEDICATION

Over the course of a lifetime associated with the military and traveling around the world I have had the good fortune of working and serving with some of the finest soldiers anywhere. Three of them stand out as representing the soldierly virtues of tactical and technical excellence, scholarship, and most important, leadership. This book is dedicated to them and their inspiring example. I would follow them anywhere. They are: Colonel French L. MacLean, Colonel Thomas A. Dials, and Colonel Peter Wells.

CONTENTS

Foreword   9

List of Maps   11

1   Urban Warfare, Past and Future   13

2   An Operational Debacle   27
Stalingrad, 1942

3   American Urban Warfare   47
Aachen, 1944

4   Urban Warfare from the Sea   67
Inchon and Seoul, 1950

5   Complex Urban Warfare   81
The Battle for Hue, 1968

6   War in the Casbah   103
The Battle of Algiers, 1956–57

7   The Long Urban War   125
Operation *Banner*, 1969–2007

8   Urban Death Trap   151
The Russian Army in Grozny, 1995

9   Invading the Urban Sanctuary   169
Operation *Defensive Shield* and the Battle for Jenin, 2002

10 Systematic Urban Warfare   **189**
"Ready First" in Ramadi, 2006–07

11 Urban Combat in the 21st century   **211**

Bibliography   **217**

Glossary   **221**

About the Author   **223**

Index   **225**

FOREWORD

This short history is meant to describe the urban battlefield as it evolved over the last half of the 20th century and into the first decade of the 21st. In describing the past, I believe, it also describes the future. Regardless of the basis of one's view of the future, whether it be focused on competition between major world powers such as the US and China, or a persistent struggle between the forces of radical Islam and the west, the 21st century is going to be a century of conflict. I believe that conflict will largely occur in cities, and the keys to understanding the conflicts of the future are illustrated in the urban battlefields of the past.

Urban areas are often absolutely critical strategic objectives. They gain the attention of the political leaders of both sides in a conflict, and often of the civilian population as well. They often have a political value that is of much greater strategic importance than the purely material military advantage they provide to either side. Thus, before and during urban combat, there must be close coordination between the tactical actions and requirements and the strategic goals and objectives. Operational-level commanders provide the link between the tactical and strategic level of war and often their understanding and integration of the two very different levels of war is critical to success on the urban battlefield.

The past illustrates many of the essential tactics of urban conflict. Many urban tactical techniques essential for success have been developed over the last half century. These include the requirement for the battle to be an all arms conflict that includes a host of equally important capabilities as diverse as the need for armor and the requirement for well-trained snipers. Another more recent tactical need that has shown itself critical in the complex urban environment is a comprehensive intelligence system adapt at analyzing and understanding the human component of the environment.

Past urban battles also describe operational and strategic requirements for successful urban battle. One of the basic operational essentials of urban battle success is isolating the enemy combatants inside the city. The history of urban combat makes plain that when the enemy is isolated then success follows. When the enemy in the urban battle is not isolated from outside support, success may be much more difficult or impossible. A corollary to this historical observation is that often the battles outside the city to isolate it from support are more difficult, consume more resources, and are more decisive, than the actual house-to-house fighting inside the city.

The battle histories described in this work are the result of research in primary sources and the most authoritative secondary sources available. Many of the battles described here, such as the battle for Stalingrad, have been the subject of multiple excellent histories by some of the finest military historians. This work in no way is a substitute for those superbly researched detailed battle histories. My intent in this work is to make three contributions. First, provide a basic understanding of the multiple dimensions of the urban battlefield, the battlefield which I believe will dominate warfare for the next century. Second, provide analytical insights regarding the urban battlefield based on the historical record of urban combat. That is, to point out critical tactical, operational, and strategic considerations which have relevance to the battlefields of today and tomorrow. Finally, this work, by examining the evolution of the military experience on the urban battlefield since 1942, will show how the urban battlefield has evolved from relatively simplistic conventional battlefield of Stalingrad and Aachen, to the purely insurgency war of Algeria and Northern Ireland, and finally to the highly complex hybrid mixture of conventional and insurgent combat found in places like the occupied territories, Chechnya, and Iraq. Thus, the goal of this book is to use military history to better understand the military affairs of today and tomorrow. American Civil War General William T. Sherman famously described war as hell. This book does not challenge his description, but makes the simple point that in the recent past and in the coming future war has been and will be not just hell, but concrete hell.

LIST OF MAPS

2.1   German Summer Offensive, 1942   31
2.2   The Sixth Army Attack into Stalingrad,
       September–November 1942   38
2.3   The Soviet Counteroffensive, November 1942   43
3.1   The Battle for Aachen, October 1944   48
4.1   The Inchon Landings, September 1950   70
4.2   The Capture of Seoul, September 1950   75
5.1   The PAVN Capture of Hue, January 1968   84
5.2   The Battle for Southern Hue, January–February 1968   87
5.3   The Battle for Northern Hue, January–Feburary 1968   91
6.1   Major Events in Algiers, 1956–57   108
6.2   Deployment and Actions of the 10th Para Division,
       Algiers, 1957   115
7.1   British Army Deployment and Major Events,
       Northern Ireland, 1969–2007   128
8.1   The Initial Russian Attack into Grozny, December 1994   154
9.1   Operation *Defensive Shield*, March–April 2002   173
9.2   The IDF Attacks Nablus, April 2002   179
9.3   The IDF Attacks Jenin, April 2002   184
10.1 Al-Anbar Province, Iraq, 2006   192
10.2 Deployment of 1BCT in Ramadi, Iraq, 2006–07   205

CHAPTER 1

URBAN WARFARE, PAST AND FUTURE

Urban Warfare – a military term that received unprecedented attention just prior to and after the invasion of Iraq in 2003 – describes the conduct of military operations in cities. As the US military entered combat in Iraq in 2003, the American military and public were both in awe of urban combat and made nervous by the challenges it posed. Supremely confident in their ability to fight and win a battle of armored vehicle maneuver, the US Army was much less confident about urban warfare. To the US Army it was a new, mysterious, and particularly nefarious type of warfare for which the US military was historically unprepared, and of which the US military was particularly wary.

That such a view prevailed in 2003 is not surprising given the generally poor knowledge of history within the general public and even among some of the professional military. The facts are, however, that urban warfare is not a new phenomenon; the US military has quite a bit of experience with urban warfare; and though, like all war, urban warfare can be brutal and costly, it is not unusually more so than warfare in many other environments. Urban warfare became the norm for US military operations in Iraq between 2003 and 2011. The nature of those operations in Iraq, including tactics, and operational and strategic context, was a natural extension of the type of urban warfare that developed over the latter half of the 20th century, since World War II. Modern urban warfare, in many respects, is not too different from urban warfare as practiced throughout the history of warfare. Given how warfare has evolved in the last decades of the 20th century, many experts believe that the complex urban battlefield will be the common environment for warfare in the 21st century. If that is the case, then military history is going "back to the future," as an examination of military history reveals that urban warfare is common, and in fact is more common in the history of warfare than classic battle in the open field.

Urban warfare has existed since men began to wage war on other men. War is fundamentally about one group imposing its will on another group. The 19th-century German military philosopher, General Carl von Clausewitz, defined war as pursuing politics by other means. The word politics comes from the Greek word politika. Aristotle described politics as "affairs of the city." In Greek the word for city is *polis*. In the modern world, as in the ancient, political discourse mostly takes place in large urban areas. Cities are where laws are passed and leadership resides. Logically then, to use force to impose political will on a group of people often requires that that force be exercised where the people live, where their leadership resides, and where they carry out their political activities – in cities. Politics, cities, and warfare are inextricably linked, and because of that connection, military forces through history have devoted much of their capability and effort to fighting for, in, and around cities.

Beyond the general nature of politics, there have been, and to this day remain, real, important military reasons for fighting in and for cities. One of the most important reasons for attacking a city was to capture the enemy's political, economic, or cultural center, thereby destroying his morale, his ability to sustain a war, and his capability to govern. In other words, the city was attacked because it was the enemy's center of gravity. This resulted in numerous battles for capital cities such as Rome and Paris. In ancient times, the Persian Empire's efforts to subdue the independent Greek city-states centered on the most important city-state and its capital, Athens. Between 492 and 479 BC, the Persians mounted three separate unsuccessful campaigns to capture the Greek cultural and economic center. The Greeks succeeded in defending Athens in a series of brilliant battles fought not in the city but on its land and sea approaches. These victories were central to the Greeks' successful resistance to the Persian invasions. In 1453, the successful siege and capture of the Byzantine capital of Constantinople by Muslim forces not only spelled the end of the Byzantine Empire but also ended Christian efforts to dominate theMiddle East. Thus, the successful attack or defense of a key city could decide the outcome of the campaign, the war, or the fate of an empire.

Attacking the urban political center of an opponent was often, but not always, decisive. The Persians eventually did capture an abandoned Athens but it did not lead to the success of their campaign. The capture of Mexico City by US forces in 1847 did not compel the surrender of Mexico. Napoleon's successful capture of Moscow in 1812 did not compel the capitulation of Russia for, as historian David Chandler explained, the French capture of Moscow allowed the Russians to seize the initiative in the campaign and then wait for "General Winter" to wreak havoc on the French army. Napoleon's focus on capturing the enemy capital and not on destroying the enemy's field army contributed directly to the failure of his Russian campaign and his disastrous retreat. Attacking an urban area as a means to defeat a nation required careful evaluation of the military situation, geopolitical factors, culture, and economics before executing operations. An incomplete understanding of the role and importance of the urban area to the opponent could lead to an extensive expenditure of time and resources with little operational or strategic gain.

A compelling reason to attack urban areas was military operational necessity. Commanders sometimes attacked an urban area to destroy an enemy force located there or because of the strategic location of the urban area. Often the urban area contained a capability that was necessary for future operations. When defending, a commander often located his forces in an urban area because of his inferior capability and the increase in combat power provided by the inherent defensive qualities of the urban terrain. These reasons compelled commanders to engage in urban operations for purely military reasons. Strategic geographic position was an important reason for deciding to attack or defend a city. Wellington's bloody siege of Badajoz in 1812 was necessary to secure the primary invasion route into Spain. During the American Civil War, General Ulysses Grant's decision to capture Vicksburg was primarily motivated by that city's strategic location on the Mississippi River. When Vicksburg surrendered on July 4, 1863, the Union gained unchallenged control of the river and divided the Confederacy geographically. This success greatly inhibited support and communications between the eastern and western Confederate states and was a devastating blow to the South's morale and prestige.

Often urban operations were required to acquire a capability for future operations. This capability may have been an advance base, logistics facilities, or a harbor. In June and July 1758 during the Seven Years' War, a 14,000-man British army under General Jeffery Amherst captured the French fortress city of Louisbourg on Cape Breton Island. This city was important as a North Atlantic base for the fleet and facilitated the blockade of French Canada. The capture of the city enabled British land and sea operations and greatly inhibited the operations of the French fleet in North America.

When defending, an army that was outnumbered often took advantage of the inherent defensive qualities of urban areas to compensate for its lack of numbers and to offset other advantages enjoyed by an enemy. In 1683, an outnumbered Christian force of approximately 20,000, under the command of the Holy Roman Empire, took shelter in, and defended, Vienna rather than meet an Ottoman army of 75,000 in open battle. The fortifications of the city permitted the outnumbered and less mobile European army to avoid defeat for two months until a relief force of 20,000 arrived to lift the siege and drive off the Turks. As the examples of Mexico City and Moscow indicate, urban operations did not always result in the desired outcome, even when tactical success was achieved and the city occupied. And, as the Turks found out at Vienna, offensive operations against cities often were not successful despite a significant commitment of resources. Thus, it behooved a commander to consider carefully whether urban operations were absolutely essential to the overall operation or campaign.

Occasionally, the commander could discover viable alternatives to the conduct of a deliberate urban operation. Oftentimes, the mere threat to a capital or key city was enough to compel its surrender. In the Franco-Prussian War, the French surrendered after the Prussians had laid siege to Paris but before an actual assault was mounted. Other times, the attacker could attempt a demonstration or ruse, or conduct a turning movement to entice the garrison of a city to fight in the open. A final technique attempted by armies whenever possible was to use surprise to capture a city before a defense could be organized. Attacking from an unexpected direction or by an unexpected means could achieve this.

British General James Wolfe used several techniques to achieve success and capture the French Canadian city of Quebec in 1759 without attacking it by the most obvious means. First, he achieved surprise and attacked from an unexpected direction by moving his army stealthily upriver from the city, conducting an amphibious landing by night, and scaling the supposedly inaccessible Heights of Abraham. By the morning of September 13, 1759, he had positioned his army in a double rank on the Plains of Abraham west of the city and astride Quebec's supply lines. The brilliant and unexpected maneuver unnerved the French commander, Marquis de Montcalm, who decided to attack the British in the open without waiting for reinforcements. In the ensuing battle, British firepower routed the attacking French, destroyed French military capability and morale, and resulted in the city's capitulation on September 18. In 1702, the Austrians also used surprise and an unexpected approach to capture the northern Italian city of Cremona by infiltrating elite troops into the defense by way of an aqueduct. In 1597, the Spanish captured the city of Amiens in northern France using a ruse. A small group of Spaniards disguised as peasants approached the city gateway, at which point they pretended that their cart had broken a wheel. In the confusion that followed, they rushed and captured the gate. These techniques entailed risk-taking and required boldness, imagination, and unique circumstances to be successful but avoided a costly and lengthy fight against the city's defenses.

Bypassing the urban area was a viable technique; however, it had disadvantages. It required that the attacker tolerate the urban garrison in his rear and that he maintain sufficient forces to contain the threat of forays by the city garrison. Another effect of bypassing large important cities was that it often extended the political viability of the opposition and the duration of the campaign, thus jeopardizing the chance of a quick and decisive victory. The mounted Mongol armies that invaded the Chin Empire in northern China in 1211 were not very adept at the nuances of siege warfare and were forced to bypass important large, fortified population centers. The Mongols' inability to conduct effective sieges was a major factor in the Chin's ability to resist and sustain their empire for over two decades after the initial onslaught. Though rarely defeated in open battle, the vaunted Mongol cavalry did not fully conquer the Chin until 1234, after being aided in their efforts by allied Chinese generals and armies who provided experience in siege warfare.

Cities dominated the focus of war for most of history, playing a central role in the earliest campaigns in recorded history. The first battle in history of which there is any significant historical record was between the Hittites and the Egyptians in 1274 BC. The battle was fought outside the city gates of Kadesh, an important transportation hub in what is today modern Syria. Capturing or destroying the enemy's major cities, and most importantly, their capital city, was the surest way to achieve victory in the ancient world. The Ancients also understood that the failure of such an attack could equal strategic defeat in the war. Therefore, the method of attack against a city was the subject of careful study and high-level discussion. Commanders very carefully considered whether to attack a city, how to attack a city, and conversely, how to defend one, before entering into battle. Attack against a city, a siege operation, was very meticulously planned before operations began.

For most of military history the importance of cities to warfare was demonstrated by large-scale siege operations. Even in ancient times, siege operations had developed into a finely honed and highly technical operation. Alexander the Great's assault on Tyre in 332 BC utilized massive engineering efforts, amphibious landings, naval and land bombardments, and 150ft (45m) siege towers. Roman siege operations were likewise characterized by elaborate planning, sophisticated engineering efforts, and specialized equipment. The Romans and other ancient military forces were also very patient in their conduct of the operations and were often willing to invest years in order to successfully capture a city – capturing a city could be that decisive.

Engineering and engineers were central to planning urban operations. Engineering was the central component of ancient urban warfare. Cities were protected by walls and towers. Professional engineers designed these protective capabilities and chose where they would be built to offer the best protection for the city. Conversely, the attacker required professional engineers to evaluate the city's defenses and develop a plan for attack. Central to that plan would be engineering equipment and capabilities. Ancient engineers developed specialized equipment and techniques to aid in the attack of the city. Equipment and techniques included battering rams, covers, ramps, tunnels, towers, ladders, and a variety of throwing machines.

Though some of the ancient specialized urban warfighting equipment was relatively simple, like battering rams, other pieces of equipment were very sophisticated and represented the cutting edge of technological capability of the time. Siege towers, which served a variety of purposes – from protected firing platform, to escalade launch vehicle, to battering ram support system – were particularly feared and complex. They could be over 100ft tall; they were usually completely mobile on their own set of wheels; they were protected against fire attacks, and all but the most powerful missile weapons; and they included their own bridge platforms (for passing troops from the tower to the wall) and firing systems (catapults and ballistae). In the Roman period, armies employed ballistae, a term which most people associate with the concept of a large-scale crossbow for firing large arrows. Ballistae were tactical powered weapons which could be mounted on city walls. However, most often they fired not arrows but small stones weighing up to 3lb, which could be extremely dangerous. The Romans used the ballista in the attack to suppress the enemy on the defensive city walls to allow friendly troops and towers to get in close for an assault. They were also mounted on siege towers and wheeled right up to the walls of the city.

One of the characteristics of urban warfare during the ancient period that still holds true in modern operations is the issue of time. Ancient commanders realized that there were essentially two approaches to urban warfare. One approach was a quick, decisive action to capture the city. This could be accomplished by deploying the main force of the army before the city could be prepared for defense; or, it could be accomplished by deceit. Often allies within the city might be persuaded to compromise the city's defenses.

The ancients demonstrated another characteristic of urban fighting that has remained consistent through history: the burden borne by the civilian population. Unlike open battle, where the civilian population had little direct experience of the operation and only indirect experience of the consequences, the civilian population of an urban area involved in battle was directly involved in both the operation and its consequences. This characteristic of urban combat remains valid into the 21st century. Civilian casualties in city battles could be extraordinarily high. At both Tyre and Jerusalem, after the battle the entire city populations were either killed or enslaved.

The importance of urban operations did not abate in the Middle Ages. Medieval warfare revolved around campaigns designed to capture cities. Attack techniques remained relatively consistent with ancient practices. One of the most successful warrior kings of the period, Henry V of England, famous for his battlefield victory at Agincourt, conducted many more sieges than battles, and they were much more decisive in his campaigns against France. His two-year siege of Rouen, 1417–19, demonstrated how urban warfare in the medieval period was often time consuming, and the death from starvation of many women and children within the city demonstrated that fighting for cities was as brutal as ever.

As Europe entered the Renaissance, an age of scientific discovery, explorations, and invention, combat to control cities remained as critical as ever to warfare. The invention of gunpowder did not change the centrality of cities to warfare but it did change the design of cities. Ancient and medieval cities were typically surrounded by high vertical walls which forced attackers to tunnel underneath, or use towers or ladders to climb over them. Gunpowder and cannon made quick and easy work of vertical stone walls, and cities responded by lowering and widening the walls. The invention of artillery was one of the most important weapon advances in military history and was a direct response to urban fortification. Artillery was initially designed specifically to deal with the walls of medieval castles and walled cities. It was so effective that it quickly caused the demise of the castle and resulted in drastic changes in the design of fortified cities. Large numbers of artillery pieces were used to attack cities. However, artillery was not normally used against the city itself. The primary purpose of artillery was to create a breach in the surrounding wall. Secondly, artillery was used to suppress enemy fire, including enemy artillery, during the approach to the walls of the city and the final assault through and over the city walls. Artillery was not commonly used against the population or structures of a city unless a commander specifically decided to compel the city's surrender through bombardment.

Engineers remained at the forefront of siege warfare and led the response to the new gunpowder technology. Cities lowered their walls and backed the stone fronts with thick earthen embankments. Defenders mounted their own cannon on the wide top of the walls. The engineers carefully designed the trace of the walls so that each wall front was enfiladed by cannon firing from walls on its flank. The resulting design resembled a star and for several hundred years many of the major cities of Europe were surrounded by star fortifications. Engineers in the early modern period were also responsible for designing assaults on fortified cities. Engineers evaluated the defenses, carefully studying distances, angles, outlying fortifications, the thickness of walls, and lie of the surrounding terrain. Based on this, the engineer designed the siege assault plan. The generals commanding the troops made all the command decisions, but those decisions were based on the recommendations of the engineer.

The most famous engineer of this era was Sebastien Le Prestre de Vauban, the chief engineer for Louis XIV of France. Vauban was commissioned as an engineer lieutenant in 1755 and by 1759 he had participated in ten major siege operations. In subsequent years he supervised the successful assault on over 20 cities. He was an expert in both the attack on and the building of fortifications. In his career he improved the fortifications of over 300 cities and supervised the building of 37 new fortresses. His greatest contribution to the art of city combat was the creation of a formal siege methodology. His methodology consisted of choosing the point of attack; emplacing long-range artillery; building a series of protected approach trenches; emplacing close artillery batteries; building more covered trenches to approach the wall of the city; and then, once the supporting artillery silenced defending artillery and created a breach, the infantry assaulted the city's defensive wall from the cover of the approach trenches. Vauban's siege tactics remained the standard for attacking a city almost until the 20th century.

Engineers supervised two types of specialty troops necessary for urban operations: sappers and miners. The engineers generally had exclusive control of the use of miners but had to share the direction of sappers with the artillery. Often this unclear chain of command caused delays in the execution of siege operations. Sapping, the digging of trenches under almost constant fire, was extremely dangerous work. Vauban instituted a system of cash rewards based on progress and danger. With these incentives, Vauban's sappers could complete 480 feet of trench every 24 hours.

Mining remained an essential element as long as cities were defended by prepared positions and fortresses. Mining could take one of two forms. In one form, a deep mine was started well outside the fortification and dug to its foundation. Barrels of explosives were then positioned against the foundation and detonated. The result, if done properly, was the destruction of the wall and the creation of a huge crater, which became the entry point of the following infantry assault on the city. The other type of mining was called "attaching the miner." This technique was a direct mine into the base of the fortress wall. The miners quickly burrowed directly into the base of the wall as the enemy above was suppressed by fire. The miners then branched left or right under the wall. Once properly positioned, explosives were placed in the mine under the wall, and detonated, bringing down a section of wall. The infantry assault then entered the city over the rubble resulting from the collapsed wall. Mining was often used when artillery proved ineffective. Engineers, sappers, and miners were absolutely critical to successful siege operations. There were never enough of them, and delays ensued when engineers were not present, or too few in number. The failure of Wellington's first siege of Badajoz in 1811 is attributed in part to a chronic shortage of engineers. Mistakes by, or the absence of, engineers could cause significant friendly casualties. Thus, the importance of cities to warfare was recognized in the effort and cost undertaken by armies to develop and train specialized troops to meet the particular requirements for successful operations against cities.

For a short time, from the middle of the 18th century to the early part of the 20th century, the genius of Frederick the Great and Napoleon relocated decisive battle from the walls of the city to the open fields of the countryside. During this period siege operations continued to be important, but decisive battles most often occurred in the open field where commanding generals matched wits and tactical acumen using a combination of firepower and maneuver to overcome their opponents. Beginning with Frederick and Napoleon, and spurred on by admirers and biographers, the 19th century was a century of decisive open-field battle. In the 19th century decisive combat on the open battlefield represented the ultimate art of warfare.

Through the 19th century the confluence of technology and the changing nature of cities were also making urban combat and sieges less common. Beginning at the end of the 17th century, many cities began to change their design, and the fortress city became less common. This process was gradual; but by the beginning of the 20th century, the fortress city was recognized as obsolete and had essentially disappeared. This was the result of several factors. For several hundred years after the Middle Ages, city populations were relatively stable, but urban populations began to increase rapidly in the late 18th century. The walled cities began to experience significant crowding and suburbs of the city began to expand beyond the city walls, making the effectiveness of the walls questionable. Additionally, during the 18th century, cities in the interior of stable nation-states were not deemed sufficiently threatened to maintain their expensive fortification. Countries such as France intentionally allowed specific city fortifications to erode. Finally, by the time of the Franco-Prussian War in 1870, modern rifled artillery was able to reduce most city fortifications from a range of nearly two miles.

At the same time that artillery technology was improving, advances in small-arms technology occurred. Rifled repeating arms made small groups of infantry much more lethal. Small-arms technology radically changed infantry tactics. In an urban area, these developments had the effect of turning individual buildings manned by small groups of soldiers into miniature fortresses. Groups of buildings became mutually supporting defensive networks. These man-made defensive networks were much less homogenous than the city wall and hence a much more difficult target for the artillery. Additionally, the lethality of infantry meant that the integrity of the urban defense was not destroyed by a breach of the walls. Defenders now had the capability of defending effectively throughout the depth of the urban environment – a technique impossible when infantry tactics relied on massed close-knit formations to achieve effective firepower. By the end of the 19th century, the pressure of urban population growth, the effectiveness of rifled artillery, and the firepower of breech-loading rifles and machine guns led to the obsolescence of the protective city wall, and resulted in the capability to defend from within individual city buildings and blocks of buildings. The tactical challenge of the fortified building moved the urban battle from the city wall to the city streets.

Commanding generals continued to pursue the objective of the open-field battle into the 20th century. However, decisive open battle was less common as armies got much bigger, warfare became global, and technology added many more dimensions to warfare including mechanized fighting vehicles and airplanes. The size of armies and the complexity of war made decisive single open-field battles a thing of the past. World War I demonstrated that the lethality of the battlefield literally overwhelmed the capacity of armies to maneuver and attack decisively. This had the interesting effect of making urban battle essentially irrelevant. Those small towns and cities which happened to be in the way of World War I combat, particularly after 1914, were simply obliterated by the massive and sustained artillery bombardments which typified all operations in the war. The first two years of World War II, the years of the Nazi Blitzkrieg, seemed to indicate that sweeping gigantic battles of maneuver – Napoleon on a grand scale – might be the new major characteristic of modern war. But in fact, World War II marked the end of a relatively short period in military history where open-field battle dominated the employment of military force. Discrete field battles occurred in World War II. Most often those battles took place in and around cities and proved to be operationally decisive. World War II commanders, seeking to fight in the open whenever possible, bypassed major urban areas with their armored spearheads whenever possible. However, eventually, either the city could not be bypassed, as at Stalingrad, or the presence of the bypassed enemy could not be tolerated. Then warfare reverted to combat in the city. Since World War II, warfare has returned to its historically traditional locale, the urban battle space, with increasing frequency. This is because, as modern armies try to be more and more precise in their application of violence they focus more and more on what is absolutely critical, and the urban centers are natural strategic and operational decisive points.

World War II established modern urban battle tactics. In the years since World War II tactics have evolved but not changed dramatically. During the Cold War, modern armies encountered traditional foes in urban combat situations very reminiscent of World War II. Cold War urban battles in places like Korea and Vietnam looked very much like the World War II experience. However, modern armies have also encountered enemies that have not been armies in the traditional sense, but rather urban insurgents. Urban insurgency emerged during the Cold War and required that modern armies build on traditional urban tactical techniques and combine them with an entirely new understanding of warfare. The French in Algeria and the British in Northern Ireland pioneered the experience of 20th-century armies fighting urban insurgents amid a large civilian population.

The first years of the 21st century continued the trend of more and more combat centered on large urban centers and their populations. Recent combat has demonstrated that the world's cities may well be more the focus of operations than at any time in history. Certainly the evidence of the first decade of the 21st century is that enemies of modern armies will seek out the urban battlefields for a variety of compelling reasons. The urban battle space gives – as it always has done – maximum physical advantages to the defender; the physical environment tends to mitigate many technological advantages held by the attacker; the presence of civilians can greatly complicate the operations of attacking forces, while sometimes also providing cover and concealment to the defender; and it opens the battle to modern media scrutiny. The beginning of the 21st century also revealed that the experiences in conventional and unconventional combat of the last half of the 20th century provide a good guide to the tactics and techniques necessary for success against dedicated and deadly urban enemies of all types. Thus, it seems that understanding the future of war in the 21st century requires an understanding of the history of modern urban combat as demonstrated in the key city battles since World War II.

CHAPTER 2
AN OPERATIONAL DEBACLE
Stalingrad, 1942

Stalingrad is the most famous urban battle in history. It was one of the most decisive battles of World War II and established much of the public and professional military's view of urban combat. Some of the lessons of Stalingrad are myths, and some of them are unique to the Stalingrad battle; however some remain standards of urban combat today and the battle is a worthy starting point for the study of urban combat. The positive aspects of the battle are virtually all on the Soviet side. On the German side, in contrast, the battle provides multiple lessons for how to attack a city in precisely the wrong way. At the tactical level, the battle demonstrated many of the truisms of urban combat, but it also established many of the myths of war in a concrete jungle.

The major event of World War II in 1941 was the German attack on the Soviet Union, Operation *Barbarossa*. The campaign, which lasted through the summer, fall and into the depths of the winter, is one of the most studied and analyzed in military history. One of the critiques of Operation *Barbarossa* was that it was a strategic failure because it was not a focused attack. The Germans failed to identify a single main effort, and instead they attacked across the entire front of the Soviet Union's western border. This lack of focus meant that, though the Germans captured immense amounts of territory and destroyed huge numbers of Soviet forces, the 1941 offensive failed to accomplish anything strategically decisive and Germany entered 1942 in a very precarious situation: not only had they provoked and wounded the Russian bear, but also, in December 1941, Germany declared war on the United States. Thus, it was imperative that Germany not only win battles in 1942, but ensure that those battles, once won, led to decisive strategic victory.

The Soviets Avoid Destruction

As the summer of 1942 approached, the Germans determined to reopen the offensive on the Russian front. This time, however, they would not only focus their efforts, but their chosen objective would greatly increase their strategic capabilities to pursue the war to victory: the Caucasus oil fields in southern Russia. The Germans devoted the entire Southern front to this effort. The new offensive was called Operation *Blue*. The Germans divided Army Group South into two Army Groups, A and B. These army groups were the primary forces in the initial attack. Army Group A, attacking in the south, would be the main effort with the mission of actually capturing the oil fields. Army Group B, to the north of Army Group A, was the supporting attack with the mission of protecting Army Group A's left flank from a Soviet threat from the north. The Volga River was designated as the limit of the advance of Army Group B. The Germans envisioned Army Group B leading the attack before forming a defensive line along the Volga River to protect the main effort. Army Group A would then assume the lead and attack south into the Caucasus Mountains and secure control of the Caucasus oil fields. The success of the Southern Front offensive would inflict significant combat losses on the Soviets, gain a vital strategic resource for the Reich, and deny that same resource to the Soviet Union.

Army Group B, under the command of Field Marshal Fedor von Bock was composed of two subordinate armies, the Sixth Army under General der Panzertruppe Friedrich Paulus, and the Fourth Panzer Army under Generaloberst Hermann Hoth. Of the two, the Fourth Panzer Army was initially the more powerful formation, consisting of two panzer corps and two infantry corps, including a total of four panzer divisions. In contrast, the Sixth Army commanded two infantry and one panzer corps. The Fourth Panzer Army was initially located north in Army Group B's sector and was the main attack. The Sixth Army was in the south of the army group sector and had the task of supporting the attack of Fourth Panzer Army. The city of Stalingrad was located in the center of the Sixth Army's sector.

In late June 1942 Operation *Blue* was launched, a little later than originally planned. In July 1942, Fuhrer Directive No. 45 changed the course of the campaign and confirmed changes that had already occurred in the original plan. By this point in the campaign Army Group B commander, Field Marshal von Bock, had been relieved of command and replaced by Generaloberst Freiherr Maximilian von Weichs. The Fourth Panzer Army was de-emphasized in the new campaign plan, and XXVIII Panzer Corps and the 24th Panzer Division were moved from Fourth Panzer Army to General Paulus' Sixth Army's control. The Fourth Panzer Army itself was transferred to the control of Army Group A. The Fuhrer's order upgraded Stalingrad to a major objective in the campaign. Finally, the attacks by Army Groups A and B were directed to occur simultaneously rather than sequentially as originally conceived. The plan as directed under Directive No. 45 became the basis of the remainder of the campaign.

The Soviets expected the Germans to resume their offensive in the summer of 1942, but they didn't expect it to be in the south. Instead, the Soviets expected the Germans to resume their offensive in central Russia with the objective of capturing Moscow. The Soviet strategy in the summer of 1942, though, was largely governed by the leader of the Soviet Union, Joseph Stalin. Stalin insisted that the Red Army continue the counterattacks that had been initiated the previous winter as Operation *Barbarossa* stalled. Thus, just prior to the Germans launching Operation *Blue*, Soviet forces attacked further north. Eventually, after the initiation of Operation *Blue* the Soviet high command discerned that the German main effort was aiming south across the Don River and on to the Volga River.

The Soviet armies facing the German offensive were not the same armies that the Germans had decisively defeated the previous summer and fall. The Soviet commanders who had survived the onslaught of the previous year were a hardened and much smarter group of leaders. The ones who had failed in 1941 had been killed, captured, or arrested. Those that remained had learned important lessons about how to survive fighting against blitzkrieg. They understood that the concept of *kettleschlag* – the entrapment battle – was fundamental to German success. Thus, as the Germans launched their summer offense in 1942, they found it harder to conduct the large and successful entrapment operations that had characterized Operation *Barbarossa* the previous year. In the summer of 1942, Soviet commanders increasingly used their tank forces to slow the panzer spearheads and quickly marched their infantry out of threatening German envelopment attacks. This became easier for Soviet commanders to do over the course of the summer as Stalin realized that he could not micromanage the Red Army to victory, and increasingly turned over control of daily operations to the Soviet high command, Stafka, and individual field commanders. In the field, Stalin's de-emphasis on political control of the military was reflected by the diminished role of political commissars who had previously been practically co-commanders of Soviet military units. Over the course of 1942 commissars were clearly placed subordinate to professional military officers on all matters related to tactical and operational decisions. This change became official in all Soviet forces in September 1942, and greatly increased the flexibility and effectiveness of Soviet commanders.

The city of Stalingrad, upgraded to a major campaign objective, was in the sector of the German Sixth Army. When World War II started, the city of Stalingrad was a major industrial center with a large population of about half a million people. Today, called Volgograd, the modern city is located on the same site as the original, approximated 200 miles north of the Caspian Sea on the west bank of the Volga River. The city's layout was unusual for several reasons. First, it was not symmetrical. Stalingrad's geographic shape was that of a very long rectangle that extended about 14 miles north to south along the west bank of the river, and was at its widest only about five miles from east to west. The Volga River east of Stalingrad was about a mile wide and thus a very significant obstacle.

Despite some attempts to evacuate portions of the city's population, the war industry capability of the city was deemed too important for it to be shut down. Therefore, many civilians remained in the city operating the various war-related facilities, especially the munitions and tank factories. The city was also a magnet for refugees fleeing east before the advancing German army. Soviet industrial facilities in the city continued to operate as the battle raged and only stopped as Soviet troops retreated. Thus, through the bulk of the fighting for the city environs, more than 600,000 civilians remained in the city. To the German military, the presence of the civilians did not affect operations at all. To the Russians, the civilians were a necessary part of the defense. They were organized into labor units that assisted in building defensive positions and they continued to work in the industrial facilities. As those facilities were gradually captured by the Germans the civilian population fled or were ferried to the east side of the river. Throughout the most intense fighting for the city as many as 50,000 civilians remained within the area of the battle.

Map 2.1 German Summer Offensive, 1942

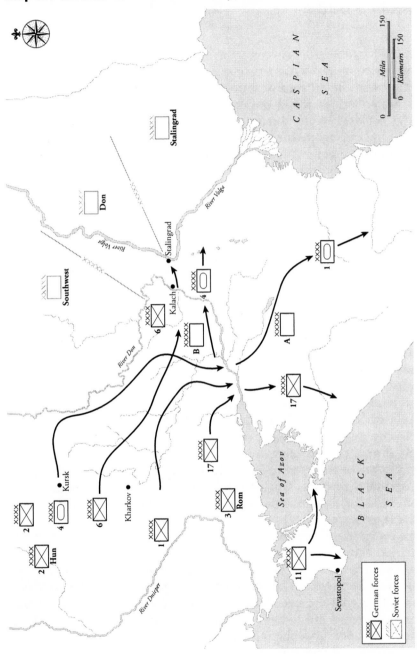

Hitler's Battle

A key to successful urban combat is anticipating the urban battle and preparing for it. The German commanders understood this. However, the operation to capture Stalingrad was not initially subject to close scrutiny because it was only a secondary objective of the campaign, and not decisive to obtaining the German army's objective for the summer campaign, the Caucasus oil fields. In fact, the original plan had no requirement to capture Stalingrad, but rather merely required the German forces to contain Soviet forces and halt the production in the factories located there.

The German army had had experience of urban warfare during the *Barbarossa* campaign and earlier in the summer of 1942. They had captured numerous Russian cities including Minsk in the Ukraine, and Sevastopol in the Crimea, and as they approached Stalingrad, the northern army group was laying siege to the former Russian capital, Leningrad. Dozens of other medium-size Russian cities had been isolated by the German panzers and then captured when the German infantry caught up with the panzer columns. Early in Operation *Blue*, the Fourth Panzer Army became involved in a tough urban battle in and around the important transportation hub city at Voronezh. Because of that experience the German army had adequate knowledge of the intricacies and challenges of tactical urban warfare. Fighting the urban battle tactically was not a concern of the German military commanders as they approached Stalingrad. However, Hitler's role in operations was a concern. Hitler, as the Nazi dictator of Germany, was the key to the German military failure at Stalingrad.

Operation *Blue* began in June 1942 and by mid-July had made important progress. The Germans, inhibited by a shortage of tanks, and fuel for the tanks they did have, found it difficult to complete the large encirclement operations that had characterized *Barbarossa* the previous year. Inadequate strength in troops, equipment, and fuel caused short delays throughout the approach to Stalingrad, which proved crucial. Still, there was significant operational success and the German Sixth Army had captured tens of thousands of Soviet troops and destroyed dozens of divisions by mid-summer. Even so, Soviet commanders managed to keep many of their major formations from being trapped and, though they lost most of their armored forces in the great retreat through southern Russia, they retained the core combat power of their divisions and avoided decisive defeat.

In the middle of July Hitler intervened in the summer campaign. He was unhappy with the rate of advance and ordered the launching of the offensive into the Caucasus as the advance to the Volga was ongoing. Thus, contrary to the original Operation *Blue* plan, which called for a sequenced advance of first Army Group B and then Army Group A attacking south into the Caucasus, Hitler Directive No. 45 ordered both army groups to attack simultaneously. This had several immediate effects. It strained the already overstrained logistics system. It also created two weaker efforts in the place of one strong attack. Finally, the two army groups' objectives were on divergent axes, so the German formations moved further away from each other as the attacks progressed, to the point where they were not within supporting distance of each other.

As important as changing the sequencing of the offensive were Hitler's changes to the orders regarding Stalingrad. Stalingrad was redesignated as a primary objective of the campaign. This change not only required the Sixth Army to capture the entire city, but required that resources which may have been used to reinforce the attack into the Caucuses were diverted to the Stalingrad battle.

The Germans began their final push to capture Stalingrad at the end of August 1942. By August 22, Sixth Army's XIV Panzer Corps had entered the northern suburbs of the city and the following day the panzers reached the Volga north of the city. The rest of the Sixth Army, and XXVIII Panzer Corps under control of Sixth Army, pushed to the outskirts of the city. The XXVIII Panzer Corps managed to break through the Soviet Sixty-Fourth Army defending the southern portion of the city and race almost to the Volga threatening to trap part of the Sixty-Fourth Army and all of the Soviet Sixty-Second Army in the city's outskirts. This success caused the two Soviet armies, the Sixty-Second and Sixty-Fourth, to give up the outer ring of the city's defenses and withdraw into the city to avoid the trap. Thus, by the end of August the Germans were firmly in possession of the outskirts of the city and threatened it from three directions: north, west, and south. It appeared the fall of the entire city would happen in a matter of weeks.

The fighting for Stalingrad proper began on September 14, as German forces attempted to force their way into the city center. The battle for the city directly involved three German army corps: the XIV Panzer and LI Corps of the Sixth Army, and the XXVIII Panzer Corps of Fourth Panzer Army. The three German corps were opposed directly by two Soviet armies: the Sixty-Fourth and Sixty-Second

Armies of the Stalingrad Front. The initial attacks were costly but successful. After about ten days of very intense fighting the two panzer and two infantry divisions of XXVIII Corps managed to destroy most of the Sixty-Fourth Army in the southern part of the city and seize about five miles of the Volga riverbank. In the center of the city, the combined forces of the LI and XIV Panzer Corps pushed the divisions of the Soviet General Vasily Chuikov's Sixty-Second Army back toward theVolga and reduced the Soviets' defensive parameter by half.

Despite the successes, the attacks of mid-September did not accomplish the Sixth Army's mission. The task of the army was the capture of the city, not just, as it had initially been, to control the city. Thus on September 27, Sixth Army renewed the attacks to eliminate the presence of the Soviet Sixty-Second Army on the west bank of the Volga. The initial attacks had severely depleted many of the veteran units of the Sixth Army, particularly in the center of the line where the most significant attacks occurred. To compensate, most of XXVIII Panzer Corps was moved from the south into the central part of the sector. This gave the Germans two strong panzer divisions (the 24th and the 14th) and two motorized infantry divisions in the center.

The Soviets anticipated the German offensive and took steps to meet it. Their excellent intelligence network inside the city informed them that the focus of the attack would be in the center and north, aimed at the major Soviet defenses based at three large factory complexes in northern Stalingrad. From north to south these were the tractor factory complex, the Barrikady weapons factory complex, and the Red October factory facilities. These complexes were huge self-contained communities which included the factories themselves and the workers' housing buildings. The buildings were massive structures constructed of steel girders and reinforced concrete. Many of the factory buildings included massive internal workshops large enough to house the emplacement of tanks and large-caliber guns to participate in the fight inside the building. After repeated air and artillery attacks, the complex and formidable defensive qualities of the buildings were actually enhanced due to extensive damage and accumulated rubble. To this the Soviet infantry added barbed wire, extensive minefields, deep protected trenches, and bunkers. By the end of September, the Soviet defensive positions in Stalingrad were every bit as formidable as the most notorious defenses of World War I.

The second major German attack into the city lasted ten days, from September 27 to October 7, and involved 11 full German divisions including all three panzer divisions. Like the first attack, it was successful and the Germans managed to capture two of the three major factory complexes: the tractor factory and the Barrikady factory. They also eliminated the Orlovka salient which was a deep Soviet defensive salient that had remained in the northern part of the city. Despite steady Red Army reinforcement which consistently frustrated a decisive German breakthrough, by the end of the attack the Sixty-Second Army was reduced to a tiny strip of the west bank of the Volga which at its widest was perhaps 2,200 yards (2,000 meters).

The third major attack to secure the city began on October 14, 1942. Three infantry divisions, two panzer divisions, and five special engineer battalions were committed to the attack – in total over 90,000 men and 300 tanks on a 3-mile front. For another 12 days the Germans ground forward, systematically reducing Russian strongpoint after strongpoint. The Soviets fed additional troops across the Volga but the defenders were running out of space. When the German offensive finally paused on October 27, they held 90 percent of Stalingrad. Only part of the Red October steel factory was outside their control. The Sixty-Second Army was fragmented into small pockets and most of its divisions were completely wiped out. All sectors of the remaining Soviet defenses were subject to German observation and attack. But the German attacks ended without achieving their objective: capture of the city of Stalingrad. As the month came to a close, shortages of troops, ammunition, tanks, and pure exhaustion of the remaining troops made further offensive operations by the Germans impossible.

Winter arrived in Stalingrad on November 9 as temperatures plunged to -18°C. The fighting, however, did not stop. The Germans were no longer capable of large-scale offensive operations but small raids and attacks continued as they attempted to eliminate the remaining Soviet strongpoints. On November 11, battle groups from six German divisions, led by four fresh pioneer battalions, launched the last concerted German effort to secure the city before the coming of winter. It, like all previous German offenses, took ground and punished the Soviet defenders, but ultimately fell short of its objective. In the LI Corps, under General Walther von Seydlitz, 42 percent of all battalions were considered fought-out and across the entire Sixth Army most infantry companies had fewer than 50 men and companies had to be combined in order to create effective units. The 14th and 24th Panzer Divisions both required a complete refitting in order to continue operations in the winter. In short, by mid-November the combat power of the German Sixth Army was almost completely spent after more than two months of intense urban combat.

The Soviet Trap

The German high command, and Hitler in particular, were desperate for a victory at Stalingrad. Desperation does not make for good military decision-making, and over the course of the campaign the German decision-making evolved from taking great risks to simple gambling. By October, the Germans were gambling that the Soviet high command was incapable of simple and obvious military judgment, which was all that was required to recognize early in the battle what an operational opportunity the shaping of the battle could provide to the Soviet high command.

Early in September the senior leadership of the Soviet Union, Premier Joseph Stalin, and generals Aleksandr Vasilevsky and Georgi Zhukov met and identified the operational opportunity that the German disposition at Stalingrad presented. The opportunity was obvious from the map. The Sixth Army was extended deep into Russia at the end of a very long supply line. Long flanks were exposed both north and south of the advance to Stalingrad. An examination of German force distribution reinforced the vulnerabilities of the geometry of the Army Group B front. The vast preponderance of the German combat power, 21 divisions, was concentrated at the very tip of the salient, in Stalingrad. The flanks were comparatively lightly held. Moreover, the bulk of the units holding those flanks were inferior allied units: Italian, Hungarian, and least effective of all, Romanian. These allied formations had been injected into the line in July and August to relieve German formations for employment in Stalingrad. Further exasperating already precarious operational dispositions was the fact that neither Sixth Army nor Army Group B held any significant operational reserves to respond to an emergency. In addition, the units that were best suited to constituting a reserve, the mobile panzer and panzer grenadier divisions, were seriously understrength, short on fuel, and many were decisively engaged in the Stalingrad street fighting and therefore unavailable. The primary Army Group reserve was XLVIII Panzer Corps. The corps consisted of the German 22nd Panzer Division and the Romanian 1st Armored Division. Both units were understrength, and the Romanian division was absolutely no match for Soviet armor. The Germans could not have offered Stalin and Zhukov a more lucrative and tempting target if they had consciously tried to do so.

Through all of September and October the Red Army prepared for Operation *Uranus*, the counteroffensive against Army Group B. The Russians carefully moved units forward at night to avoid German detection. They used intelligence gathered from captured prisoners and a partisan intelligence network to carefully plot German dispositions. Secrecy was extreme and even senior commanders, such as General Chuikov in Stalingrad, were unaware of the preparations for the counterattack. The German command was the most unaware of what was happening. German intelligence not only was completely unaware of the massive Soviet buildup north and south of Stalingrad, but they were convinced that the Red Army had no significant operational reserves. The performance of German intelligence throughout World War II was consistently poor, and often, as at Stalingrad in November 1942, had disastrous consequences.

In preparation for Operation *Uranus*, the Soviet Army reorganized its command structure. Three front commands were created in the Stalingrad area. The Southwest Front, under General Nikolai Vatutin, was far to the north and west of Stalingrad. The Don Front, under General Konstantin Rokossovsky was located directly north of Stalingrad. The Stalingrad Front, under General Andrei Yeremenko, had responsibility for Stalingrad itself and units to the south of the city. The plan called for the Southwest and Don fronts to launch attacks deep into the rear of Sixth Army. The Southwest Front's Fifth Tank Army would attack the Romanian Third Army over 100 miles west of the Sixth Army's main forces in Stalingrad itself. Simultaneously, the Stalingrad Front would counterattack 50 miles south of the city, aiming at the 51st and 57th Corps of the Romanian Fourth Army.

On the morning of November 19, the attack began. All across the Southwest Front Soviet artillery blasted huge holes in the Romanian lines which were quickly driven through by Russian armor and horse cavalry. The Soviet operational technique was simple: massive artillery bombardment shocked and suppressed the defending Romanian infantry; Soviet armor rolled over the still shocked Romanians who were woefully short of antitank guns and had no armor reserve. Soviet horse cavalry followed closely behind the armor to protect its flanks. Finally, Soviet infantry moved forward and mopped up the remaining isolated Romanian positions. The

Map 2.2 The Sixth Army Attack into Stalingrad, September–November 1942

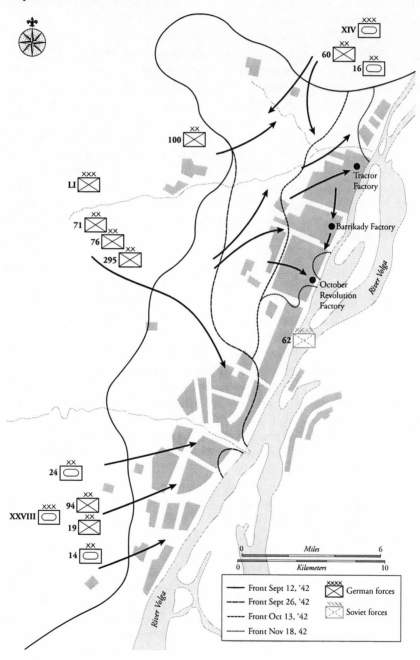

XIV

60

16

100

LI

71

76

295

Tractor Factory

Barrikady Factory

October Revolution Factory

River Volga

62

24

94

XXVIII

19

14

Miles		
0		6
Kilometers		
0		10

——— Front Sept 12, '42

– – – Front Sept 26, '42

- - - Front Oct 13, '42

········ Front Nov 18, 42

German forces

Soviet forces

River Volga

Soviet assault tactics were extremely effective against the poorly equipped and led Romanians, and Soviet armor formations quickly penetrated and fanned out into the Romanian and German rear areas. The objective of the Southwest Front was the west bank of the Don River and the Sixth Army logistics base at Kalach on the east bank of the Don River. Kalach and the vital bridge over the Don located there were captured on November 22, a mere three days after the attack began.

On November 20 the Stalingrad Front launched its attack on the Romanian Fourth Army. The pattern to the northwest was repeated south of Stalingrad. The Romanian forces were quickly overrun by Soviet armor formations which proceeded to advance rapidly against light opposition to the west and northwest. On November 23, four days after the beginning of the offensive, armored forces from the Don Front linked up with forces from the Stalingrad Front just east of Kalach and effected the complete isolation of the Sixth Army and attached troops around Stalingrad.

The battle for Stalingrad was decided on November 23 when the Red Army managed to isolate the German Sixth Army in and around the city. In three months of combat prior to the end of November, the German forces had been unable to isolate the Soviet Sixty-Second Army in the city and therefore the battle had raged on. The Germans had never contemplated isolating Stalingrad by attacking across the Volga River. In contrast, in four days the Soviets surrounded the city and sealed the fate of the Sixth Army. Approximately 250,000 Axis troops were trapped in the *kessel*. Over the next two and a half months the Soviets gradually pressed against the perimeter of Sixth Army while the rest of the German army watched on helplessly. Finally, the bulk of the German troops surrendered on January 31, 1943. The remaining holdouts, after enduring a withering Soviet artillery barrage, surrendered on February 2. In all the Russians took in almost 100,000 prisoners as the five-month battle for the city ended. In total, the losses at Stalingrad were immense. In the battle and campaign, which included the Soviet counterattack, the Germans lost 400,000 men, and the Soviets lost 750,000 killed, wounded, and missing. Allies of the Germans – the Italians, Hungarians, and Romanians – lost another 130,000, 120,000, and 200,000 respectively. Thus total casualties on both sides exceeded one million men. Of the 600,000 civilians who lived and worked in Stalingrad and its suburbs, no one knows how many died, although 40,000 were reported killed in the initial air attacks against the city. Hundreds of thousands of civilians became casualties over the course of the five-month battle, and those remaining became refugees. Only 1,500 civilians remained in the city at the end of the battle. In terms of raw casualty numbers, the battle for Stalingrad was the single most brutal battle in history.

The German Tactical Approach

Though the German army had acquired experience of urban fighting during the fall of 1941, the individual divisions in Stalingrad had to develop their own version of city fighting for the unique Stalingrad situation. Stalingrad was different from other cities for several reasons. One was the massive amount of destruction that had been inflicted upon the city, destruction which continued and increased over time. The second was the nature of the buildings in Stalingrad. They were massive concrete affairs which, when surrounded by rubble following artillery and air bombardment, were virtual fortresses. The Germans found that the most effective tactic was to combine infantry and armor into teams. These teams were supported by artillery and closely supported by the Luftwaffe. Stalingrad was the last great performance by the fabled German Stuka dive-bombers.

Typically, German attacks followed a pattern: Luftwaffe air bombardment, followed by a short artillery barrage, and then the advance of German infantry followed closely by panzers in support. This pattern generally ensured success. Panzers, though not optimized for city warfare, were absolutely critical to it, and the three panzer divisions that fought at Stalingrad were a key part of most of the Sixth Army's tactical successes. The problem the Germans had tactically was that they simply did not have enough panzers, infantry, and artillery to execute the tactics they employed with sufficient vigor to overcome the Russian defenders quickly. In the course of the German attacks in Stalingrad, virtually all the attacks were successful. However, they were never as fast as the Germans wanted or expected them to be, and were always more costly than the Germans could afford. The German army could be, and was, successful in urban combat in Stalingrad, but at an unacceptable price in time and casualties.

In the rubble of Stalingrad, the disparity between German and Soviet tactical capabilities, which was very prominent in the open battles of maneuver on the Russian steppe, was reduced significantly. The German army excelled at operational warfare: the close coordination of all arms at the division and corps level of command to achieve rapid and decisive effects across great distances. In urban combat, the important distances were blocks – divisions and corps could not maneuver, and command and coordination at the highest levels was relatively simple and not very important. Thus, the strengths of the German military machine were fairly irrelevant to the battle. Instead, the battle devolved to tactical competence at the battalion level and below, combat leadership, and the psychological strength of the individual soldier. The Wehrmacht had these characteristics in great abundance. However, so did the Soviet army. Thus, unlike in operational maneuver warfare, in urban combat the two sides were both fairly competent, and thus very evenly matched. These organizational circumstances were a recipe for a long and bloody battle. The Red Army, and in particular the Sixty-Second Army, augmented the natural strength of the Russian infantry in close combat and the urban terrain with several innovative tactics which made them more formidable in urban combat than the Germans expected.

Soviet Shock Groups

One of the most effective and feared German weapons at Stalingrad was the venerable Stuka dive-bomber. Weather permitting, all major German attacks were preceded and closely supported by the Stukas of Luftflotte IV under Generaloberst Freiherr Wolfram von Richthofen. To lessen the effectiveness of this weapon, as well as of German artillery, General Chuikov ordered that all front-line units stay engaged as closely as possible to the Germans. The Sixty-Second Army "hugged" its German adversaries so that German bombardment could not engage the front-line Russians without hitting their own troops. This resulted in there being virtually no "no-man's land" on the Stalingrad battlefield. Across the entire front Red Army positions were literally within hand-grenade range of the German positions. Thus, attacking Germans were often confronted by defenders who were unaffected by the pre-attack artillery or air bombardment.

After the initial penetration of the city, the Soviet armor of the Sixty-Second Army was not used in a mobile manner. The tanks, instead, were dug deep into the rubble and heavily camouflaged. Often they were invisible from more than a few yards away. They were placed on the routes most likely used by German tanks and supporting vehicles, and invariably were able to fire the first shot. The short ranges, careful preparation, and ability to fire first gave the Russian tank crews better than even odds despite the general superiority of German crews. In total the German and Soviets together employed over 600 tanks inside the city.

One of the most innovative and effective ideas developed by the defending Red Army was the idea of shock groups. Shock groups were non-standard small assault units organized to conduct quick attacks on specific German positions. They often attacked at night. Typically they consisted of 50–100 men. They were lightly equipped so that they could move quickly and silently through the city. The groups were led by junior officers; they used a variety of weapons but relied heavily on sub-machine guns and grenades. They also included engineers for breaching doors and other obstacles, snipers, mortar teams, and heavy machine guns to defend the newly won positions. Shock groups relied extensively on the initiative of the junior leaders to determine how best to assault an objective. Many of the men in the group were volunteers who relished an opportunity to take the fight to Germans, despite the Sixty-Second Army's overall defensive stance. Because of this aggressiveness and the latitude allowed the junior leaders, shock groups were both very effective and also very much a departure from standard Soviet tactical practice which was typically very controlled. The departure from standard doctrine which shock groups represented in the Soviet army indicated the desperate measures that were permitted on the Soviet side during the battle. They proved to be a very effective tactic during the second part of the battle, after September, and were an indicator of the tactical parity that existed in close urban battle. Though shock groups were copied by other Soviet armies in subsequent urban combat during World War II, as the Soviet Union gained the operational and strategic initiative the groups became more and more standardized, larger and more heavily equipped (to include tanks and artillery). As the war progressed, they were permitted less freedom of action. Soviet shock groups, as they existed by the end of the war, bore little resemblance to the highly effective organizations developed during the battle for Stalingrad.

One of the major special tactics that the Russians developed and utilized in the Stalingrad battle was snipers. Though the Red Army had a small number of trained snipers as part of its organizational structure, in Stalingrad the employment of snipers became a largely

Map 2.3 The Soviet Counteroffensive, November 1942

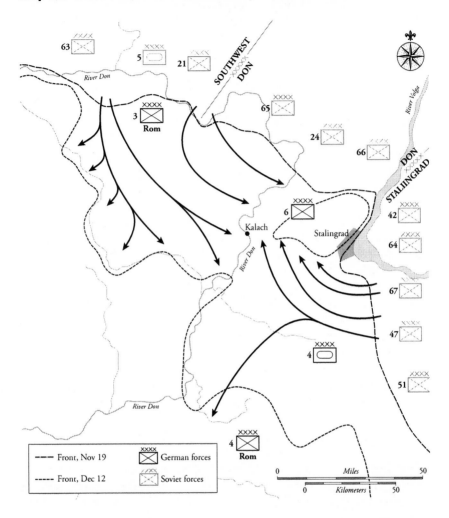

ad-hoc movement initiated by individual soldiers and eventually embraced and encouraged by commanders. Early during the battle self-motivated snipers acquired rifles with telescopic sights and then got permission from their commanders to go on individual "hunting" missions. Red Army commanders, including the army commander General Chuikov, saw the snipers as brave and angry soldiers whose frustration and hatred could be channeled by the army into a useful outlet. Thus, sniping became a sanctioned individual mission and the success of snipers was widely publicized both within Stalingrad and throughout the Soviet Union to encourage morale among the soldiers at the front and the civilians at home. Sniping was inordinately successful in Stalingrad for many reasons: the density of troops in the built-up area; the protracted nature of the battle, which led to troops becoming careless, and allowed snipers to learn the patterns of the enemy; the terrain, which allowed snipers to stalk and hunt targets with both cover and concealment; and the proximity of the enemy, which made effective sniping relatively easy – many targets were less than a hundred yards away. The Russian command carefully tracked the progress of individual snipers and trumpeted their success in propaganda. The most famous of the snipers, Private Vasily Zaitsev, had well over 200 sniping kills, and was one of several snipers who killed more than a hundred Germans. The effectiveness of the Russian snipers was not only a major morale booster to the Sixty-Second Army, it had tremendous adverse psychological effects on the German troops who never knew when a shot would crack and a man would drop to the ground.

Armor, for both the Soviets and the Germans, proved to be extremely important to successful city fighting. Soviet armor was primarily used in stationary firing positions. Though stationary, the armored vehicles were heavily camouflaged and carefully sited to cover avenues that the attacking Germans could not avoid. Unlike antitank guns and machine-gun positions manned by infantry, the stationary tanks were immune to all but a direct hit by artillery and often required an enemy tank or assault gun to knock them out. They were important anchors in the Russian defensive scheme. German tanks were equally invaluable. They provided the firepower and shock action necessary for German infantry to overpower skillfully defended Russian defensive positions – particularly bunkers and dug-in Soviet tanks. Their firepower made up for the relatively low numbers of infantry in the German force. They provided an important psychological advantage that boosted German infantry morale and intimidated defending Soviet infantry. Finally, their mobility meant they could be rapidly repositioned to weight a particular sector or exploit success. It was no coincidence that the major successes achieved by the Germans in their four major attacks in the interior of Stalingrad included major components of German armor. Rather than having a limited role in urban operations, Stalingrad demonstrated that armored forces were key and essential to successful urban operations.

Losing the Battle

The battle for Stalingrad was simultaneously a tribute to Soviet army skill and endurance, and an example of the incompetence of German senior leaders. German commanders executed Operation *Blue* poorly. A large factor in that poor execution was the inept strategic and operational guidance and orders of Adolf Hitler. Several senior officers were removed from their positions because of their conflicts with Hitler. Among these were the chief of the Army General Staff, General Franz Halder, and the commander of Army Group B, General Fedor von Bock. In both cases it was directly due to Hitler's refusal to act in accordance with a real appraisal of the battlefield. Hitler personally took command of Army Group South and gave very specific operational and tactical guidance down to battalion level through much of the battle. He made the key flawed decisions to launch operations into the Caucasus before the Volga line was secure; to elevate Stalingrad from a secondary campaign objective to a primary campaign objective; to require all of Stalingrad be captured not just controlled; and to hold fast as the Sixth Army was surrounded and later not to break out when the 6th Panzer Division and Field Marshal Erich von Manstein's Army Group Don was only 20 miles away. It is doubtful that any army could recover at the tactical level from the terrible position the Sixth Army ended up in as a result of Hitler's amateurish involvement in operations. However Hitler did not single-handedly set up the conditions for the Stalingrad defeat. Collectively the senior German military was also guilty of incompetence for ignoring the weaknesses of the allied armies protecting Sixth Army's flanks; not understanding the limited capabilities and strength of XLVIII Panzer Corps, the Army Group reserve; and completely underestimating the Soviet military's competence, strength, and intentions prior to the launching of Operation *Uranus*. It was the sum of the failures of Hitler and other senior leaders that led to the debacle at Stalingrad. The great lesson of Stalingrad is that urban warfare, for all of its painful brutality at the tactical level, is often won or lost due to operational and strategic decisions made at levels above the tactical and often immune to the conditions of the concrete hell of urban warfare.

CHAPTER 3

AMERICAN URBAN WARFARE

Aachen, 1944

Eighteen months after Stalingrad, on the opposite side of the European continent, the US Army was tested in major urban combat of when the Americans approached the German city of Aachen in October 1944. The battle for Aachen demonstrated many of the characteristics of urban warfare seen at Stalingrad. It also highlighted some of the basic requirements of successful urban operations that were missing in the Stalingrad battle. Finally, Aachen demonstrated some uniquely American characteristics of urban operations. Though not conducted on the same scale as Stalingrad, the battle for Aachen was nonetheless one of the key battles on the Western Front of World War II as the Allies sought, and the Germans contested, the capture of the first German city of the war.

Drive to the German Border

The Western Allies opened the Western European Front on June 6, 1944, when troops were landed at Normandy. For the next seven weeks German and Allied forces dueled in the hedgerows of Normandy. The terrain suited the German defense and the Allies were continuously frustrated in their attempts to break out of their beachheads. Finally, on July 25 the American First Army's Operation *Cobra* succeeded in breaking out of the beachhead. In the next weeks a battle of maneuver ensued. A German panzer counterattack was defeated at Mortain, August 7–13, 1944. Meanwhile, the Americans activated General George Patton's Third Army which quickly captured the Brittany

Map 3.1 The Battle for Aachen, October 1944

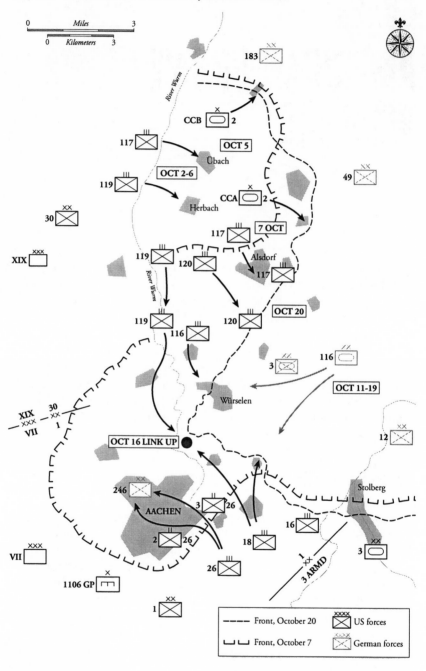

Peninsula, turned east, and dashed through light resistance across central France.

Meanwhile, the failed German counterattack left the German Seventh Army dangerously exposed to the American armored spearheads spreading out in all directions through the gap in the German lines. In orders reminiscent of Stalingrad, Hitler ordered that the German army not withdraw, and fight for every piece of French soil. This set up the German Seventh Army to be enveloped by elements of the US First and Third Armies which hooked north and east behind the Germans. Simultaneously the British launched an offensive on the opposite side of the front designed to envelop the Seventh Army from the north. As the Allied pincers began to close, the German command recognized the danger and belatedly began to withdraw. Though some of the German Seventh Army escaped the trap at the Falaise pocket, the bulk of it was destroyed and the American and British forces then turned and began to pursue the rapidly retreating Germans toward the German border.

By the middle of September the US Third Army was approaching the German fortress complex in Lorraine centered on the famous city of Metz. The US First Army liberated all of Northern France, Luxembourg, and southern Belgium and was approaching the German frontier defenses, known as the Siegfried Line, along the German–Belgium border. The British 21st Army Group had pursued the Germans north, liberating western Belgium and Antwerp. The British were poised to liberate Holland and cross the Rhine. It was at this point in the offensive, after seven weeks of continuous high-tempo offensive operations, that the bane of all senior commanders – logistics – began to dominate operational decision-making.

Though the breakout from the Normandy beachheads had been wildly successful, the Germans had managed to either defend or destroy virtually all the major port facilities along the French coast. Thus, the two Allied army groups, the 12th US Army Group and the British 21st Army Group, were both primarily reliant on logistics brought over the Normandy beaches. The volume of supplies that the Allies could move over the beaches was limited. Further, the French railroad system had been effectively destroyed by Allied airpower. Thus, most of what was brought ashore was moved forward by truck. There were simply not enough trucks for the job, and thousands of miles traveled quickly began to wear out the trucks that were available. Thus, by mid-September 1944, the Allied spearheads began to grind to a halt for lack of fuel. It was at this time that the leading combat elements of the US First Army reached Aachen, which was virtually undefended.

The supreme Allied commander, General Dwight Eisenhower, was acutely aware of the logistics problems. He also understood that the German army was in full retreat, that the western defenses of Germany were largely unmanned, and that there was an opportunity to possibly end the war before Christmas. Eisenhower had the logistics capability to sustain one of the three major axes being pursued by his armies, but the cost of doing so was stopping the other two offensives in their tracks. For a variety of valid, if arguable, reasons, Eisenhower determined to back his northern attack led by the British Field Marshal Bernard Montgomery's 21st Army Group. Offensive operations in the US 12th Army Group were suspended and the US First and Third Armies halted. The US forces in the vicinity of Aachen reverted to the defense.

The Aachen terrain corridor was a stretch of relatively open ground that could give large formations access into northern Germany. To the north of the Aachen area was Holland and that approach was characterized by numerous canals, estuaries, associated bridges, and marshes. It was not a promising approach for large mobile formations. South of Aachen lay the Hurtigen and the Ardennes forests. These dense forests lay over steep hills and ravines, had a very limited road network to the east, and thus were excellent for defensive operations and unsuited to large mobile operations. The next eastward avenue suitable for the movement of large mobile formations was far to the south in the Lorraine. It was in this area that Patton's Third Army operated. Thus, the best approach route into Germany in the northern part of the front was through Aachen, and it was in the northern part of the front that the bulk of the Allied combat power lay.

The Plan to Capture Aachen

Aachen had a special place in German history and in the ideological underpinnings of the Third Reich. Hitler declared the city a *"festung"* city, a fortress city, and that it was to be defended to the last. Toward this end the Nazi government evacuated most of the citizens as the US forces approached. When the initial impulse toward Aachen in September failed to take the city, the Nazi propaganda machine began to portray Aachen as a reverse Stalingrad. According to Nazi propaganda, the US Army would be lured into a battle for Aachen and destroyed.

The failure of Field Marshal Montgomery's offensive to cross the Rhine in September – Operation *Market Garden* – is well documented. Less well known is what German officers on the Western Front came to call "the miracle in the West." Warfare at all levels, tactical through strategic, is often a matter of simple choices which slow or speed a campaign or battle. Minutes, hours, and days often spell the difference between victory and defeat, or swift victory and slow destruction. The delay caused to the American advance by logistics problems, lasting through the last two weeks of September 1944, was the breathing space that the German command needed to reorganize units, bring forward supplies, and shuffle reinforcements to the west. Thus, at the end of September 1944, when the US armies were ready to resume their advance, they faced a much more formidable foe.

When offensive operations began again on the Western Front in October 1944, not only were the German forces no longer in full retreat, but General Eisenhower had adopted a new strategy for the front. Eisenhower determined that with the failure of Operation *Market Garden* any single thrust deep into Germany was too risky. Instead he adopted a broad-front strategy. Eisenhower's concept – to attack simultaneously with all Allied armies from Holland to the Swiss border – was bold and insightful. It leveraged the Allies' great advantage in resources, and somewhat mitigated any advantage the Germans may have had in tactical skill and equipment. Within the context of this broad-front strategy, General Courtney Hodges planned for his US First Army to resume offensive operations in early October. His initial major objective was the German city of Aachen, which lay on the tri-border point between Holland, Belgium, and Germany. Hodges' concept was that the Aachen battle would penetrate the Siegfried Line, and open up the Ruhr industrial area to Allied occupation as a prelude to crossing the Rhine River.

The approach to the Aachen, and the battle itself, was controlled directly by the US First Army. This was required because the Aachen sector of the front was split by a corps boundary. The XIX Corps was positioned north of Aachen while the southern portion and the main part of the city were in the zone of the VII Corps. The First Army plan to capture the city was relatively simple. The XIX Corps would attack north of the city and drive east and then southeast to encircle the city from the north. After success in the north, the VII Corps would launch its attack northeast to link up with the XIX Corps. Once the two corps had linked up and isolated the city, elements of VII Corps' 1st Infantry Division would assault the city directly to capture it.

Aachen lay in the sector of the German LXXXI Corps, under General der Infanterie Friedrich Köchling. The corps was part of the rebuilt German Seventh Army, part of Army Group B under Field Marshal Walter Model who was tasked by Hitler with stabilizing the situation on the Western Front. The entire front was commanded by the venerable German Field Marshal Gerd von Rundstedt. Having staved off a coup de main seizure of the city in early September, the German command recognized that Aachen had to be held as long as possible for several reasons. First was the importance of the Siegfried Line defenses, two belts of which ran to the east and west of the city. Second, the political symbolism of an ancient German city resisting the Allied assault was extremely valuable propaganda. Finally – and this was a factor which influenced all German operations in the battle – the German counteroffensive planned for the west, Operation *Wacht am Rhine*, later known as the Battle of the Bulge, was to be launched out of the German Eifel Mountains into the Ardennes forest south of Aachen. A successful penetration at Aachen would place the Allies deep in the northern flank of this planned attack and make it very vulnerable to counterattack.

The German LXXXI Corps defended the Aachen sector with four infantry divisions: the 183rd and 49th Divisions; the 246th Division, which had responsibility for the city itself; and the 12th Division, which defended west of the city in the vicinity of Stolberg. The corps had a number of separate panzer and assault gun units in reserve, notably the 506th Heavy Tank Battalion, equipped with King Tiger tanks. The mission of these mobile forces was to counterattack against any penetration of the infantry division defensive lines. Available, but not released to the corps, was the Army Group B reserve of the 116th Panzer Division and the 3rd Panzer Grenadier Division, both organized under I SS Panzer Corps. Field Marshal von Rundstedt had control of the mobile reserve and would only release it under extreme circumstances.

Enveloping the City

In early September the German Seventh Army was in disarray and the West Wall defenses were largely unmanned. As the German army retreated, the German command assigned the defense of Aachen to the 116th Panzer Division. This unit, however, was only a shadow of itself after the losses of August. The German commander decided to give up Aachen without a fight. The American VII Corps, however, determined not to attack directly into the city and the 3rd Armored Division leading the corps advance bypassed Aachen to the south and advanced east and northeast beyond the city into the outskirts of the town of Stolberg. Elements of the 3rd Armored were positioned on the western edge of Stolberg when offensive operations ceased to permit priority of supplies to *Market Garden* in September. As September ended, the US First Army sat immobilized on the German frontier. The VII Corps' 3rd Armored Division was positioned east of Aachen near Stolberg. The Corps' 1st Infantry Division was positioned east and south of the city. The boundary between VII Corps and XIX Corps ran roughly through the western portion of the city. North of the city was the area of operations of the 30th Infantry Division whose front generally followed the Wurm River which flowed northwest from northern Aachen.

The battle for Aachen began on October 2, 1944, with the attack of the 30th Infantry Division across the Wurm River, north of Aachen. The American plan was simple, tactically sound, and reflected a solid understanding of urban warfare. The attack involved three divisions and supporting troops. In phase one of the attack, the 30th Division attacked north of the city to drive east and then southeast to secure the town of Wurselen, about 9 miles northeast of the city proper. The 2nd Armored Division supported the attack of the 30th and protected the 30th's northern flank from counterattack. In the second phase of the attack, the 1st Infantry Division attacked from the south to the north to secure Aachen's eastern suburbs and to link up with the 30th Division in Wurselen. Phase two's objective was the complete isolation of the city. The final phase of the attack was an attack by two battalions of the 1st Division's 26th Infantry Regiment. This attack was from east to west to capture the city center itself. Phase three was timed to occur after the completion of phase two.

At 9am on October 2, the US XIX Corps began its attack with a massive aerial bombardment of German positions, followed closely by an artillery attack which included 26 artillery battalions firing almost 20,000 rounds of ammunition. The 30th Division attacked with two regiments, the 117th and 119th, abreast. The regiments had to penetrate a line of West Wall pillboxes and bunkers, and then attack through a series of small but substantial towns en route to the division's objective for linkup with VII Corps. Over a period of five days, October 2–7, the two infantry regiments, augmented by reinforcements from the division's 120th Regiment, made slow but steady progress. The Germans opposed every step of the 30th Division's advance and each successful American attack was met with a focused German counterattack. General Köchling, the commander of LXXXI Corps, supported by field marshals Model and von Rundstedt, used every available unit in the corps sector to attempt to stop and reverse the American advance. All three of the understrength assault-gun brigades in the corps were used to counterattack the Americans, including the heavy King Tiger tanks of the 506th Heavy Tank Battalion. Infantry battalions were withdrawn from both north and south of the 30th Division penetration to help contain the US attack. An entire infantry regiment and six powerful antitank guns were pulled from Aachen itself to reinforce the forces fighting the 30th Division attack. In addition, the Germans assembled massive amounts of artillery to continually pound the American forward positions and the Wurm River crossing sites.

The Americans met each German counterattack, and the XIX Corps committed the 2nd Armored Division in support of the 30th Division in order to keep the 30th Division's attack moving and to protect the lengthening north flank of the division. By October 7, the 30th Division had secured Alsdorf and the southern regiment was poised 3 miles from the objective of Wurselen. The German LXXXI Corps had expended all of its resources in its unsuccessful effort to stop XIX Corps' attack. At that point in the battle the US VII Corps launched its attack.

By October 7, most of the German LXXXI Corps' reserves were fully committed to the battle. This included all of the mobile elements from the assault-gun brigades, the 108th Panzer Brigade, and the 506th Heavy Tank Battalion. These were impressive formations on paper, but only actually fielded 22 assault guns, four heavy Mark VI (Tiger) tanks, and seven medium Mark V (Panther) tanks. Not an inconsequential force, but only a fraction of what the unit titles represented. It was roughly the size of a weak American armored combat command. On October 5, von Rundstedt released his theater reserves, the rebuilt 116th Panzer Division and the 3rd Panzer Grenadier Division, both divisions under command of the I SS Panzer Corps headquarters, to enter the Aachen battle. The panzer division, though not at full strength, was equipped with 41 Mark IV and V medium tanks. Both divisions had their full complement of infantry, artillery, and antitank guns. It was a significant counterattack force but would take several days to enter the battle.

On October 7, the VII Corps' 1st Infantry Division occupied positions on the west, south, and east sides of Aachen. The Germans were supplying the city garrison along two highways which entered the city from the north. When the 30th Division captured Alsdorf on October 7 they captured one of the two highways leading into Aachen, leaving the German LXXXI Corps a single line of communications and supply into the city. The 1st Infantry Division was arrayed with all three of its regiments on line over a 12-mile front. From east to west the regiments of the division were aligned with the 16th Infantry Regiment west of Stolberg, the 18th Regiment in the suburbs just east of Aachen proper, and the 26th Regiment bending the line south along the perimeter of the city. The 1st Division's line was filled south and west of the city by 1106th Combat Engineer Group whose engineer battalions were in the line occupying foxholes as infantry.

In the darkness of the morning of October 8, the 18th Regiment spearheaded the 1st Division's attack to complete the encirclement of Aachen. The 16th Regiment would guard the flank of the 18th Regiment and link the division to the 3rd Armored Division defending further east in Stolberg. The 26th Regiment's 1st and 2nd battalions would remain in position facing downtown Aachen. The 18th Regiment's objective was a series of three hills which dominated the approach into Aachen. The attacking companies were led by special assault squads armed with flamethrowers, bangalore torpedoes, and explosive satchel charges, and specifically trained to attack German pillboxes and bunkers. In addition, a company of mobile tank destroyers and a battery of self-propelled artillery guns supported the regiment by taking the bunkers under direct fire as the assault teams closed in. Eleven artillery battalions fired in support of the assault. In 48 hours the regiment succeeded in taking all of its objectives with very few casualties. The assault teams, supported by fire from tanks, tank destroyers and direct fire artillery, closed in on the bunkers under the protection of a heavy artillery barrage. As soon as the artillery lifted, the bunkers were attacked before the defenders could recover. In this manner the first two objectives were taken. The final hill was captured by a night assault during which the US infantry infiltrated around the German bunkers and occupied the crest of the hill in darkness. The next morning the Americans mopped up the German positions from the rear. By October 10, the 18th Regiment was firmly in position north of Aachen and awaiting the linkup with 30th Division attacking south from the north. The attacks of the 1st Infantry Division left only one narrow corridor into Aachen in German hands. As the 18th Regiment consolidated its new positions,

CONCRETE HELL

the Germans ordered the theater reserves, the 116th Panzer Division and 3rd Panzer Grenadier Division, to counterattack at Aachen.

The German reserves began positioning for their counterattack on October 10. The first attack took place on that day against the 30th Division, and included elements of the 116th Panzer. By October 15, the 3rd Panzer Grenadier was in position to attack. The attack came early in the morning and was not aimed directly at the 18th Regiment but further east, at the left flank of the 16th Regiment which had not participated in the attack to close the circle and was therefore rested and in good defensive positions. The Germans attacked in the early morning with two Panzer Grenadier regiments supported by 10–15 Tiger tanks against a single US infantry battalion of the 16th Regiment. However, the Americans were prepared and as the German infantry advanced across open ground, six American artillery battalions laid down a preplanned barrage on the exposed infantry. The artillery stopped the German infantry but the Tiger tanks rolled into the American positions and began firing on the foxholes from point-blank range. American artillery continued to pour into the German attackers as well as work back into the supporting positions preventing reinforcement and the bringing forward of supplies and ammunition. The US artillery also fired on several of its own company positions, while the infantry hugged the bottom of their foxholes, to prevent the Germans from overrunning the battalion. Air support arrived in the form of a squadron of P-47 fighter bombers in the early afternoon. The aircraft strafed the exposed German troops and finally broke the German attack. Though the American infantry could do little to stop the German tanks, the American artillery completely demolished the German infantry attacks and the German tanks were loath to advance without infantry support. That night the Germans attacked again with the same result. The attacks were broken up by heavy artillery fire even as they reached the US positions and the infantry fought hand to hand. By October 16, the 3rd Panzer Grenadier division had lost a third of its strength in attacking the lone US battalion and withdrew to regroup. Thus ended the most dangerous threat to the eastern US positions.

As the 1st Infantry Division attacked and then defended against the German counterattack, the 30th Division began its attack south from Alsdorf to link up with the 1st Division. The division attacked with all three regiments on line. The 117th Regiment in the north attacked to further establish the northern flank and protect the regiments further south. The 120th Regiment in the center attacked to secure high ground northeast of Wurselen and thus dominate approaches to the town from the north and east. The attack of the 120th would support the attack of the 119th Regiment which would attack southeast into the northern part of Wurselen, the division objective. Control of Wurselen would effectively close the last route into Aachen and put the 30th Division approximately a mile from the westernmost element of the 1st Division's 18th Regiment. Patrols would seal the linkup and close off German access to Aachen.

The attack to link up began inauspiciously on October 8 when the northern 117th Regiment attacked headlong into the German counterattack made by Mobile Group von Fritzschen, a hastily assembled but potent organization formed by LXXXI Corps around the 108th Panzer Brigade. The German force included numerous halftracks, several infantry battalions, Panzer IVs and Vs of the brigade, and Tiger tanks of the ubiquitous 506th Heavy Tank battalion. The objective of the mobile group was to recapture Alsdorf. Though the Germans were beaten back with severe losses by the 117th Regiment, they were successful in stopping the attack of the 117th Regiment. During the night the German infantry reverted to the defense, the 506th Tiger tanks moved south to join the attack against the 1st Infantry Division on the opposite side of Aachen, and the 108th Panzer Brigade moved south to continue the attack to expand the corridor into Aachen. On October 9, the 108th Panzer Brigade attacked again but ran into the attack of the 120th Infantry Regiment in the center of the 30th Division line. The Germans successfully blocked the American attack and seized the town of Bardenberg.

The German attack that seized Bardenberg on October 9 caused great concern in the 30th Division because it effectively isolated two battalions of the 119th Infantry Regiment which had previously secured the northern portion of the division's objective, Wurselen. On October 10, the 119th Infantry attacked to retake Bardenberg but were unsuccessful in a daylong fight with German panzers and halftracks in the town. Meanwhile the 120th Regiment captured the road leading into the town, effectively isolating the German forces. At night the Americans withdrew from the edges of Bardenberg to allow American artillery to bombard the town. The next day a fresh American infantry battalion attacked the town and in a daylong fight captured it, in the process destroying 16 German halftracks and six tanks. The fighting in Bardenberg absorbed all of the reserves of the 30th Division and on the same day division intelligence reported identifying elements of the 116th Panzer Division in the area.

General Leland S. Hobbs was justifiably concerned with his division completely committed, no reserves, soldiers tired after ten days of continuous offensive operations, and a fresh German panzer division in the area. The general ordered his center and northern regiments to halt and defend, and determined to focus the division's efforts on the attack to secure the primary objective at Wurselen.

On the morning of October 12, the 30th Division's attack on Wurselen had not even begun when another German counterattack hit the division. This attack was led by the panzergrenadier regiment of the 116th Panzer Division, but also included an infantry battalion of the 246th Volksgrenadier Division in Aachen, elements of the 1st SS Panzer Division (Kampfgruppe Diefenthal), remnants of 108th Panzer Brigade, and Tiger tanks of the 506th Heavy Tank Battalion, all under the control of the I SS Panzer Corps which took over responsibility of the northern German defense against the 30th Infantry Division from the LXXXI Corps. Indications to the US XIX Corps commander, General Charles H. Corlett, were that the 30th Division might be fighting two panzer divisions. All throughout October 12, the regiments of the 30th Division successfully fended off the German attacks with the help of supporting artillery and fighter-bombers.

The 30th Division resumed the attack through Wurselen on October 13 and made only very limited progress for three days. The town was defended by the 60th Panzergrenadier Regiment of the 116th Panzer Division supported by the division reconnaissance battalion and the engineer battalion as well as numerous small detachments of panzers. The American attack was on such a narrow front that the German defensive concentration was very effective and in three days the Americans barely advanced 1,000 yards. Frustrated with the slow pace of the attack through Wurselen, on October 16 the 30th Division opened a new attack, this time along the banks of the Wurm River. The attack, aided by diversions all along the 30th Division line, made rapid progress and at 4.15pm a patrol from the 119th Regiment linked up with the 1st Infantry Division, isolating the German garrison in Aachen.

For most of the time that the two-week battle over access to Aachen raged around the city, things inside the city were relatively quiet. As the Germans and Americans traded attack and counterattack outside the city, over 5,000 defenders of the 246th Volksgrenadier Division under Colonel Gerhardt Wilck waited in the center of the city for the American assault. Wilck's force was almost entirely infantry but he did have other arms to assist in the defense including five Mark IV tanks, and over 30 artillery pieces. In addition he had access to several battalions of artillery support outside of the city. Wilck's infantry varied greatly in quality. They included fortress garrison units and policemen who possessed minimum combat skills, as well as a company of German paratroopers and a battalion of SS panzergrenadiers. The latter two organizations were the best infantry found in the German army. Wilck's force had ample time to set up their defense and was not surprised when the Americans began their attack.

The American forces designated for the attack into Aachen were the 1st and 2nd battalions of the 26th Infantry Regiment, 1st Infantry Division. On October 10, as the 30th Division began to make what was thought to be a quick attack to link up with the 1st Division and complete the isolation of the city, the VII Corps commander ordered that the city garrison be given a surrender ultimatum. This document, issued by General Clarence Huebner, commander of the 1st Division, promised the destruction of the city if it was not surrendered within 24 hours. On October 11, the time in the American ultimatum passed and US artillery bombardment and air strikes on the city commenced. For an entire day the bombardment continued, with over 100 guns firing over 500 tons of ammunition into the city. On October 12, the attack on the city center commenced with the 3rd Battalion, 26th Infantry (3/26) attacking on the right, and the following day the 2nd Battalion (2/26) attacked on the left. The objective of 3/26 was to cover the right flank of 2/26 and clear the industrial areas on the north side of the city. The 2/26 had the mission of attacking straight into the heart of the city center across a significant frontage of 2,000 yards filled with destroyed and partly destroyed buildings, each of which had to be cleared by the infantry. It would be a slow, systematic attack.

Prior to beginning the attack, the American commanders analyzed the situation and identified four challenges: high ammunition expenditures; command and control; thousands of civilians in the combat zone; and maximizing armor support without losing too many tanks. The ammunition problem was solved by building up battalion ammunition caches close to the assault positions so that resupply would be readily available during the attack. The command and control problem was solved by developing a specific map code where each major building and street intersection was assigned a unique code so that units could provide quick pinpoint information regarding where they were and where they needed artillery fire. The problem of civilians was answered by deciding to evacuate the entire civilian population as the units advanced through the city. This solved multiple problems: it prevented enemy combatants from hiding within the civilian population; it reduced the attacking unit's administrative burden of dealing with the population; it reduced the possibility of the population interfering with operations; and it provided maximum protection to the population once they came under American control. The attackers planned to reduce the vulnerabilities of the American tanks by minimizing the exposure of the tanks on the major city streets. The idea was to move the tanks down side streets whenever possible, keep the infantry in close proximity of the tanks, use buildings as cover for the tanks whenever possible (firing around building corners), and finally, suppressing all enemy positions by fire whenever the tanks had to move from one firing position to another.

The Americans also adjusted their combat organization specifically for the fight in the city. In 2/26, which planned for the attack into the city central, the commander reorganized his battalion to create three self-contained assault companies. The battalion broke up its heavy weapons company and was reinforced with antitank guns from the regiment's antitank company, and distributed these capabilities among the three infantry rifle companies: each company was provided with two additional 57mm antitank cannons, two heavy machine guns, two bazooka teams, and a flamethrower. The battalion's attached armored support was likewise distributed among the assault companies: each company was assigned three tanks or self-propelled tank destroyers, which were then allocated, one to each of the company's platoons. The battalion planned to attack with all three companies and no reserve. Any reserve would have to be provided by higher headquarters.

The attack technique of the American battalions going into Aachen was represented by the philosophy of 2/26 commander, Lieutenant Colonel Derrill Daniel, who told his subordinates to "knock them all down." The basic philosophy of the battalion was to use firepower to destroy the enemy before they had to clear buildings and engage in a short-range infantry fight. Collateral damage to buildings was not a consideration in the fight, and civilian casualties were only a secondary consideration. The Americans were perfectly content to knock a building down on top of its defenders if that prevented American casualties.

By October 15, three days after beginning the assault, the two American battalions in the attack had battered their way deep into the city. American infantry avoided the streets and instead burrowed their way from building to adjacent building through the building or basement walls. American armor moved steadily down the streets but only stopped in areas protected by buildings and within a surrounding screen of American infantry support. German handheld antitank weapons, *panzerfausts*, were very effective against the unwary tank that exposed itself. The Americans found that many German bunkers, and even some buildings, were relatively impervious to the tank fire supporting the infantry. To increase the fire support to the infantry, both American battalions brought forward 155mm self-propelled artillery guns. These proved to be incredible psychological weapons as well as being capable of bringing down a multistory apartment building with a single round. In some cases just the threat of using the artillery gun on a position was sufficient to induce the Germans to surrender.

Offensive operations inside the city were delayed on October 15 as the 1st Division confronted the 3rd Panzer Grenadier Division counterattack. On October 16, the 30th and 1st Infantry Divisions isolated the city. The attack resumed again on October 18, in the pattern that existed before. The two American battalions methodically moved from objective to objective using a combination of artillery, mortar, machine-gun, and tank fire to suppress the Germans prior to a rapid infantry assault. Both battalions were unhurried in their operations and took time to methodically clear each objective as it was won. This included clearing underground sewer systems and conducting room-to-room searches for enemy who had remained behind. The 26th Infantry was joined in the Aachen battle by a two-battalion task force of the 3rd Armored Division attacking on the north flank of the 3/26 Infantry, and a single battalion of the 28th Infantry Division filling the growing gap between the advancing 2/26 and the 1106th Engineer Group. On October 18 and 19 the relentless advance continued, block by block, objective by objective. On the 19th the German defenses began to crumble as the German troops recognized the inevitable end and surrenders increased dramatically. By October 20 the city center and the northern zone of the city had been taken and the pace of the American attack increased. The only remaining resistance existed in the western and southwestern suburbs, areas low on the Americans' priority list of objectives. Finally, on October 21, Colonel Wilck, against Hitler's orders to resist, surrendered his headquarters and all German troops under his command, just prior to an assault by 3/26.

The US Army took 19 days to capture Aachen and its 20,000 remaining inhabitants. The 30th and the 1st US Infantry Divisions captured approximately 12,000 prisoners. Though no accurate count of German casualties was possible, they were certainly in the area of 15,000 in addition to those taken prisoner – casualties in the 3rd Panzer Grenadier Division alone were at least 3,000. Over 20 different German infantry and panzer battalions were used in futile counterattacks to retake lost ground and push the Americans back across the Wurm River. During the battle the US artillery fired an average of 9,300 artillery rounds a day and the Germans were estimated to have used 4,500 rounds a day. American losses were significant: the 30th Division suffered approximately 3,000 casualties in 19 days of combat, roughly 20 percent of the division strength but almost a third of the division's infantry strength. Aachen was an important battle in which, ironically, both sides achieved their objectives. The Germans had managed to keep the Americans from capturing the city for almost three weeks, until nearly the end of October, and protected their ability to stage for the coming counteroffensive – the Battle of the Bulge. The Americans were able to take the city, breach the West Wall, and secure a start position for their final offensive into Germany and across the Rhine River.

American Tactics

Aachen demonstrated and validated many important lessons regarding conventional urban combat. Many of the issues illustrated at Aachen were identical to characteristics of urban warfare highlighted in the earlier Stalingrad battle. Aachen validated the important role of the fight outside the city to the fight inside the city; like Stalingrad, the decisive operations occurred well outside the city, making the final reduction of the city center somewhat anticlimactic. The battle validated the critical role of armor in urban warfare – tanks were a key element in all operations. The US infantry always attacked with tank support. The only serious threats to US domination of the battlefield came from the various German armor units thrust into the battle by the German LXXXI Corps. The Tiger tanks of the 506th Heavy Tank Battalion were a dangerous nemesis. The most serious German counterattacks against the American attack were by the mobile formations of the I SS Panzer Corps.

Aachen also illustrated the continued necessity for tailoring unit organizations for urban combat at the lowest levels. The squad-level bunker-assault teams, and the combined-arms task forces built on the infantry companies of 2/26 were good representations of the benefits of building units tailored for the battle before the battle. Like the Germans and Soviets on the Eastern Front, the Americans understood that combined-arms assault teams were the required organization for urban combat. In Aachen the US infantry platoons advanced from one building to the next only after a preparatory barrage of artillery or mortars. The infantrymen led, supported closely by flamethrowers and tanks. The entire force avoided the open streets as much as possible. An important concern was not fretting away the numbers of the assault platoons by requiring them to occupy and guard the houses they captured. Other supporting arms, antitank guns, machine-gun crews, and even headquarters personnel, were dropped off by the advancing assault troops to guard captured buildings against reoccupation by the Germans.

Aachen confirmed the critical role of artillery in urban combat. The experienced American infantry assaulted defended positions close behind their supporting artillery barrage. A well-timed artillery attack did not kill many defenders but it allowed the attackers to close in on the building or bunker and assault it while the defenders sheltered from the barrage. American artillery, unlike Soviet artillery, and to a much greater degree than German, was responsive to forward observers and could quickly mass fire at any designated point within range. Thus, even small-scale assaults could be preceded by accurate artillery barrages. Aachen also demonstrated the fantastic effects that artillery in a direct-fire role could achieve. The employment of the self-propelled 155mm guns in support of the infantry demonstrated that those effects were not only material but psychological.

Aachen validated several characteristics of urban warfare which were valid regardless of what army was participating in the battle. These included the need for tanks, the requirement to use small combined-arms assault teams, the amount of time necessary to capture a city from a skilled and determined enemy, and the important role of the battles outside the city to ensure success inside the city. It also identified some aspects of urban warfare which were unique to American forces. American forces tended to substitute firepower for manpower, and though they did not change their operating methods, they did make plans for the civilian population even though it was considered hostile.

One of the uniquely American characteristics was the substitution whenever possible of firepower for manpower. The US forces made liberal use of artillery and airpower whenever possible. This permitted the Americans to conduct very intensive offensive operations without a major numerical advantage in infantry. Although American infantry did not outnumber their adversary, they made up for numerical parity with lavish quantities of artillery and airpower and virtually limitless supplies of munitions. This not only reduced the number of infantry required, it also reduced the number of casualties incurred by the attacking force.

The liberal use of firepower by the Americans would also seem to equate to a disregard for civilian casualties equivalent to the attitudes of the Germans and Soviets on the Eastern Front, but this was not the case. Though the Americans did not change their operational approach to account for civilian casualties, they made a major effort to remove civilians from the battle area once they came under American control. Civil Affairs specialists were positioned immediately behind the battle area to take charge of the civilian population, process it, and evacuate the population to camps under army control. Thus, though US forces in Aachen placed concern for enemy civilian casualties as a lower priority than mission accomplishment, it was still a priority of the command.

When the 26th Infantry Regiment assaulted Aachen on October 13, the two infantry battalions in the attack were outnumbered by Colonel Wilck's defenders at least three to one. Despite all the advantages that the Americans had in airpower, the odds on the ground should have favored the German defense. That the American infantry were successful, and at a relatively low cost in casualties, was astounding. The success of the attack can be attributed to the application of a variety of urban fighting techniques, blended in a near-perfect combination by the soldiers of the US 2nd Armored Division, and 30th and 1st Infantry Divisions with their supporting units. Aachen demonstrated that it was very possible to capture a relatively large urban area, heavily defended by good-quality troops, with a comparatively small number of infantry.

Comparison with Stalingrad

The major difference between the American approach to Aachen and the German approach to Stalingrad was the use of maneuver to set favorable conditions for urban battle. The Americans fought and maneuvered outside of the city to isolate the city from support before reducing it. This greatly reduced the burden on the battalions that eventually assaulted the city center. Because the city was isolated, the Americans could choose to attack the city from any number of directions. In contrast, the Germans had to defend everywhere. Because the city was isolated, the Americans could attack the city from the east, when the city's defenses were designed to protect from attacks from the west. Finally, because the city was isolated, the psychological stress on the defenders was significantly greater than on the attackers. These were all advantages that the Americans had at Aachen, and that the Germans did not have at Stalingrad. This aspect of the American approach to Aachen demonstrated the ideal operational conditions for city fighting: don't fight for the city until you control access to the city. Despite the simplicity of this concept, subsequent chapters will show that its application is not always obvious to modern armies, or easy for them to achieve.

CHAPTER 4
URBAN WARFARE FROM THE SEA
Inchon and Seoul, 1950

After World War II the American military jettisoned the vast bulk of the superb ground force that had fought and won the war. By 1950 that force was a hollow shell of its former self. The only remaining remnants of the combat-experienced ground forces were the non-commissioned officer and officer leadership of the skeleton divisions that remained in the force. The bulk of the force in 1950 was draftees with no experience, and in some cases their equipment wasn't even the best of the World War II equipment. In the late summer of 1950, this force found itself in the midst of another large-scale urban battle against a wholly unanticipated foe in a theater of operations that many Americans had never heard of and would have a hard time finding on a map.

A Hot Cold War

In June 1950 the forces of Communist North Korea launched a surprise attack on the forces of South Korea. The military forces of the North, well trained and equipped by the Soviet Union, vastly outnumbered those of the South. In addition, though there were US Army advisors with the Republic of Korea's (ROK) military, the US vision for the ROK Army (ROKA) was as a large military police force; which meant that there were no heavy weapons, tanks, heavy artillery or antitank weapons among the small South Korean force. Because of this, and the surprise of the attack, the North Korea People's Army (KPA) was very successful, and in just six weeks managed to push the combined South Korean and American defenders back to a small perimeter at the toe of Korea around the important port city of Pusan.

At the end of the first week of the surprise attack, the US military entered the war decisively on the side of South Korea. The most effective and responsive weapon that the US had in Asia was the US Air Force, and air attacks against the advancing North Korean columns began on June 27. However, air attacks could slow, but not stop the North Korean advance. Therefore, the US Eighth Army, stationed in Japan, began to deploy to Korea. The problem was that the Eighth Army in 1950 was a shadow of the great American army that had fought its way across the Pacific Ocean under General Douglas MacArthur during World War II. Still under MacArthur's command – MacArthur was the Supreme Commander Allied Powers in Japan, and Commander US Forces Far East – the Eighth Army was greatly debilitated by post-World War II defense cuts. The Eighth Army had four divisions organized into two corps. However, each of the army's infantry divisions comprised only two regiments instead of the doctrinal three. Likewise, each regiment had only two battalions, and each battalion only two companies. Similarly, division artillery was reduced to two battalions, all the medium and heavy artillery had been removed from the force at all levels, and each battalion only had two firing batteries of light howitzers. The medium-tank battalions supporting each infantry division was similarly reduced to light-tank battalions of only two companies each. Finally, if the numbers alone were not bad enough, budget and facility constraints greatly inhibited training, leaving the units in a poor state of readiness. Though a formidable force on paper, the Eighth Army and all its subordinate forces were in reality only about 50 percent as capable as the World War II version of the army. This army was thrown as fast as possible into the path of the advancing North Koreans.

General Walton Walker commanded the combined US and South Korean armies on the peninsula. In the last weeks of August 1950 he managed to stem the North Korean onslaught around the city of Pusan. However, in the first eight weeks of the war the Communists captured over 80 percent of the land of South Korea. Clearly, Walker and his commander, General Douglas MacArthur, could not sit passively on the defensive. As early as the end of July, as Walker fought desperately to maintain a toehold in Korea, General MacArthur was thinking in terms of a counterstroke.

End Run to Seoul

MacArthur, in keeping with the operational thinking he had developed during the Pacific campaign of World War II, was keen to avoid the hard campaign that a counterattack back up the mountainous Korean peninsula would entail. He set his staff to investigating the various possibilities of an amphibious operation to bypass the major North Korean forces and land in their rear. This would avoid the tremendous casualties of a frontal assault, save invaluable time, and guarantee the complete destruction of the bulk of the North Korean army. The only problem was there was no suitable landing site for a major amphibious thrust along Korea's very formidable coastline. The closest that the planners could identify was the city of Inchon on Korea's west coast.

The command faced several significant problems executing a major amphibious assault at Inchon. These included the difficulty of the local tides, lack of suitable beaches, the difficulty of achieving surprise, and a shortage of trained troops available. MacArthur carefully considered the problems but also weighed the points in Inchon's favor. The difficulty of the operation would lend itself to surprise and thus lessen opposition to the landing. Inchon's geographic position put it close to Seoul. Thus, a successful landing at Inchon could easily lead to a quick conquest of Seoul. Seoul was MacArthur's ultimate objective. The city's geographic location put it astride the only important north–south maneuver corridor on the peninsula. Control of Seoul meant control of South Korea. More important than its position, which was extremely important, was that Seoul was also the capital city of South Korea. To many, the loss of Seoul had represented losing the war in the first week: recapturing Seoul represented snatching victory from apparent defeat. MacArthur recognized that the political and psychological importance of Seoul were beyond measure. MacArthur understood that the value of Seoul outweighed the operational risks inherent in an amphibious assault and therefore determined that the operation proceed over the objections of key subordinates and experts on amphibious operations.

To execute the operation to capture Seoul the Americans assembled a new unit, separate from the US Eighth Army fighting the battle at Pusan. This new unit, X Corps, was tailored for the amphibious operation, and reported not to Eighth Army, but directly to General

Map 4.1 The Inchon Landings, September 1950

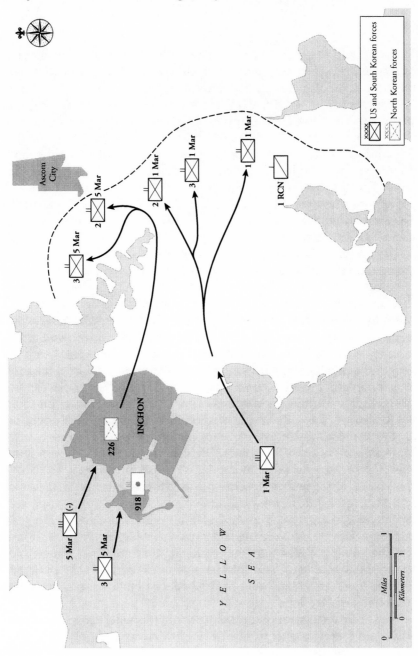

MacArthur's Far East Command. The two major subcomponents of the X Corps were the 1st US Marine Division, and the US Army 7th Infantry Division, all under the X Corps commander, Major General Edward Almond. In addition to the two infantry divisions, the corps had the direct support of the Marine Air Wing of the 1st Marine Division. It also included two ROK military units: the ROK Marine Regiment attached to the 1st Marine Division, and the ROK 1st Infantry Regiment attached to the 7th Infantry Division. These latter two units were critical for a variety of reasons, not the least of which was to improve the flagging prestige and morale of the ROK military, and also to highlight the important political objectives which were an important goal of the operation.

Seoul was a city of over a million people when the war broke out – the fifth largest urban population in Asia. It was the ancient capital of the Korean peninsula and thus was extremely important to both North Korea (the Democratic People's Republic of Korea – DPRK) and to South Korea. As the North Korean forces poured across the border in the summer of 1950, the population had panicked and attempted to flee. However, over a million people – largely without automotive transportation – cannot quickly pick up and move. So, as the Americans began to execute operations to recapture the capital, there were hundreds of thousands of South Korean civilians still living in Seoul under the occupation rule of North Korea.

The initial landing area at Inchon was opposed by about 2,000 troops. The KPA had a total of about 16,000 troops in the Inchon–Seoul area. This was a relatively light defensive force given the area's strategic importance, but it reflected the North Korean high command's focus on the battles in the south around the Pusan perimeter. In addition to the 2,000 troops positioned in the area of Inchon, another 2,000 troops of the 87th Infantry Regiment were positioned to defend the major suburb of Seoul at Yongdungpo. Additionally, Seoul was garrisoned and defended by the Seoul Defense Division, a unit of approximately 10,000 troops. The remainder of the initial KPA forces around the capital were various support units. Not part of the Seoul garrison, but able to respond quickly to any threat to the city or an amphibious landing, was the KPA's theater reserve, the 105th Tank Division, equipped with T-34/85 tanks. This unit was the premier unit of the KPA, equipped with over 50 tanks, supporting artillery, and antitank and infantry subunits. It was refitting near Seoul when the landings at Inchon occurred.

The March to Seoul

On September 15, the 1st Marine Division landed two regimental combat teams (RCTs), the 1st and the 5th Marine Regiments, south and north of the city of Inchon respectively. The landings, unusually, took place late in the afternoon, due to the tides. The two regiments secured their initial objectives quickly, overcoming relatively light resistance in Inchon itself. The North Korean defenders were surprised, shocked by the pre-invasion naval and air bombardment, and gave up all resistance during the night. The next day the 5th Marines marched through the abandoned city of Inchon to link up with the 1st Marines and begin the 18-mile movement to the capital of Seoul. The 1st Marines were directed to advance directly west with the objective of securing Yongdungpo, the major suburb of Seoul on the west bank of the Han River. The 5th Marines veered north to secure Kimpo Airfield, the major air terminal of the capital and the largest and most modern airfield on the peninsula, also on the west side of the river.

By September 17, the 5th Marines were in position to attack Kimpo Airfield. Fighting through scattered North Korean strongpoints, the RCT secured the southern edge of the airfield by the end of the day. To the south the 1st RCT fought its way through a series of North Korean roadblocks on the main Inchon–Seoul highway. By nightfall the 1st RCT had advanced about two miles.

During the night the North Koreans defending Kimpo staged several small-scale counterattacks against the Marines, all of which were beaten off successfully. In the morning of September 18 the Marines advanced across the airfield against light resistance and by 10am the airfield and surrounding villages were secure. On September 18 the first troops of X Corps' 7th Infantry Division began to land at Inchon. Their mission was securing the major highway south of Seoul that was the lifeline of the North Korean army fighting desperately at Pusan.

As the Marines closed in on the west bank of the Han River north of Seoul, the plan to recapture the city developed. The first phase of the plan involved securing a bridgehead on the east bank and bringing the entire west bank under control of the Americans. On September 20, the 5th Marine RCT crossed the Han north of Seoul and then wheeled right and began to attack the city from the north to the south. Simultaneously the 1st RCT entered Yongdungpo and began a building by building attack to clear the west bank of the Han. By September 23, the 1st RCT had accomplished its mission and was prepared to join the 5th Marines on the east bank.

The river assault of the 5th RCT was only lightly opposed. The Marines were mounted in LVTs (Landing Vehicles Tracked), literally amphibious armored personal carriers. These vehicles and crews were provided by the Marine 1st Amphibious Tractor Battalion, and the US Army's 56th Amphibious Tractor Company. In addition, some Marines at Inchon and at the crossing of the Han River rode in army DUKW amphibious trucks of the 1st Amphibious Truck Company. Importantly, X Corps had no assault-bridging capability, so they could not put a military bridge over the Han. This meant that it was very time-consuming to move the important M-26 tanks of the 1st Marine Tank Battalion across the river to support the 5th RCT. Finally, as the plan was fashioned, four RCTs would participate in the battle of Seoul, each attacking in a set sequence. The sequencing of these attacks was all determined by the requirement that all four RCTs be moved across the river by the same single LVT battalion. Thus, the Han River obstacle shaped the assault on Seoul more than any other single factor.

The intent of the attack of the 5th RCT was to get behind the defenses of Seoul as the assumption was that the North Korean forces would be oriented south and southwest towards the approaches directly from Inchon. What the planners of the operation failed to account for was that the area northwest of Seoul was a former Japanese army training area, and had been improved by the South Korean army as a defensive line, so the positions were oriented north against attack from North Korea. Those prepared defensive positions were still in place and the North Korean army occupied them in defense against the attack of the 5th RCT. In addition, the North Korean army moved approximately 10,000 troops into these positions just prior to the Marines crossing the Han. Thus, though the 5th RCT covered 4 miles on the afternoon of river crossing, September 20, it then ran into stiff resistance. It would take the Marines five more days to fight their way across the last four miles of ridges between their landing site and Seoul.

On September 24, the 1st RCT crossed the river, assaulting directly from Yongdungpo into the heart of the city. With three battalions abreast, the 1st RCT attacked directly east through a series of roadblock barricades that the North Koreans had constructed on the major thoroughfares through the city. The 5th RCT wheeled left, and advanced on the left flank of the 1st RCT as both Marine units systematically cleared barricades, buildings, culverts, and sewers. Both regiments used their M-26 Pershing tanks extensively. Typically a single tank led a Marine infantry platoon as it systematically cleared the interiors of the buildings. The Marine tanks were virtually unstoppable, and easily brushed aside North Korean infantry, and also made short work of a few Soviet-built T-34/85 tanks found in the city.

On September 25, two additional regiments entered the battle for Seoul. One was the 32nd Infantry Regiment of the US Army's 7th Infantry Division. The other was the 1st ROK Infantry Regiment, attached to the 7th Infantry Division. These two regiments, using the same LVTs as the 1st and 5th RCTs, crossed the Han River into the southern part of Seoul. Thus by September 25, the four allied regiments were on line advancing across Seoul. On the night of September 25–26, the North Korean army mounted a last major counterattack against the 5th, 1st, and 32nd Regiments. The attack against the 1st Marines was led by T-34 tanks and self-propelled assault guns. In the morning the two Marine regiments counted almost 500 enemy dead as well as nine destroyed armored vehicles and eight antitank guns in front of their positions. The steady advance of the three major regiments, supported by the 17th ROK Army Regiment, continued on September 26, and on September 27 the major portion of the city was cleared of communist forces and the X Corps lead elements were pursuing the enemy north through the mountains toward the 38th parallel. It had required 12 days for the X Corps to achieve its objective after landing at Inchon.

The only other major combat formation involved in the battle for Seoul was the 7th Marine Regiment of the 1st Marine Division. This regiment was still en route to Korea when the initial Inchon landings occurred. It landed at Inchon on September 21. The 7th Marines' role in the Seoul operation was to isolate the city and prevent North Korean forces from escaping the city to the northeast. As the 5th Marines attacked into the city from the north the 7th Marines passed behind them and attacked east. Unfortunately, the direction of attack to the east was across numerous valleys divided by very rugged mountains aligned north to south, and the area was virtually unsupported by roads. Thus, though not strongly opposed, the attack proceeded very slowly. It was only on September 28 that the northeast escape routes were closed, and by then some of the best North Korean troops defending Seoul had escaped.

Map 4.2 The Capture of Seoul, September 1950

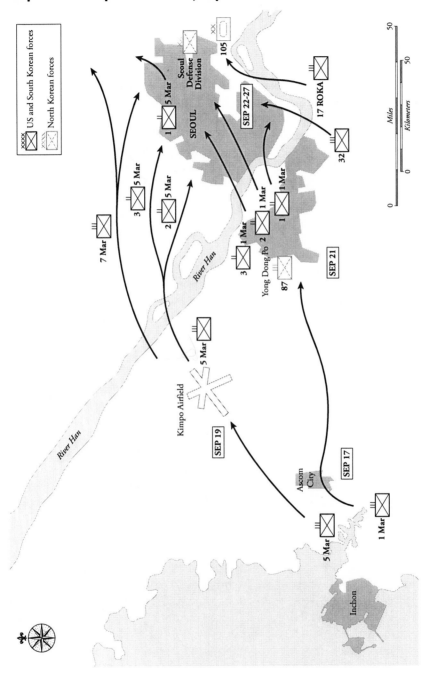

75

On September 29, 1950, General Douglas MacArthur and South Korean president, Syngman Rhee, arrived in the capital and General MacArthur declared the city secure. In fact, significant fighting continued as the American units in the city, aided by South Korean forces, continued to systematically clear buildings and streets. Nonetheless, the city was declared secured exactly 90 days after the outbreak of hostilities. The major portion of the 1st Marine Division moved to the eastern portion of the city and prepared to pursue the North Korean army north. Earlier, on September 26, at Suwon, 30 miles south of Seoul, elements of the US Eighth Army linked up with X Corps' 7th Infantry Division. Between Seoul and Pusan, the North Korean army was completely shattered.

A Fluid Battle

Large urban areas are very difficult objectives to seize except at great cost both in resources and time. The key to the successful capture of a large city, quickly and with minimum expenditure of resources, is to seize it before it is adequately defended. This is extremely difficult to do and can only be accomplished through one of three types of operations: airborne assault; amphibious attack; or a deep rapid armored thrust. General MacArthur recognized that a counteroffensive launched from the Pusan perimeter alone would likely devolve into a long and costly battle of attrition through the Korean mountains, and through numerous large urban areas, including Seoul. The Inchon landing operation, at some significant risk, avoided a war of attrition and resulted in the fall of Seoul in just over 10 days with minimum losses. Unlike most World War II urban battles, the battle for Inchon and Seoul was a battle of maneuver. This was primarily because the attacking force was able to achieve strategic surprise and thus the defender did not have the time to assemble forces and could not establish a comprehensive defense of the entire city area.

The US Marine approach to urban warfare in Seoul was relatively straightforward. Seoul was a huge city which, with Yongdungpo, covered about 80km^2 (30 square miles). Despite having more than 20,000 troops available, the North Korean Army had insufficient manpower to defend a continuous line of buildings. The North Korean forces in the city choose to defend fortified barricades oriented on the major avenues and significant natural and city terrain features. The fight for the city became known as the battle of the barricades. Along the city streets the North Korean army erected barricades, constructed of whatever material the North Koreans could find within the city. This included rubble and dirt-packed rice bags, bricks, household furniture, old cars and buses, and any other obstacle-making device they could find. These were torn down by the US and ROK infantry and engineers, or driven over by US tanks. The Marines developed a standard approach to the barricades: artillery fire on the area followed by mortar fire on the position; machine-gun and bazooka fire to suppress the enemy while engineers cleared mines; and finally, with the mines removed, the tanks moved forward. The powerful US M-26 tanks were often able to simply plow through the assorted debris. With the tanks came the Marine infantry armed with semiautomatic rifles, fixed bayonets, and grenades. Marine scout-sniper teams overwatched all operations and took a deadly toll on any enemy not behind cover. Each barricade was stoutly defended by North Korean infantry supported by antitank guns, machine guns, and snipers; and took about 45 to 60 minutes to reduce. Thus the movement through the metropolis was of necessity slow, but steady.

A potentially major threat to the US operation was the Soviet-built T-34/85 tanks of the North Korean People's Army 105th Tank Division. In the march from Inchon to Seoul, 53 of these lethal machines were thrown into counterattacks against the Marines. These tanks had been extremely effective combat vehicles against the best German armor in World War II just five years before. They also furthered their reputation in the first weeks of the North Korean invasion. However, after the initial encounter, the Marines were completely nonplussed by their arrival on the battlefield. They were easily destroyed by a combination of Marine close air support, Marine M-26 tanks, and antitank weapons. By the time the Marines secured the west bank of the Han River, 48 had been knocked out by the Marines and five were found abandoned. In the battle for Seoul itself, the 1st Tank Battalion destroyed 13 T-34 tanks or Soviet-built self-propelled guns and 56 antitank guns, for the loss of five Pershing tanks and two Shermans (most of the American tank losses were to mines and at least one was lost to one of the frequent attacks by North Korean sappers armed with satchels of explosives). Importantly, North Korean armor was of sufficient strength that it could have completely disrupted the US operation, had the US not enjoyed close air and armor support. Thus, armor and close air support were again proven to be very important factors to successful urban combat.

The relatively small size of the US attacking force was possible due to effective air, naval, armor, and artillery support. The air support of the Marines in the Inchon–Seoul operation was particularly effective and noteworthy. Marine aviation units perfected the art of close air support during the Korean War, beginning in the Inchon–Seoul battles. That support was far more responsive and closely coordinated than that achieved by the Marines in World War II. Six Marine squadrons (four day-fighter and two night-fighters) supported the 1st Marine Division and X Corps during the operation. They were controlled by the 1st Division's 1st Marine Air Wing. They had no other mission other than close air support of the ground forces. Initially the Marines flew in support from two navy escort carriers, the USS *Badoeng Strait* and the USS *Sicily*, but once Kimpo airfield was captured, the five F4U Corsair squadrons and the one F7F Tigercat squadron operated from that base, literally minutes from their targets. Close air support was coordinated by Marine Tactical Air Control Squadron 2, which commanded tactical air control parties (TACP) located in each Marine infantry regiment and battalion headquarters. When the US Army 32nd Infantry Regiment entered the battle for Seoul, a Marine TACP was attached to the regiment to give it the benefit of close air support. During the 33-day campaign, September 7–October 9, the Marine aviation units flew almost 3,000 ground-support sorties, including over a thousand in support of the Army's 7th Division.

Aviation support was critical to the advance from Inchon to Seoul. It was particularly critical to the 5th RCT's difficult attack south on the east side of the Han River. However, once units entered the city proper the use of close air support became increasingly difficult because of the difficulty of identifying the front line from the air and the danger to the friendly civilian population. Still, even as the battle raged inside Seoul, close air support played an important role aiding the advance of the 7th Marine Regiment through the mountains north of Seoul, isolating the city from reinforcements, and destroying KPA units attempting to retreat from the city.

Politics and Urban Warfare

One of the major characteristics of the fight for Seoul was the intense pressure put on the Marine division to capture the city quickly. This pressure was resented by the Marine officers because speed often caused them to take risks with the lives of their Marines. Often this was viewed as General MacArthur placing politics before the tactical considerations of urban combat. However, there were good reasons to take the city quickly. First, the military advantages of cutting off the bulk of the KPA south of Seoul were obvious. Second, and perhaps most important, were the psychological and political advantages to be gained by recapturing the city less than three months after its capture by the KPA in June. The capital of Seoul defined the allied government of the Republic of Korea and restoring that city to allied control was extremely important strategically to the prestige and legitimacy of the South Korean government. MacArthur understood how strategic Seoul was to the South Korean government, as well as to the UN cause and to the US home front, which desperately needed positive war news. Thus, like many important capital cities in warfare, the strategic value of the city was worth the tactical sacrifices necessary to capture it, and capture it quickly.

Another characteristic of the battle for Inchon–Seoul was the integration of South Korean forces into the battle. There is no doubt that South Korean forces were not necessary to the battle. However, General MacArthur insisted that the ROK Marine Regiment and the 17th ROKA Infantry Regiment be integrated into operations and participate in the recapture of Seoul. Again, this insistence demonstrated that the fight for a capital city such as Seoul was as much about perceptions and information operations, as it was about tactics. The role of ROK infantry and Marines in the battle was small, but the prestige incurred by the ROK government was huge, and the battle did much to boost the morale and confidence of the ROK military which eventually would assume the largest burden of combat operations in the war and would prove itself capable of fighting not just the KPA, but also the Chinese Army effectively.

A final characteristic of the campaign for Seoul and the battles for Inchon and Seoul was the nature of the assaulting force. The assault force, X Corps, was a unique organization. Though its composition was strongly influenced by the lack of available forces in the early days of the Korean conflict, it was also uniquely tailored to the needs of modern urban combat. The X Corps was a true joint-service force, and a combined allied force, and thus had capabilities not found in a typical army corps. As a joint force it had unique amphibious, naval support, and close air support capabilities which were all critically necessary to the strategic situation, and the tactical problems involved in the recapture of the Korean cities. The leveraging of the capabilities of air and naval power reduced the need for large numbers of infantry, and reduced the casualties among the attacking US and ROK Marines and infantry. The navy ensured strategic surprise and supported the force logistically, and with naval gunfire. The air component augmented artillery fires, protected the force from North Korean airpower, and helped isolate the urban battlefield. Both air and naval forces provided a psychological boost to the assaulting US and ROK Marines and infantry, and demoralized the KPA defenders. As a combined US and ROK force, X Corps represented the unique political nature of the Korean conflict, and maximized the strategic gains that the recapture of the ROK's capital represented. Neither a single-service corps, nor a completely American corps, could have conducted the operation as effectively, or achieved the same strategic success that the uniquely joint and combined allied X Corps was able to achieve. In many ways X Corps represented an ideal urban fighting organization.

CHAPTER 5

COMPLEX URBAN WARFARE

The Battle for Hue, 1968

Almost 20 years would pass before American military forces found themselves involved in a situation where urban combat skills were again important. Ironically, the next major city fight involving US forces came during the Vietnam War, a war known for its sharp conflicts in the mountains, jungles, and rice paddies. Vietnam was not a war generally associated with urban fighting, but in the winter of 1968, when the North Vietnamese launched the famous Tet Offensive, one of the major objectives of the offensive was to bring the war into the major urban centers of South Vietnam. One of the most decisive, hard fought, and dramatic of the 1968 battles was the battle for the city of Hue which began in the early morning of January 31.

Hue was one of the oldest and most revered cities of Vietnam, North and South. It was the ancient imperial capital of Vietnam, and also the center of the Catholic church of Vietnam. It remained, under the government of the Republic of Vietnam (RVN), the capital of Thua Thien Province. It was South Vietnam's second largest city, covering an area of 67km² (26 square miles), and home to a population of approximately 280,000 people. Hue was a coastal city, positioned where the Perfume River empties into the East China Sea. The river bisected Hue from east to west, dividing it into a northern and southern half. The northern portion of the city was older, and was dominated by the 18th-century Imperial Palace and citadel. The southern portion of the city was more modern and consisted of the main government buildings as well as Hue University. The Perfume River was crossed north to south by two important bridges. One was a railway bridge located in the western portion of the city and the other was a highway bridge supporting Highway One, the primary north–south roadway. Though not a major port, Hue also included a US Navy facility that permitted the offloading of supplies. Because of the bridges, highway, and port, Hue was an important transportation center along the logistics line that connected the major military logistics bases further south and the important military positions such as Kha Shan, north of Hue along the Demilitarized Zone (DMZ) between North and South Vietnam. Though there was no doubt that Hue was an important urban area to the South Vietnamese government because of its size, history, military significance, and governmental role, an agreement between the two opposing governments, the southern Republic of Vietnam and the northern Democratic Republic of Vietnam (DRV), declared Hue an open city that would not be used for military purposes by either side. For this reason, despite some warning that a major North Vietnamese offensive might be looming, the South Vietnamese and American militaries were not overly concerned with defending Hue itself.

The Tet Offensive

Prior to the launching of the Tet Offensive, the American command in South Vietnam, under US Army General William Westmoreland, was satisfied with the progress of the war. The year 1967, the second full year of the major American military commitment to Vietnam, had been a year full of battles. American casualties were high, but intelligence estimates were that the North Vietnamese Army and the Viet Cong had suffered significantly worse. As the year ended the US commander traveled back to the United States to give President Johnson a personal, upbeat assessment. It was thus in December 1967 that General Westmoreland declared that he "could see the light at the end of the tunnel," implying that the end of the war was not far off. Because of this assessment, the Tet Offensive came as a complete strategic surprise to the US and South Vietnam, despite some military indicators of an impending attack.

North Vietnam also recognized that South Vietnamese and American military operations were generally achieving success in their efforts to expel the North Vietnamese military from South Vietnam, and subdue the Viet Cong. Because of this, the DRV determined that the situation in the South would continue to deteriorate unless they made a bold move. General Vo Nguyen Giap, commander of the People's Army of Vietnam (PAVN), received permission from the DRV government to launch a general offensive in the South in 1968, supported by a general uprising of South Vietnamese communists. The PAVN scheduled the offensive to begin during the Tet holiday, a time when much of the South Vietnamese army would be on home leave. The objective was to use a combination of PAVN regular troops, in conjunction with the Viet Cong, to strike at key targets, mostly urban areas, throughout the South. American and South Vietnamese army forces would be destroyed as they counterattacked. Simultaneously, a spontaneous general uprising of the South Vietnamese population against the RVN's government would ensure the destruction of the South Vietnamese government.

The city of Hue was assigned as the objective of the Tri Thien Hue Front command. The North Vietnamese plan to take the city was relatively simple. Viet Cong guerrillas, in civilian garb, would infiltrate the city in the days before the attack. They would observe targets and position themselves for the attack. On the night of the attack, the Viet Cong would spearhead the attack on the civilian targets and join with two battalions of PAVN sappers to attack military and government positions in the city. Two full regiments of PAVN infantry would then flow into the city to prepare it for defense against the inevitable counterattack. A third PAVN infantry regiment had the task of ensuring that the PAVN line of communications into Hue remained secure.

A Battle in Four Phases

The Viet Cong and PAVN launched their attack in the early, dark hours of January 31, 1968. It was timed to coincide with hundreds of other attacks all over South Vietnam, and achieved complete surprise. The initial attacking force, numbering perhaps as many as 10,000 PAVN and Viet Cong troops, captured most of the city with virtually no resistance. The PAVN 6th Regiment entered and secured the Citadel area north of the river aided by Viet Cong in South Vietnamese army uniforms who overwhelmed the Citadel's west gate guard detail. The PAVN 4th Regiment quickly secured the south side of the river. The PAVN troops had received special training in urban fighting and immediately began to dig in and prepare defenses. Outside of the city, the PAVN 5th Regiment set up

Map 5.1 The PAVN Capture of Hue, January 1968

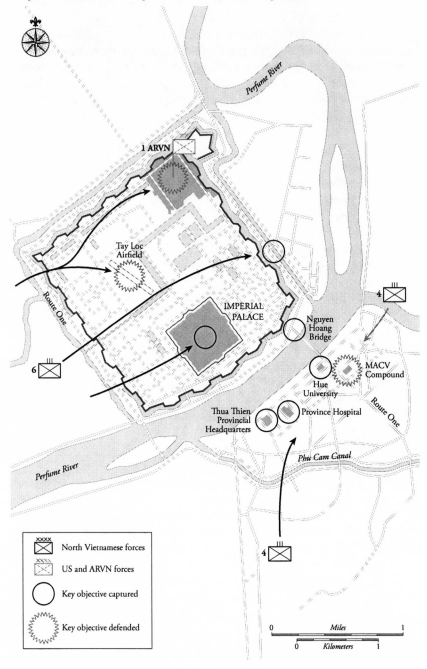

1 ARVN

Tay Loc
Airfield

Route One

IMPERIAL
PALACE

Nguyen
Hoang
Bridge

4

MACV
Compound

Hue
University

Route One

6

Thua Thien
Provincial
Headquarters

Province Hospital

Perfume River

Perfume River

Phu Cam Canal

4

North Vietnamese forces

US and ARVN forces

Key objective captured

Key objective defended

0   Miles   1

0   Kilometers   1

defensive positions to protect the attackers' line of communications and supply into the city. At the same time that regular troops prepared for the inevitable counterattack, a special cadre of political officers moved through the city with a list of several thousand individuals to be placed under arrest.

Though the attack to capture Hue was a remarkable feat of arms that used stealth, intelligence, and boldness to seize the city with almost no fight, the execution of the assault was not flawless. The North Vietnamese had identified literally hundreds of large and small objectives inside the city, but the three most important were the headquarters of the 1st Army of Vietnam (ARVN) Infantry Division in the northeast corner of the Citadel; Tay Loc airfield, also in the citadel just to the north of the Imperial Palace; and the Military Assistance Command Vietnam (MACV) compound, which housed the 1st ARVN Division's American advisors, located on the south side of the river. The commander of the South Vietnamese division, Brigadier General Ngo Quang Truong, had had several indicators of an impending attack and therefore had his division on full alert. His headquarters was fully manned and operating, as were all of his units, although over half of the division's strength had been released on leave for the Tet holiday. General Truong was mistaken in his assumption that the North Vietnamese attack would not be directed at Hue itself, because of the city's unique status and importance. Nonetheless, when the PAVN attack came, Truong's division was alert and ready to respond.

The PAVN 6th Regiment's attack through the Citadel moved rapidly from the southwest to the northeast. Little resistance was met until the North Vietnamese attacked Tay Loc airfield. The airfield was defended by the 1st ARVN Division's reconnaissance company, an all-volunteer elite unit that, though outnumbered, held the airfield against repeated PAVN attacks. The 6th Regiment's assault did not slow at the airfield but rather flowed around it and ran into Truong's alert 1st ARVN headquarters. Like at the airfield, Truong's headquarters troops resisted fiercely inside their walled compound. The PAVN attack had been preceded by a rocket bombardment of the entire city. That bombardment alerted the personnel of the MACV compound on the south side of the city. Thus, when sappers and troops of the PAVN 4th Regiment assaulted the MACV position they were met by a hail of fire from the first of the compound's defenders to get to their positions. A machine gun on top of a 20ft tower, manned by a US Army advisor, mowed down the first wave of attackers.

Similarly, a key bunker occupied by several US Marine advisors was manned and firing to stave off the first assaults on the compound gate. Though both positions were rapidly silenced by the PAVN, they delayed the attack just long enough that the remaining garrison was able to man defensive positions, beat back the attack and inflict severe casualties. Thus, though the PAVN attack was very successful in capturing 95 percent of the city, it failed to capture the three most important military objectives in the city. Although the airfield and two compounds were small failures compared to the wide success of the PAVN almost everywhere else, they were to prove decisive as these positions became the basis of the counterattack to retake the city.

By the morning of January 31, the PAVN was firmly in control of Hue, and PAVN soldiers openly patrolled the streets of South Vietnam's second largest city. Fighting raged at the airfield, while the PAVN were content to bombard the 1st ARVN headquarters and MACV compound with rockets. The ARVN and MACV radioed for reinforcements but all over South Vietnam chaos dominated on the first full day of the Tet Offensive. The requests for assistance were lost in the avalanche of reports that deluged all major headquarters across the country. Slowly, however, a response was formed and the outline of the battle for Hue emerged. The remaining battle would occur in three distinct phases which were related, but generally independent of each other. One battle occurred on the north side of the river between the ARVN and the PAVN 6th Regiment. A second battle occurred on the south side of the river between the PAVN 4th Regiment and US Marines. A third and final battle integral to the operation to recapture the city occurred to the west and north of the city between the PAVN 5th Regiment and elements of the US 1st Cavalry Division.

The Initial American Counterattack

Marine Lieutenant General Robert Cushman III was responsible for American forces in the vicinity of Hue. He was not sure of the situation in Hue but was aware early on January 31 that there was a need for reinforcements in the city. He ordered that Task Force (TF) X-Ray – located at the large US Marine base at Phu Bai, the closest US headquarters to the city – reinforce US forces in the city and relieve the besieged MACV compound. Brigadier General Foster LaHue, the assistant division commander of the 1st Marine Division and

Map 5.2 The Battle for Southern Hue, January–February 1968

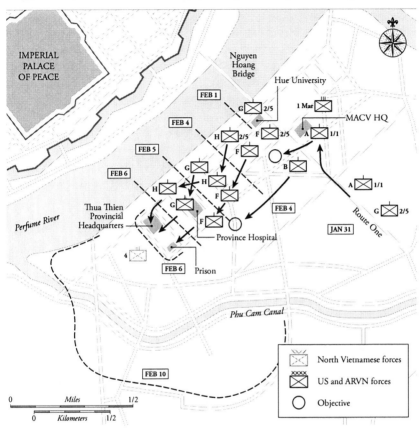

commander of TF X-Ray, was unaware of the scale of the attack in Hue, and thus responded by dispatching A Company, 1st Battalion, 1st Marine Regiment (A/1/1) to relieve the MACV compound.

A Company, with no other guidance than to relieve the MACV compound, and no real intelligence as to the situation in Hue, loaded into trucks and moved up Highway One toward Hue, about 10 miles away. On the march to Hue the infantry company was joined by four M-48 tanks of the 3rd Marine Tank Battalion. Together the small task force moved toward Hue, encountering significant sniper fire, and occasionally stopping to clear enemy-occupied buildings along the road. As the company crossed the Phu Cam Canal and entered the southern part of Hue it was caught in a hail of rifle, rocket, and machine-gun fire. Advancing slowly and carefully the Marines dismounted and, working with the tanks, moved slowly against increasing resistance toward the MACV compound. Just short of the compound the company was pinned down by intense fire and the company commander was wounded. The company radioed Phu Bai for support.

Task Force X-Ray responded to the call for help from the Marine company in Hue by dispatching Lieutenant Colonel Marcus J. Gravel, commander of 1/1 Marines, his battalion headquarters, and G Company, 2nd Battalion, 5th Marine Regiment (G/2/5) to reinforce A/1/1. Gravel, still with no specific knowledge of the situation in Hue, loaded up his Marines in trucks, and along with two Army M-42 "Duster" self-propelled dual 40mm antiaircraft guns, made the run to Hue. The Marine reinforcements linked up with A/1/1 and together the two infantry companies, supported by tanks and antiaircraft guns, pushed on to the MACV compound which they successfully relieved late in the afternoon. Upon reporting to X-Ray the success of the mission, Colonel Gravel was ordered to continue to attack north across the Perfume River bridge and link up with the ARVN forces fighting on the north side of the river. As medical evacuation helicopters arrived to remove the MACV and Marine wounded, Gravel ordered the relatively unscathed G/2/5 to continue while A/1/1, which had incurred significant casualties including all of its officers, was left to secure the MACV headquarters compound and the helicopter landing zone.

Gravel had gained an appreciation of the PAVN strength in Hue during his move to the MACV compound. Upon receipt of the new orders he protested, but was told to "proceed," clearly indicating that the true situation in Hue was still not understood in Phu Bai. The company moved north from the MACV compound, fighting through enemy snipers until it reached the southern bank of the Perfume River. There G/2/5 encountered the Nguyen Hoang Bridge over which Highway One connected the old city on the north bank with modern Hue on the south bank. The Marine tanks, now joined by several M-41 light tanks of the ARVN 7th Armored Cavalry Squadron, deployed on the south bank and supported the rush of infantry across the bridge.

The Marines of G/2/5 proceeded across the bridge cautiously and were halfway across when the opposite bank erupted with fire directed at the exposed infantry. In the initial volley 10 Marines were killed or wounded on the bridge as the allied tanks returned fire, desperate to suppress the PAVN machine guns which covered the bridge. With the aid of the suppressive fires, Gulf Company pushed forward across the bridge while gathering its dead and wounded. On the far side of the bridge the Marines encountered the closely packed housing that surrounded the massive Citadel walls. PAVN fire increased as the Marines entered the labyrinth of buildings. Enemy fire came from all directions, front, flanks and even from the rear as the company attempted to advance. To Colonel Gravel it was obvious that a single infantry company was grossly insufficient for the task of attacking into northern Hue, and there was the very real danger that the company might be cut off and surrounded. On his own initiative he ordered the company to withdraw back to the south bank, itself a very difficult task to accomplish under constant and intense enemy fire. By 8pm the Marines were again consolidated on the south bank of the river. Gulf Company had managed to bring all of their dead and wounded back to the south bank in their withdrawal, but the attempt to cross the bridge was costly: 50 Marines had been killed or wounded on and around the bridge, a third of the company's strength. As night fell at the end of the first day of fighting in Hue, the Marines were engaged, but they were outnumbered and the situation was in doubt on the south side of the river. Meanwhile, demonstrating the lack of understanding of the situation at higher headquarters, that same night General Westmoreland, commander of all US forces in Vietnam, reported that the PAVN only had three companies fighting in Hue and that the Marines would soon have them cleared out.

On February 1, the 1/1 Marines' new mission was to attack west to secure the Thua Thien Provincial Headquarters and the province prison, six blocks from the MACV compound. The mission was assigned to G/2/5, commanded by Captain Chuck Meadows. The company, which had taken significant casualties in the failed foray across the bridge, now took on what appeared to be a simple six-block movement to rescue South Vietnamese forces still holding out in the provincial headquarters. However, the attack stalled immediately. Depleted by casualties from the day before, it took all the company's resources to advance, one building at a time. Each building and each room in each building was defended by the enemy. A long, hard day of fighting, aided by the M-48 tanks, resulted in an advance of less than one block, and further casualties. That evening a third Marine company, Fox Company, 2/5 Marines, entered the battle and took over the advance from Gulf. In its first combat, Fox suffered 15 casualties and four dead in its lead platoon. As darkness fell Gravel ordered the attack to pause for the night. The Marines' first full day in Hue ended in frustration.

On February 2, the third day of the battle, Hotel Company of the 2/5 Marines (H/2/5) arrived by convoy and was immediately assigned to join A/1/1 securing the university. Later, all four companies, including F/2/5 and G/2/5, expanded the secure base around the MACV and attempted to attack to relieve the prison. The attack failed when one of the lead platoons was immediately pinned down. That night the PAVN 4th Regiment counterattacked but was easily repulsed.

With four Marine companies in Hue, the headquarters of 2nd Battalion, 5th Marines (2/5), was ordered to the city. The battalion commander, Lieutenant Colonel Ernie C. Cheatham, and his staff, researched and attempted to acquire any and all types of munitions and equipment the battalion might need in urban warfare, having been previously engaged in jungle warfare. Cheatham found and read several field manuals which offered suggestions for conducting operations in cities. The night before moving to Hue the battalion acquired CS riot-control gas and protective gas masks for the battalion, loaded up its 106mm recoilless rifles and an abundance of ammunition, and the battalion's 81mm mortars. The battalion also located large numbers of 3.5in. rocket launchers, known during World War II as bazookas. The weapons had been shipped to Vietnam but had seen little use and had recently been replaced by the lighter but less powerful Light Antitank Weapon (LAW). Cheatham's officers picked up numerous rocket launchers and ammunition because the manuals indicated that it was an ideal weapon for busting through building walls.

On February 3, the 1st Marine Regiment Headquarters, under Colonel Stan Hughes, arrived in Hue to take over the battle, bringing with it Lieutenant Colonel Cheatham and the headquarters of 2/5 Marines. The 2/5 Marines took over the attack from 1/1 with orders to clear the city south of the river. Cheatham attacked west with two companies leading: H/2/5 on the right with its right flank on the river, and F/2/5 on the left sharing a boundary with A/1/1. The attack, however, made no progress. The attacks failed due to a huge volume of fire aimed at the two lead companies. The entire attack was further hindered by the requirement to keep the attacking companies on line. If H Company was successful in its attack but F was not, as occurred on the afternoon of February 3, then H Company had to withdraw because it had insufficient troops to both attack and cover its exposed flank.

Map 5.3 The Battle for Northen Hue, January–February 1968

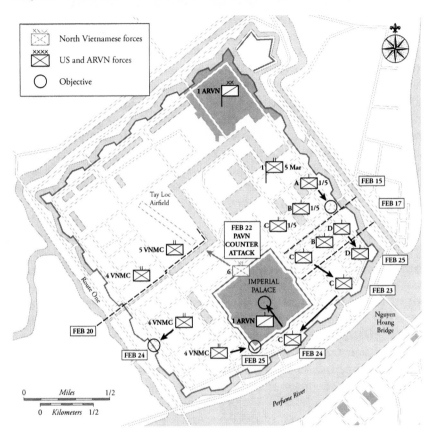

On the fifth day of the battle, February 4, the Marines south of the river began to make progress, and were achieving local superiority. At 7am the 2/5 Marines resumed the attack with H and F companies. The objective of the attack remained the provincial headquarters and prison, but the major obstacle in front of 2/5 was the government treasury building facing F Company. The treasury was a strong concrete structure with limited access, specifically designed to keep thieves out. Several attempts by F Company to get into the building on the previous day had failed. The renewed attack, however, made use of CS gas. The Marines positioned an M-38 gas launcher, capable of rapidly firing 64 30mm CS gas pellets, in front of the building and then doused the building with a barrage of CS. Tank and 106mm recoilless rifle fire then pounded into the building followed by a close assault by a platoon of Marine infantry wearing gas masks. Using fragmentation grenades and automatic rifle fire, the Marine infantry smashed through the front door and systematically cleared the large three-story building. Most of the enemy withdrew as the CS, against which they had no protection, wafted through the building. A few stragglers were killed by the Marines and the building was quickly secured. F Company's success facilitated the advance of H Company, which captured the French consulate where almost 200 friendly civilians were taking cover.

Simultaneous with the 2/5 attack, A/1/1 attacked with support of tanks and captured the Saint Joan D'Arc school and church buildings. Late that afternoon, B/1/1 arrived by convoy in Hue, along with the last platoon of A/1/1 giving Colonel Gravel's 1/1 Marines two reasonably fit companies (A and B) and the ability to attack alongside 2/5 and protect that battalion's southern flank. In the course of the afternoon 1/1 consolidated its position around the school and church complex and in the process killed almost 50 PAVN troops. No-one in the unit had ever heard of inflicting 50 casualties on an enemy unit in a few hours in Vietnam; let alone have the bodies of the enemy strewn around their position as evidence. A Company also took two PAVN officers prisoner during the day.

The Marines continued the attack on February 5. In the previous four days they had covered two of the six blocks to their objective. Now several new factors came into play in favor of the Marines. Restrictions on the use of artillery and close air support fire were lifted as the higher headquarters gained a better understanding of the significant threat inside the city. The US Navy destroyer USS *Lynde McCormick* arrived offshore to provide naval gunfire support to the Marines. Most important, however, the Marines, who had no urban warfare training or experience, developed effective tactical techniques for fighting successfully from one building position to another heavily defended building position. Marine commanders were now adept at coordinating company and battalion mortar fires, suppressive small-arms and machine-gun fire, CS gas, 3.5in. rocket launchers, recoilless rifle and tank fire, and assaulting infantry into a carefully choreographed assault sequence that could systematically capture buildings and blocks of buildings with the fewest casualties.

On February 5, 2/5 Marines moved G Company into line on the right, setting up a three-company frontage that increased the combat power available to each company as it attacked. The attack began early and quickly captured a city block of ground in front of the battalion with little resistance. This brought the battalion in front of the Hue City Hospital complex of buildings, which civilians reported had been turned into a fortified position as well as serving as the regimental hospital for the 4th PAVN Regiment. Lieutenant Colonel Cheatham determined that, despite 1/1 Marines on his left flank not being able to keep up, he would continue the attack into the hospital. Cheatham's men used all the techniques they had learned in Hue to systematically take down one hospital building after another. Now that the battalion had three full companies in the attack, it also had the capability of maneuvering within the blocks of buildings. Thus, the right flank company, Gulf, attacked first straight ahead, and then, once it had advanced forward of H Company, it turned left and attacked across the front of H Company. This not only took the enemy buildings from the flank, but it also cut off PAVN troops still in defensive positions facing H Company. F Company advanced slowly and bent its line backwards to deny the battalion left flank and remain linked to 1/1 Marines. By the end of the day, 2/5 Marines was one block from its objective, the Provincial Headquarters building and prison, and had all three of its rifle companies on line prepared to attack.

The morning of February 6 began with the companies of 2/5 Marines clearing and consolidating the buildings of the hospital complex which they had secured the previous day. Their objective – the block occupied by the provincial capital – had three major features: the provincial capital in the northern portion, the provincial prison in the middle, and more hospital buildings at the southern end of the block. The 2/5 companies were arrayed north to south: H, G, and F; with H and G having traded positions in the line as a result of the previous day's cross-front attack. The penetration of the objective block began with F Company, which attacked the hospital building at the southern edge of the block as an extension of consolidating its positions. The southern portion of the block was not heavily defended but the company took several casualties from PAVN troops firing from the high prison walls which bordered the company's right flank. With F Company set, G Company in the center bombarded the prison with mortars for over two hours, then breached the walls of the prison early in the afternoon and quickly overran the defenders. The final assault of the day was H Company's attack directly through the front door of the provincial headquarters.

The company preceded the attack with a hundred-round mortar bombardment of the building and 60 rounds of 106mm rifle fire. Then the building was liberally bombarded with CS gas. The lead Marine platoon then assaulted the building through the gas clouds wearing gas masks as the mortar and rifle fire ceased. Boards were used to cross over concertina wire strung around the building. Once inside the front door, the Marines quickly cleared the building using fragmentation grenades and rifles.

Following the assault on the provincial headquarters, the Marines tore down the Viet Cong flag flying above the building and replaced it with the stars and stripes. However, though the Marines would realize later that the day's assault had broken the back of the 4th PAVN Regiment's defense of southern Hue, it would require several days of dangerous clearing operations to confirm that the PAVN had given up the southern part of the city. By February 10, the southern part of the city was considered secured: the Marines had cleared the last of the PAVN snipers and rearguard, and recovered hundreds of discarded weapons, and tons of equipment. Thousands of Vietnamese civilians came out of hiding and a civil affairs collection and assistance point was set up by the US and South Vietnamese military to handle them. However, the battle for Hue was far from over, and attention shifted to operations north of the river.

The Battle in the Old City

While the US Marines fought systematically against the PAVN 4th Regiment for control of southern Hue, the ancient old city north of the river was the subject of an even more desperate contest between the ARVN 1st Division and the PAVN 6th Regiment. Like the PAVN 4th Regiment, the 6th was very successfully seizing most of its objectives in the early morning of January 31, but also like the 4th Regiment, the 6th failed to take the key military objective in the old Citadel part of the city, the headquarters compound of the ARVN 1st Division. This compound, like the MACV compound in the south, became the base of the ARVN counterattack.

General Truong was a shrewd military leader, who unlike many ARVN generals had made his rank and reputation in the ARVN through combat success and competence. He recognized that the most important terrain in the Citadel was his headquarters and immediately after beating back the initial PAVN attempts to capture it, he took steps to secure it completely against future PAVN attack. Toward this end he ordered that the division reconnaissance company and the division ordnance company, which were successfully defending Tay Loc airfield and the ordnance compound respectively, abandon their defensive battles and withdraw to reinforce the division headquarters position. He also immediately ordered his closest subordinate units, elements of the ARVN 7th Armored Cavalry Squadron, and the ARVN 3rd Regiment, to counterattack into the city. Further, he informed ARVN I Corps of the situation in Hue, and obtained operational control of the ARVN 1st Airborne Task Force, a group of three ARVN paratroop battalions. He immediately ordered these units to counterattack into Hue as well.

General Truong's forces were a mixed lot of some of the best and some of the average ARVN military. The airborne units, and later the ARVN Marines who came under his command, were exceptional units. His own reconnaissance company and the armored cavalry squadrons were also very capable military units. However, his regular ARVN infantry battalions were modestly capable at best. At least one of his battalions was made up almost exclusively of new conscripts who were not completely trained. Though of comparable size to their US equivalents, the ARVN units were not nearly as robustly equipped and supplied. For example, the ARVN armored units were equipped with the M-41 light tank. The tank's 76mm cannon and exposed .50cal. machine gun were not nearly as capable as the 90mm cannon and the protected cupola machine gun of the US Marine M-48 tank. More importantly, the US tanks could take numerous hits from virtually all weapons in the PAVN arsenal and continue to operate, while the M-41 was easily knocked out by the PAVN's lightest anti-armor weapons. Thus, though individually very competent, and numerically sufficient, a lack of training, leadership, and equipment, meant that the fight to retake Hue was much more difficult for the ARVN division than for the US Marines.

Beginning on February 2, the ARVN 1st Division began to call battalions and regiments back to Hue to begin to organize the counterattack to recapture the city and destroy the 6th PAVN Regiment. The geographic objective of the ARVN attack was the Imperial Palace, located virtually in the center of the old Citadel. The first objective of General Truong was to secure the division compound area, which was the vital communications link inside the Citadel, and which they would use as a base for the assault to retake the city. On February 3, the ARVN began to attack to liberate northern

Hue from the PAVN 6th Regiment. The first objective was the Tay Loc airfield which elements of the ARVN 3rd Infantry Regiment and the 7th Armored Cavalry Squadron were able to secure after difficult fighting. General Truong made clear to the ARVN I Corps, his immediate headquarters, that without reinforcements he would be unable to recapture the city. In response General Truong was reinforced with the ARVN Airborne Task Force, an elite unit which was the ARVN's strategic reserve. The task force consisted of three small airborne infantry battalions, and General Truong assigned them to attack southeast from the ARVN 1st Division compound, along the old city's northeast wall. Simultaneously, the ARVN infantry began to attack west and southwest from the vicinity of the Tay Loc airfield. The ARVN units in the north and west of the city were unable to make much progress, but the ARVN airborne infantry, the best of the ARVN, fighting against the more vulnerable elements of the PAVN 6th Regiment in the eastern portion of the city were able to make fair progress at heavy cost. By February 13, the Airborne Task Force had advanced about half the distance from ARVN 1st Division compound in the northeast corner of the city to the southeast corner of the city.

By February 12, almost two weeks since the initial attacks, the ARVN had recaptured about 45 percent of the Citadel. The ARVN battalions of the ARVN 1st Division were, however, exhausted, and severely depleted by casualties. The ARVN Airborne Task Force had likewise expended a significant amount of its strength. Both the South Vietnamese and the US commands agreed to provide reinforcements, particularly because the decisive fighting on the south side of the river appeared to be over.

The American command chose the 1st Battalion of the 5th Marine Regiment (1/5 Marines) to reinforce the ARVN in the old Citadel portion of Hue. On the ARVN side, three battalions of Vietnamese Marines (VNMC) were identified to reinforce Hue. It took two days to move 1/5 Marines under Major Robert H. Thompson from positions in the field south of Ben Hua to northern Hue. The battalion had to cross the Perfume River on US Navy landing craft. The plan was for the US Marines to attack along the northeastern wall of the Citadel, relieving the Vietnamese Airborne Task Force, while the VNMC attacked along the southwestern wall. The wall itself was an ancient fortification that was up to 20 feet thick and flat on top. In places, the city had mounted the walls, and buildings occupied the top of the wall. The objective of both attacking forces was the walled Imperial

Palace compound located in the center of the southeastern wall just north of the river.

The 1/5 Marines began their attack on the morning of February 13 and were immediately surprised when they were engaged by enemy firing down from the top of the Citadel wall as they marched southeast to relieve the ARVN airborne infantry. The Marines took casualties and immediately deployed into tactical formations and the lead elements of A Company attacked the wall. Subsequent to the successful, but costly attack by A Company, the Marines determined that the ARVN had pulled out of city during the night without coordinating, and the ARVN positions had been reoccupied by the PAVN 6th Regiment.

The beginning of the attack demonstrated the difficulty that the Marine battalion would experience in its attack. The old city presented more difficult tactical problems to the Marines than those encountered in the newer, southern part of the city. Buildings in the north were smaller, more numerous, and closer together. The streets were also much narrower. These conditions increased the cover for the PAVN, decreased the Marines' options for maneuver, and made employing tanks and the Ontos recoilless rifle vehicles much more difficult. It took the Marines the entire first day of the attack to secure the original positions given up by the withdrawing ARVN paratroopers.

The casualties of the first day of the attack hit A Company the hardest, and as the attack began again on February 14, the battalion attacked with B Company on the left, wrestling with the dominating Citadel northeastern wall, and C Company on the right fighting along the outside wall of the Imperial Palace; A Company became the battalion reserve. From February 14 to February 17, B Company and C Company fought doggedly forward, achieving one hard-fought block a day. After four days of continuous fighting, the battalion was two-thirds of the way to the southwestern wall of the Citadel, only two blocks away. But the advance was costly. The battalion suffered tremendous casualties and the battalion, with permission from the commander of Task Force X-Ray, stood down to rest, replenish supplies and bring forward replacements.

The attack resumed on the night of February 20 with a large patrol from A Company infiltrating PAVN lines to occupy positions two blocks south along the southwestern wall. From there they directed artillery, mortars, and air strikes as the battalion attacked on the morning of February 21 with three companies abreast, D Company having reinforced the battalion during the pause in the attack.

The new attack was as slow, methodical, and fiercely fought as the previous week's attack. The Marines continued to call on all the tools in their arsenal – tanks, Ontos, recoilless rifles, CS gas, artillery and close air support – and advanced one block a day. On February 23, the battalion achieved the southern wall and the northern bank of the Perfume River. The battalion then immediately turned right (west) and secured the gate to the palace. At that point the battalion halted as higher command insisted that ARVN forces be permitted to attack into the palace grounds. For the US Marines, the battle of Hue ended on February 23.

On the opposite side of the city, the VNMC attacked parallel to 1/5 Marines with the objective of securing the western portion of the Citadel and the Imperial Palace. However, the VNMC were having a hard time. Of the three VNMC battalions in Hue, one entire battalion was committed to securing the northwestern corner of the city where there were significant numbers of bypassed PAVN and Viet Cong units threatening the line of communications for the units attacking south. The three VNMC units had been moved to Hue directly from two weeks of hard fighting in the heart of the South Vietnamese capital city Saigon. En route to Hue they had replenished their supplies and received replacements, including hundreds of conscripts fresh from basic training. Thus, the VNMC units were much less experienced than the Americans. Like similar ARVN units, they lacked many of the heavy weapons employed by their American counterparts. Further, the VNMC units were supported by ARVN M-41 light tanks. The ARVN tank guns could not penetrate the concrete building structures of Hue and the tanks were easily destroyed by the standard PAVN B-40 rocket – of which the PAVN seemed to have an endless supply. Finally, in the VNMC zone of attack was the Chu Huu city gate, in the southwest corner of the city. This was the PAVN 6th Regiment's line of communications and supply and therefore the regiment was determined to hold it against VNMC attacks at all costs. The result was that, similar to 1/5 Marines to the east, the VNMC battalions were unable to advance rapidly. Finally, as 1/5 Marines achieved the banks of the Perfume River on February 23, the PAVN and Viet Cong began to abandon the city. The VNMC quickly broke through the PAVN defenses and captured Chu Huu gate on February 24, sealing the escape routes of the remaining Communist forces. On February 25, the VNMC battalions secured the southwest corner of the palace walls and linked up with 1/5 Marines and ARVN units along the river.

Operations North of the City

The sudden collapse of the PAVN defense of Hue on February 23 and 24 was strongly influenced by the efforts of the 3rd Brigade of the US Army 1st Cavalry Division operating northwest of Hue along National Highway One. The Vietnamese and US high commands were slow to understand the situation in Hue and slow to react in a comprehensive way. Finally, several days into the battle, the magnitude of the PAVN attack was recognized and the higher command took steps to isolate the PAVN forces in Hue. The ideal force to isolate the PAVN in Hue was the airmobile units of the US Army, but in the midst of the nationwide Tet Offensive the highly mobile helicopter infantry were in great demand. The mission eventually given to the Cavalry was to not only isolate Hue, but also to ensure that Highway One north of Hue was clear. The Cavalry assigned the mission to one battalion: 2nd Battalion, 12th Cavalry, 3rd Brigade of the 1st Cavalry Division (2/12 Cavalry).

The 2/12 Cavalry airmobiled into a landing zone about six miles north of Hue. From there the battalion began moving south toward Hue parallel to Highway One. It had not gone very far when it began to take fire from a small village. The battalion quickly organized what it assumed would be a routine attack on the hamlet but when that attack was vigorously repulsed the American soldiers realized that they were encountering a large, well-organized enemy force. As the cavalrymen organized a hasty defense in an exposed rice paddy, only their firepower prevented them from being overrun. What the cavalry troopers had uncovered was the PAVN 5th Regiment, which was defending the Thung Front headquarters as well as guarding the supply route to PAVN forces in Hue.

Thus began a hard fight for dominance over the northwestern approaches into Hue. Initially, the numerically superior and well dug-in PAVN had the advantage, and 2/12 Cavalry almost didn't survive the early part of the battle. However, 2/12 was able to establish a defendable position and then slowly the 3rd Brigade built up its combat power in the area. Eventually the brigade had five airmobile battalions deployed in a ring around the PAVN 5th Regiment and the Front headquarters. On February 23, the US Army began closing the ring only to find many of the positions completely abandoned. The Thung Front and the PAVN 5th Regiment had escaped the trap that the Americans were building, but in the process of making good that escape they abandoned the PAVN 6th Regiment and its attachments in Hue to their fate. Not coincidentally, on February 23 the Marines and South Vietnamese troops in Hue began making progress in attacks to secure the Citadel. Part of the reason for the collapse of the Hue city defenses was the cutting of their supply lines when the 3rd Brigade forced the retreat of the PAVN 5th Regiment.

New Maneuver Techniques

Both the US forces and the PAVN demonstrated unique maneuver capabilities in the urban battle for Hue. The PAVN used a tried and true technique – stealth – on an unprecedented scale, while the US introduced a new maneuver technology: the helicopter. The initial success of the PAVN attack on the city was largely the result of surprise. The PAVN was incredibly effective at moving the equivalent of an entire infantry division through what was essentially hostile territory virtually onto the urban objective without being detected. This phenomenal achievement was the result of detailed planning, outstanding intelligence, effective tactical security to avoid detection, and patience. The result was that the PAVN was able to seize one of the most important urban centers in South Vietnam, almost without opposition, despite the close proximity of large ARVN and US military formations. The seizure of Hue by the PAVN is one of the great achievements in the history of urban warfare and demonstrates well the lesson that the best way to seize a city is to do so before it can be defended.

The most unique aspect of the American response was the employment of helicopters in the battle. Helicopters played numerous roles in the battle. The most important role did not occur until late in the battle with the airmobile maneuver of the 1st Cavalry Division's 3rd Brigade into the area north of the city, completing the isolation of the PAVN forces in Hue itself. This capability, utilized late in the battle but achieving decisive results, represented a new way of introducing forces into an urban battle, and a quick way of achieving isolation of a city area. However, it is a technique that can incur significant risk. The 3rd Brigade almost suffered the loss of 2/12 Cavalry because the initial airmobile operation was conducted without sufficient intelligence regarding the situation on the ground.

Tactical Victory, Strategic Defeat

The battle for Hue was not an inconsequential battle. It was an important battle in the Vietnam War in that it represented the strategic success of the North Vietnamese Tet Offensive. Like the larger offensive, the PAVN's defense of Hue, though tactically unsuccessful, represented a strategic victory. The PAVN demonstrated, after three years of US intervention in the conflict, that it had the capability to capture South Vietnam's third largest city and hold that city for more than three weeks against the best troops possessed by the United States and South Vietnam. That demonstrated the North's capabilities, and also the ineffectiveness of US strategy to that point in the war. After the Tet Offensive, US strategic thinking increasingly focused on how to end the war, rather than how to win the war.

The battle for Hue also represented continuity in the nature of urban combat and perhaps signaled an increased importance for battle in cities. As important as any tactical lesson, Hue again demonstrated that at the operational level of war the most important aspect of urban warfare was isolating the city. Until the 1st Cavalry Division accomplished the isolation of Hue, the PAVN defenses remained strong. The battle for Hue also demonstrated that the tried and true conventional military approach to urban combat remained the same. City combat required aggressive small-unit leadership, an application of a wide variety of weapons types and techniques, and patient persistence. The US Marines, and to a lesser extent the ARVN and VNMC, systematically recaptured the city, block by difficult block. Urban combat in Hue also demonstrated that indirect fire and air support were important, and that armored firepower in the form of the main battle tank was essential to attacking in an urban environment.

The political lessons of urban combat were as important as the tactical and operational military lessons of the battle. Like Stalingrad, Aachen, and Seoul, the battle for Hue was dominated by strategic political considerations. The North Vietnamese understood the political strategic situation perhaps better than their opponents. The PAVN would not allow the 6th Regiment to withdraw from the city even after the expected uprising failed to occur and after it became apparent that US and South Vietnamese forces would destroy the regiment if it remained. The PAVN high command understood the immense psychological and propaganda value of the Viet Cong flag flying over the Citadel, the cultural center of both Vietnams, for weeks. The ARVN and US forces in the city began the battle at a tactical disadvantage because the city's cultural value initially curtailed the use of air and artillery firepower. In the latter stages of the battle the US Marines were prohibited from finishing the battle due to the political need to demonstrate that victory was achieved by ARVN force of arms.

Hue was a turning point in Vietnam War despite being a tactical defeat for the PAVN. The battle was an indicator of an important trend in city fighting: strategic victory in urban combat may not be directly related to tactical victory on the street. In Hue the US Marines and ARVN won the battle on the streets, but the strategic battle of perceptions was won by the PAVN. Hue demonstrated that controlling a major population center, a city, for any significant period of time can be strategically decisive for a weak adversary and may lead to strategic victory even when combat power is insufficient for achieving that end.

CHAPTER 6
WAR IN THE CASBAH
The Battle of Algiers, 1956–57

The challenges of city fighting faced by the US military in Korea and Vietnam were difficult and tested the valor and ingenuity of soldiers and commands; yet, they were a confirmation of the type of urban combat that had originated in World War II. The veterans of conventional urban combat in Stalingrad and Aachen would have been very familiar with the combat environment in Seoul and Hue. However, the decades after World War II saw the rise of a relatively new type of war, "people's revolutionary war," and its application in urban centers around the globe. One of the first examples of revolutionary war practiced in an urban environment was in Algeria in 1956. There, the National Liberation Movement (FLN) was fighting a nationalist insurgency against the French government. In 1956 the insurgent leadership determined to move the main focus of the insurgency into Algeria's capital and largest city, Algiers. The battle of Algiers, between the FLN and the French army in 1956 and 1957, was one of the first large-scale attempts by an insurgency to overthrow an existing government through operations inside a large city.

"People's revolutionary war" was a theory of warfare formally developed by the leader of the Chinese Communist movement, Mao Tse Tung. Mao's Chinese Communist movement began a struggle for power with their opponents, the Kuomintang under Chiang Kia-shek, in the 1920s. The Kuomintang was a powerful organization with a competent military arm and in the late 1920s it forced the Communists from China's urban areas. For the next 20 years Mao organized and planned the return of the Communists as they nurtured their strength in China's isolated mountains and rural areas. During the Japanese occupation of China (1933–45), the Kuomintang focused on China's war with Japan. Mao and the Communists were given a respite to regain their strength. After World War II, the Communists led a revolt against the Kuomintang and ultimately defeated them in the Chinese Civil War in 1948.

During his decades-long struggle with the Kuomintang, Mao developed a theory of revolutionary war which guided his strategy. Mao's theory of people's revolutionary war was based on a political base of popular support. The strategy had three major lines of effort: political agitation, guerrilla warfare, and conventional warfare. These phases of the revolution also may be called the strategic defense, when a political base was established; the strategic stalemate, when limited military operations occurred; and the strategic offense, when the revolutionaries could revert to mobile conventional war. The goal of revolutionary warfare, the end state, was the replacement of the reigning government system with that of the revolutionary. In the first political phase of the theory the revolutionary force worked among the people establishing a base of popular support. This was the main effort of the revolutionary movement, and though the immediate priority of the revolution may later shift, Mao maintained that the revolutionary must always have the popular support of the people and thus political considerations and the political end state always guide operations, regardless of short-term priorities. Violence may occur during this initial phase but the aim was to support the buildup of popular support. After a political base was established, the revolutionary shifted to the guerrilla warfare phase. In this phase the revolutionary attacked the instruments of government power on a small scale without decisive engagement. Guerrilla operations had several objectives but the most important was to delegitimize the government and demonstrate its ineffectiveness. Secondary objectives in this phase included continuing to build popular support, train military members and commanders, and erode the military capability of the government. Once the military power of the revolution was sufficient the revolutionaries entered the third phase of the revolution, the strategic offensive, and directly challenged the military forces of the government on the battlefield. The final phase would result in the overthrow of the government and its replacement by the revolutionary leadership.

This theory guided Mao's strategy in his confrontation with the Chinese Nationalist government. Mao's theory of revolutionary war inspired the strategy adopted by the Vietnamese revolutionaries under Ho Chi Minh, and it was the strategy that the Vietnamese pursued successfully against the French in Indochina. Many in the French military were thus very familiar with the writings of Mao, and some had even been exposed to the revolutionary war strategy while prisoners of war of the Vietnamese after the French defeat at Dien Bien Phu in 1954.

After World War II, as most European powers were divesting themselves of their foreign colonial holdings, the French were interested in reasserting their traditional control over their overseas possessions. French policy was in sharp contrast with the aggressive nationalism that became popular in the former colonies during the war. The French compromised and bowed to independence movements in many of the colonies, most notably Morocco and Tunisia. However, the French government thought that it was in their interest to retain their colonial investment in Indochina, and the French believed that Algeria was not a colonial holding but rather an integral part of France. Therefore, the French government made a stand against nationalistic movements in both Vietnam and Algeria. In Vietnam the French faced a sophisticated Maoist insurgency that ultimately led to their military defeat at the battle of Dien Bien Phu. By 1955, French military forces were withdrawing from Vietnam and based on the Geneva Agreement of 1954, the temporarily independent states of North and South Vietnam were established by the United Nations.

At the same time that the Vietnamese were fighting the French in Indochina, unrest was occurring in French North Africa. Soon after the end of World War II, a political movement began among the Muslim population of the French province of Algeria to win autonomy from France. Because of its proximity to the French Mediterranean coast, Algeria had been established by the French not as a colony, but as an integral part of France. The major problem with this arrangement was that, though Algeria was a province of France, Muslims – who comprised 90 percent of the population – did not enjoy the full rights of French citizens. A small minority (about 10 percent of the total population) of European colonists in Algeria, known as Colons, did have full citizenship rights, and this minority ruled the province. Because of their position of power, the Colons had a vested interest in maintaining the status quo.

Violence began in Algeria in 1945 and continued with increasing frequency and force for almost a decade. In late 1954 the FLN was in open revolt against French rule, and the capabilities of the FLN insurgents were too sophisticated and powerful for the French police to handle. In 1954 the French government began to employ the French army against the insurgents. For the first two years of the insurgency, the FLN fought the French army primarily in the hinterlands of the country. This strategy was classically Maoist. The rationale of the FLN was that insurgent forces could lose themselves in the difficult mountainous terrain and survive with the support of the friendly Muslim rural population. However, the problem with that strategy was that conducting hit and run raids against mostly military targets in isolated areas of the country had little or no political, military, or economic effect. In 1956 the political leadership of the FLN determined to change their strategy. They decided to move the focus of the insurgency nto Algiers, Algeria's largest city, the center of the economy, and the capital of the province. The strategy envisioned attacking prominent public targets that French politicians, the French population, and the international community, particularly the United Nations, could not ignore.

The city of Algiers was the most important in the province. It was captured in 1830 when the French invaded Algeria, and became the center for all French operations in the region. In the 1950s the city had a population of about 900,000, of which two-thirds were Muslims and about 300,000 were Colons. The city was divided into a large new colonial city, and the Casbah. The modern city comprised perhaps 80 percent of the city area and was designed in a southern European architectural style. The Casbah was the old Muslim quarter of the city. It was positioned on the heights above the port and was small, covering approximately 1km^2 (0.4 square miles), but housing over 100,000 residents. The buildings of the Casbah were stone, brick, and concrete, tightly packed next to each other, and three to five stories tall. Each building housed an extended family unit, and other relatives often lived in the neighborhood. Most of the Casbah was inaccessible to vehicles, the buildings being separated by steep narrow cobblestone lanes. The Casbah became the center of the FLN movement in Algiers.

The FLN organization in Algiers mirrored the larger FLN national organization and followed a classic insurgent cell structure. The FLN was organized in three-man cells with only one person having any knowledge of the larger organization and that person's knowledge being limited to a single contact in the next higher organization. The FLN political leader in Algiers was Larbi Ben M'Hidi. Ben M'Hidi was also part of the national executive leadership of FLN. He was assisted by Saadi Yacef who was his executive for operations. Before the campaign against the French began in Algiers, Yacef took charge of preparing the Casbah as a base. His network of 1,400 operatives included bomb experts, masons, and numerous other special experts. Yacef purged the Muslim population within the old city of known French sympathizers. He also supervised the building of a network of hides and caches throughout the district. These positions were built into residences by creating false walls and tunnels that facilitated the storing of weapons and explosives, and the hiding and escape of insurgents during French army search operations.

A chain of events precipitated the initiation of hostilities in Algiers. On June 19, 1956, two known FLN operatives were executed by the French for their involvement in the murder of several French civilians. The prisoners were executed by guillotine, and were defiant to the end. In sympathy with the executed prisoners, mobs of Muslims rioted throughout Algiers and randomly killed Europeans. This violence was encouraged by M'Hidi and the FLN. On orders from Yacef, FLN operatives roamed around Algiers and gunned down 49 French civilians in retaliation for the executions over a three-day period. This action was designed to build popular Muslim support for the FLN. The Colons themselves responded to the Muslim violence with a terrorist bombing of a suspected FLN home in the Casbah, which killed over 70 Muslims, most of them not associated with the FLN. The FLN then made a decision to begin a deliberate campaign of violence against the French civilian population in Algiers. The campaign had several purposes: to bring international attention to the grievances of the Muslim population of Algeria, to establish the FLN as the legitimate authority representing the Muslim population, and to demonstrate the ineffectiveness of the French authorities.

The Battle

The campaign began at the end of September 1956 with the most famous attack, the Milk-Bar bombing. The Milk-Bar attack was an unprecedented intentional assault on the civilian Colon community. The attack occurred on September 30, 1956, and consisted of three

Map 6.1 Major Events in Algiers, 1956–57

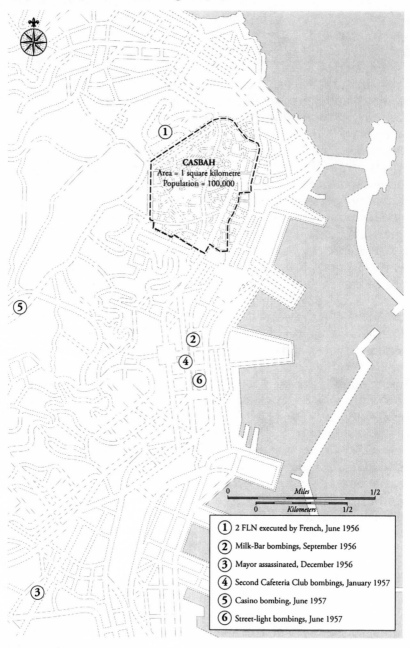

CASBAH
Area = 1 square kilometre
Population = 100,000

0   Miles   1/2
0   Kilometers   1/2

(1) 2 FLN executed by French, June 1956

(2) Milk-Bar bombings, September 1956

(3) Mayor assassinated, December 1956

(4) Second Cafeteria Club bombings, January 1957

(5) Casino bombing, June 1957

(6) Street-light bombings, June 1957

closely spaced bombings at businesses that catered to the young wealthy Colon population. Yacef used three female bombers to carry out the attacks. Two were 22-year-old law students at Algiers University. They were specifically chosen because they were all generally attractive, and most importantly, somewhat European in appearance so could easily blend in with the European Colon population. Dressed in typical European style, the three left the Casbah separately. They met Yacef's bomb-maker outside the Muslim quarter and were each issued their bombs. The explosions were planned to occur in rapid succession. The first occurred at the Milk-Bar, which was a youth hangout, and which was filled with mothers and young children drinking milkshakes at the time of the bombing. The second detonation followed within a minute, at the Cafeteria club, another favorite spot of young Colons. Together these two bombs killed three and wounded over 50, including numerous children. The third bomb, emplaced at an Air France travel agency, failed to go off because of a faulty timer.

The bombings terrified the Colon community and received international attention. Yacef and B'Hidi determined that the bombings had achieved the type of success they desired: the European community distrusted and feared any Muslim as a potential terrorist. The Muslim community was on its guard against rampaging European mobs. The FLN determined to increase the terror campaign to further separate the two populations and in December they followed up the September attacks with the assassination of the civilian mayor of Algiers. The Colon community was outraged, and further angered when a FLN bomb exploded at the mayor's funeral. Though this bomb did not cause any casualties, the funeral procession turned into a mob which rampaged through the city, attacking and killing any innocent Muslims they encountered. The FLN responded with more assassinations, and this finally drove the civilian governor-general of Algeria, Robert Lacoste, to take desperate measures.

In January 1957, due to the inability of the civil authorities to make any progress toward defeating or arresting the bombers and assassins, French officials turned government authority in Algiers over to the military commander of French forces in Algeria, General Raoul Salan. Salan promptly deployed the elite 10th Parachute Division to Algiers and gave the division commander, General Jacques Massu, the task of defeating the FLN organization in the city. Effectively, the civilian administration of the city was replaced by the military command of Massu.

The 10th Parachute Division was a relatively new organization in the French army but one superbly manned, and experienced in the ways of counterinsurgency warfare. The division consisted of four parachute regiments, each about a thousand men strong: the 1st, 2nd, and 3rd Régiments de Parachutistes Coloniaux (RPC), made up of French colonial troops, and the 1st Régiment Étranger de Parachutistes (REP), the Foreign Legion parachute regiment. The total strength of the division was 4,600 paratroopers. The division's subordinate commanders and staff were some of the foremost counter-revolutionary experts in the French service, with extensive experience in the art of resistance fighting. Leading the 10th Parachute Division was General Jacques Massu, one of France's foremost soldiers. He graduated from St Cyr and served on colonial duty in western Africa before World War II. During World War II he joined the Free French 2nd Armored Division and participated in the liberation of Paris. He was a founding member of the first French army parachute unit, and he served with the paras in Indochina. In 1956, at the age of 47, he was the first commander of the 10th Parachute Division and led it during the Suez Crisis in Egypt.

Massu's staff were exceptionally experienced counterinsurgency experts. They were also ruthless fighters who recognized few limits in their efforts to defeat the FLN. Massu's right-hand man was his chief of staff, Colonel Yves Godard. Godard was 44 years old at the time of the Algiers battle. In 1940, he had been captured by the Germans. After escaping German captivity on his third attempt, in 1944, he returned to Paris and then joined the French Resistance. Godard returned to the regular army in 1948, and was assigned to a secret intelligence unit, the 11th Shock Unit. He later led that unit to Indochina.

Godard had two outstanding assistants. One was 48-year-old Major Roger Trinquier. Trinquier was one of the originators of the *"Guerre Revolutionnaire"* doctrine, the French army's answer to insurgency. He served in China from 1938 to 1945, and there became an expert on revolutionary warfare. Later, he formed the first battalion of colonial paratroopers, 1st bataillon de parachutistes coloniaux (1st BPC). He spent most of the years 1948 to 1954 in Vietnam, and most of that time he spent gathering intelligence and leading pro-French guerrillas against the Viet Minh deep in enemy-controlled territory. During the battle of Algiers he was a special deputy to Massu, and chief of the informant system in Algiers. Later he commanded the 3rd RPC and was subsequently recalled from Algiers for involvement in political agitation.

Massu's other intelligence chief was Major Paul Aussaresses. Aussaresses served with Free French special services in World War II. During World War II he was imprisoned briefly in Spain, and participated in Jedburgh operations in occupied France and Germany. After World War II he formed the 11th Shock Unit, a secret intelligence and direct-action unit. He served in Indochina with the 1st RPC and conducted intelligence operations behind Viet Minh lines. He served in Algeria as an infantry brigade intelligence officer, in the 1st RPC, and as Massu's special deputy for "action implementation." Aussaresses was in charge of French interrogation efforts. Aussaresses left Algeria in 1957 and continued an uneventful military career in the army, eventually retiring as a general.

The four regimental commanders of the 10th Parachute Division were as impressive in their experiences as the staff. Colonel Georges Mayer commanded the 1st RPC. He was a graduate of St Cyr and one of the original members of the two airborne companies created by the French Army in 1937. He fought in World War II in Alsace and also in Indochina. Colonel Albert Fossey-Francois commanded the 2nd RPC. He was a literature student before World War II and joined the special services during the war. He had commanded his regiment, the 2nd RPC, in Indochina. Perhaps the most impressive of the parachute commanders was the 3rd RPC commander, Colonel Marcel Bigeard. Bigeard enlisted in the army before World War II, and was captured as a sergeant in the Maginot Line defenses in 1940. He escaped from the Germans and joined a colonial infantry unit. The army commissioned him as a lieutenant in 1943, and he joined the paratroopers and jumped behind German lines in 1944. As a major and battalion commander he jumped with the 6th BPC into Dien Bien Phu in Vietnam. He was promoted to lieutenant colonel during the battle and became a prisoner of the Vietnamese when the command surrendered. Probably because of his reputation, the 3rd RPC was responsible for operations in the Casbah. The last of the para commanders also had a very impressive record. Lieutenant Colonel Pierre Jeanpierre commanded the Foreign Legion Parachute Regiment, the 1st REP. He served in the French Resistance during World War II, was captured by the Germans and spent the last year of the war in the Dachau concentration camp. Jeanpierre went to Indochina with the French Foreign Legion 1st REP and fought with them there until 1954. He was second in command of the 1st REP until March 1957 and was then appointed commander. During the battle of Algiers his regiment captured Yacef, and he was wounded during that action. Jeanpierre was killed in action leading his regiment in Algeria in 1958. Combined with Massu and his experienced staff, the officer leadership of the 10th Parachute Division was a formidable group. Their combined experiences and leadership made the 10th Para one of the most experienced, and most effective, counterinsurgency forces ever fielded.

The Guerre Revolutionnaire Doctrine

At the beginning of the war, French forces in Algeria did not completely understand the nature of the enemy with which they were engaged. The initial actions of the FLN were viewed as criminal terrorism to be dealt with by the police. By 1956 the French government recognized the scale and effectiveness of the insurgency, and the French response was large but conventional military operations. These proved generally ineffective against the insurgency, which by then had been active for two years, was well organized, had a large popular support base in the Muslim population, and was skilled in conducting hit-and-run guerrilla operations. Beginning in 1956 the French started to adjust their tactics and operational approach. This was mainly due to the arrival in theater of experienced officers and troops from Indochina who understood the Maoist approach to revolutionary warfare. The new French leaders began to informally articulate a counterinsurgency doctrine known as *guerre revolutionnaire*, and the tactics, techniques, and procedures to implement it.

Guerre revolutionnaire was not a formally adopted doctrine of the French army. Rather, it was a counterinsurgency doctrine articulated by influential French officers and disseminated unofficially through discussions, and private and professional writing. The crux of the new doctrine was that the objective of the army was the support and allegiance of the people. This support had to be won by providing a promising alternative ideology to the population. That ideology was a liberal French democratic ideology with strong Christian overtones. The tactics that supported the French doctrine were in general very effective. These tactics rested on five key counterinsurgency fundamentals: isolating the insurgency from support; providing local security; executing effective strike operations; establishing French political legitimacy and effective indigenous political and military forces; and establishing a robust intelligence capability.

The French doctrine demonstrated that they had a solid theoretical understanding of Maoist revolutionary war. The battle for Algiers was the first clear large-scale application of guerre revolutionnaire against the FLN.

The leaders of the French paratroopers, in particular the staff officers, knew that the most important key to successful operations against the FLN was intelligence. This was the primary responsibility of Godard, Trinquier, and Aussaresses. They quickly created a very sophisticated and robust human intelligence (HUMINT) system in the city. This system was multilayered, including local loyal Algerians, turned former FLN members, paid informers, and aggressive interrogation and detention practices. It was linked to strategic intelligence operations in France as well as to the intelligence operations of other nations – notably Israel. It was managed by the key division staff officers personally, and included unit intelligence officers in each regiment. The key to the success of the intelligence system was the rapid dissemination of critical information to strike units. The French standard was to strike at targets identified through their intelligence system within hours of uncovering the information. High-stress interrogation techniques and torture were an integral part of this system – and its major defect. The failure of the French to recognize this flaw had immense strategic consequences.

The French adapted their operations and tactics, techniques, and procedures in recognition of the importance of intelligence. They adjusted their organizations to ensure that the most competent and qualified officers were assigned to the intelligence positions. The intelligence staff positions became in effect the key operational staff positions in battalion-level organizations and higher. The French ensured that intelligence was linked tightly to mobile reaction units. They understood the fleeting nature of good intelligence and thus developed the ability to react to acquired intelligence quickly with their mobile units. The French recognized that human intelligence was most important. They built multiple, overlapping layers of HUMINT networks to provide and cross-check information. They also understood that the environment in which the insurgents operated was the population. The French army therefore sought to organize that environment. This took the form of a very detailed and accurate documentation of the population. Censuses were conducted and identification cards were issued that enabled files to be established on the civilian population and gave the army the ability to track individuals within the population.

Counterinsurgency Tactics

Tactically the 10th Parachute Division used the quadrillage system to organize the city. They divided the city into quadrants and assigned one to each of the four regiments. The regiments then became experts on the people and the layout of their assigned area. The regiments also controlled access to their quadrants through checkpoints and patrolled their quadrants constantly. The intent was to isolate each part of the city from external influence. The quadrillage system also ensured that nothing could happen of significance within the city without the paratroopers being immediately informed.

As each regiment took charge of their zone, their operating environment was carefully cataloged. The paratroopers went door to door and forced the population to submit to a detailed census which created a huge database of residents, their occupations, family, and addresses. This database was invaluable in subsequent search operations and interrogations. In addition, the physical layout of the city was studied. The paras established a coded organizational system for the unstructured Casbah. They mapped, and assigned each block and house in the Casbah a designation. The letter–number codes were then painted prominently on all the buildings. This allowed quick and accurate targeting of patrols and raids anywhere in the city and, combined with the population data, gave intelligence officers and commanders an accurate understanding of the human terrain of the battle space.

The FLN Returns

In the fall of 1956 the FLN established itself in the Casbah, built its organization, and prepared itself for operations. The Milk-Bar bombings and subsequent operations demonstrated the ability of the FLN to carry out campaigns. However, the real battle for Algiers began in January 1957 with the arrival in the city of General Massu and his division. The first contest between the paras and the FLN was the general strike action called for by the FLN in January 1957.

Ben M'Hidi believed that the bombings and assassinations had demonstrated the effectiveness of FLN operations within the city. They had also firmly driven a wedge between the European and Muslim populations of the city. What had not been demonstrated,

Map 6.2 Deployment and Actions of the 10th Para Division, Algiers, 1957

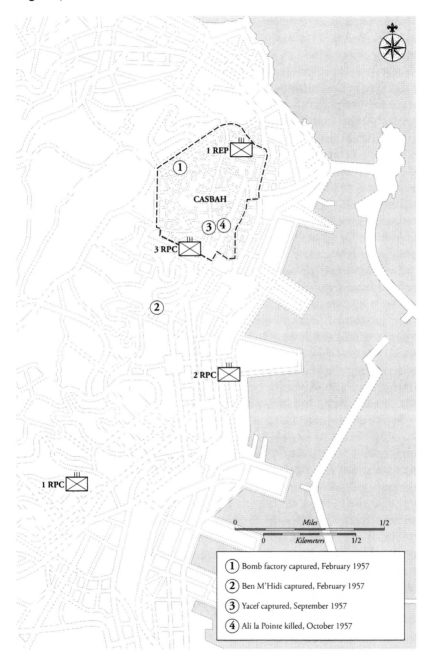

1 REP

CASBAH

3 RPC

2 RPC

1 RPC

0   Miles   1/2
0   Kilometers   1/2

(1) Bomb factory captured, February 1957

(2) Ben M'Hidi captured, February 1957

(3) Yacef captured, September 1957

(4) Ali la Pointe killed, October 1957

however, was the extent to which the general Muslim population was under the control of the FLN. This, according to M'Hidi's plan, was to be demonstrated by a city-wide general strike that would last eight days, beginning on January 28, 1957. The strike, timed to coincide with the beginning of the UN session in New York, would demonstrate to the Algerian population, the French, and to the world the willingness of the Muslim population to follow the FLN's leadership, thus firmly establishing the FLN's legitimacy. The strike would benefit the FLN's case for Algerian independence to the United Nations.

The French completely understood the threat of the strike to the legitimacy of French rule in Algeria. Thus, the French government directed Massu to break the strike at all cost. On Monday morning, the first day of the strike, Muslim shops throughout the city remained shuttered and closed, Muslim children did not go to school, workers at the post office, the telegraph and telephone service, and the railroad failed to show up for work. It appeared that the strike was a total and complete success. Then the French army moved into action.

Massu ordered his paratroopers to deploy throughout the city, and each regiment quickly swarmed over its assigned sector. Armored cars hooked up to the fronts of the closed businesses and ripped the doors off their hinges. Shop owners were faced with the option of appearing and protecting their stock or having the local population pillage their stores. Once the owners showed up, paratroopers ordered them to stay open or be subject to immediate arrest. Fleets of trucks followed the paratroopers who began to systematically move through the Muslim neighborhoods and roust the population. Using their census data as a guide, working-age males were gathered, quickly organized by workplace, and then trucked to work under guard. Any who resisted were arrested, but faced with imprisonment by the French, most of the strikers – like the shop owners – reluctantly complied. Within a few days, the same tactics were used with schoolchildren. The French army literally herded the children from their homes to the schools. Thus, within a few days, the strike was broken, and the city, to all appearances was back to normal. The French, and importantly, the FLN, both recognized that the FLN plan had failed in a very dramatic and public way. Colonel Godard remarked that the FLN's mistake was to declare the strike effective for eight days. Godard conceded that had the FLN called for a one- or two-day strike, it would have appeared to be very effective, and the paras could not have made their presence felt fast enough to claim a victory. As it was, the failed strike seemed to indicate that the French government still had effective control over the city and its population.

The strike was a major setback to the FLN in its campaign to demonstrate its claim as the legitimate representative of the Muslim population. However, it did not diminish the FLN's operational capability. As an alternative to the strike action, Yacef supervised another bombing campaign. Two days before the strike began the FLN hit downtown Algiers with a patterned attack of three simultaneous bombings. The attack was designed based on the successful Milk-Bar attack. Three young women were chosen as the bombers. The targets were popular entertainment and eating establishments, including the Cafeteria club for the second time. This time all three bombs detonated killing five and wounded 60, including a young Muslim who was lynched on the spot by outraged mobs of Colons. Two weeks later, on a Sunday, young girls aged 16 and 17 planted bombs in two crowded sports stadiums that detonated and killed ten and injuring 45. Despite their success, however, it was getting harder and harder for Yacef and his organization to operate.

The FLN was forced to use women bombers because it was virtually impossible for a Muslim male to travel unchallenged anywhere in the city. The French army's grip on the city grew tighter as patrols and checkpoints began to bring in more and more Muslims for questioning. Each interrogation was carefully conducted to create a picture of the FLN organization, and new information was quickly used to provide more focus for patrols, raids, and arrests. Careful police action at the scene of the bombings was also important. Police investigations led to the information that at least some of the bombers were women, and from that point on army and police checkpoints subjected all women to the same intense searches as men. Police investigation also led to the identification and arrest of the stadium bombers. Those arrests, and the arrests of several couriers by checkpoints and patrols, combined with intense interrogations, gave the French paras the leads they needed to begin to systematically track down and deconstruct the FLN network.

An example of how the French interrogation system worked is the capture of a locksmith working for the FLN. He was stopped and searched by a routine patrol of the 3rd RPC, and found to have bomb blueprints in his possession. He was then turned over to the division special interrogation branch. After three days of intense interrogation he gave away the address of Yacef's bomb factory in the Casbah. However, with three days' notice the FLN had time to break down the hidden factory and hide all evidence and the raid on the residence netted no results. A week later however the paras captured a bomb courier and the mason who built many of Yacef's hides in the Casbah. Both talked under torture and they gave away the exact location of the primary bomb factory and the bomb-maker. Raiding paras managed to capture almost a hundred completed bombs, thousands of detonators, and hundreds of pounds of explosive. As important, they rounded up many of the FLN associated with the bombing network, and had positively identified names of most of the others. It had taken Yacef 18 months to create his network in Algiers but by the end of February 1957 it had been essentially destroyed by the French paratroopers.

The same intelligence that the paras used to track down the bombers of the FLN was also helping them close in on the leadership of the organization. By the end of January 1957 Yacef himself had barely eluded capture several times. On February 9, a top lieutenant of B'Hidi was captured. On February 15, the FLN leadership agreed that their campaign in Algiers was on the verge of failing and they determined that the political leadership should depart the city to avoid capture. They also decided to leave Yacef behind to continue the campaign as best he was able. On February 25, Ben M'Hidi moved out of the Casbah and into a suburb of the city. That move caught the attention of a Muslim informer in Trinquier's network. The paratroopers quickly raided the home and captured M'Hidi in his pajamas. A little over a week later the French army announced that M'Hidi killed himself while in captivity. Most of the population of Algeria understood that the French army killed him. More than 40 years later, in 2001, Major Paul Aussaresses admitted in his account of the battle of Algiers to having shot the FLN leader.

The capture of M'Hidi, the retreat of the FLN leadership, and the loss of key operatives, safe houses, and the bomb-making network were major setbacks for the FLN. However, Yacef, the operations chief, was still at large and active. Through the spring of 1957, even as paratroopers were withdrawn from the city, Yacef laboriously rebuilt the damaged FLN network in the city. In June the FLN felt strong enough to strike back. The first attack was a four-bomb attack where the bombs were installed in the iron bases of street lights. The light casings enhanced the effects of the explosives and the bombs killed eight and wounded over 90 civilians. For the FLN, however, the attacks were a strategic mistake because the bombs, located in busy public places, indiscriminately killed Europeans and Muslims alike, and created discord in the Muslim community. This strategic error was not repeated a few days later when a massive bomb was exploded in Algiers Casino, an upscale entertainment venue catering to well-to-do Colons.

The casino bombing of June 9, 1957 killed nine and wounded 85. The bomb was placed under the bandstand and because of its positioning many of the wounded suffered leg amputations. Nearly half of the dead and injured were women. In reaction the Colon community went on a rampage through Muslim neighborhoods. Mobs broke into and pillaged Muslim businesses as police and soldiers stood idly by. The mob, estimated at over 10,000 in number, was finally brought under control by Major Trinquier who brandished a tricolor from his jeep, got their attention and led them to the French commander, General Salan. Salan addressed them and then ordered them to disperse, which they did. In addition to hundreds of businesses destroyed, five Muslims were killed, over 50 injured, and 20 cars burned. The casino bombing and the Colon reaction drove the two communities irrevocably apart and pushed the Muslim community into the arms of the FLN.

By the time of the casino bombing the various actions of the French had restricted the safe havens of the FLN exclusively to the Casbah. With the FLN again active, the para regiments were redeployed throughout the city, and a subordinate of Trinquier, Captain Leger, deployed a new intelligence asset into the battle. Leger, a member of the elite 11th Shock Unit and an Arab expert, recruited a group of former FLN members and deployed them into the general Arab working population, clad in the typical blue dungaree dress of the working class. These spies, known as Leger's "Blues," achieved astounding success as they mingled with their former associates and reported back to the French. The first success of the "Blues" was locating Yacef's new bomb-makers. On August 26, they were both killed in a stand-off after being trapped by the paras in an apartment.

The French intelligence net, the "Blues," and incessant patrols and checkpoints by the paras made it impossible for Yacef to operate. In late September a courier carrying a message from Yacef to the FLN outside of Algeria was captured by the French on an informer's tip. The courier, under intense interrogation, gave the French the location of Yacef's final hideout. On September 24, the house was surrounded by Colonel Jeanpierre's 1st REP and a search revealed a hollow wall behind which Yacef was hidden. As the paras started to break down the wall Yacef threw a grenade out of a hole and wounded three paras including Colonel Jeanpierre. At that point Colonel Godard arrived and took charge of the operation. He ordered the entire house set for demolition and informed Yacef if he didn't surrender they would blow the building up with him inside. At that point Yacef surrendered himself and a female companion. Neither Yacef nor his companion were tortured and, though sentenced to death by several military tribunals, Yacef was eventually pardoned by French President de Gaulle. Two weeks after Yacef's capture, a "Blue" led the paras to the hideout of Yacef's deputy, Ali la Pointe. On October 8, after fruitless negotiations, the paras blew up the house containing the trapped FLN assassin and two companions. The explosion set off secondary explosions in a bomb cache and brought down neighboring buildings resulting in the deaths of 17 innocent Muslims, including several children.

The capture of Yacef, the deaths of his bomb-makers, and the death of Ali la Pointe effectively destroyed the last organized elements of the FLN in the city of Algiers and ended the battle for the city. The battle was a clear victory for the French army over the insurgent forces of the FLN. One commentator at the time declared that the French victory was the Dien Bien Phu for the FLN. The French army, and the paras in particular, were the heroes of the Colon community and also of the French population in general. The political influence of the French army increased accordingly. The FLN, in contrast, was at a low point. The leadership had fled the country, the Muslim population was war-weary, and it was apparent that the military arm of the FLN was no match for the French army. However, though a short-term defeat, the battle for Algiers set the conditions for the long-term victory of the FLN. The battle focused French and international attention on the city and on French tactics used to defeat the FLN. As outsiders examined those tactics it became increasingly and alarmingly obvious that a cornerstone of French tactics had been harsh interrogation techniques; techniques many considered torture.

Torture

A major weakness of the French strategy was that it was based on the assumption that the primary ideological focus of the insurgents was Marxist communism. It did not account for an ideological motive based on indigenous nationalism and anti-colonialism. The ideological and spiritual nature of the conflict was internalized by many in the French army and became one justification for torture. They saw the enemy as communist and therefore as inherently evil. The struggle was one of ultimate national and ideological survival. This extremely ideological view of the war justified any tactical technique, regardless of its legality or morality, in order to achieve success. One French officer testified that young officers were told that the end justified any means and that France's victory depended on torture. Many French army leaders believed that the extremely high stakes of strategic success or failure justified moral compromise at the tactical level.

Another justification for torture was that insurgent warfare was completely different from conventional warfare, and therefore required a different operating approach. In accordance with this view, the laws of conventional land warfare were considered inappropriate and counterproductive in the context of counterinsurgency warfare. The French also understood the primacy of HUMINT to successful counterinsurgency and they believed torture was an effective way to quickly get tactical intelligence information. This combination of perceptions led to the official condoning of torture.

A third justification for torture was that it was a controlled application of violence used for the limited purpose of quickly gaining tactical intelligence. Toward this end some French officers subjected themselves to electric shock to ensure they understood the level of violence they were applying to prisoners. What these officers did not understand was the huge difference between pain inflicted in a limited, controlled manner without psychological stress, and pain inflicted in an adversarial environment where the prisoner is totally under the control of the captor. They also failed to understand that once violence was permitted to be exercised beyond the standards of legitimately recognized moral and legal bounds, it became exponentially more difficult to control. In Algeria, officially condoned torture quickly escalated to prolonged abuse, which resulted in permanent physical and psychological damage, as well as death.

The official sanction of torture by French army leaders had numerous negative effects that were not envisioned because of the army leadership's intensive focus on tactical success. The negative results of torture included a reduction in France's ability to affect the conflict's strategic center of gravity – the Muslim population; internal fragmentation of the French army officer corps; decreased moral authority of the army; the enabling of even greater violations of moral and legal authority; and providing a major information operations opportunity to the insurgency. The irony is that even though some tactical successes can be attributed to the use of torture, the French had numerous other effective HUMINT techniques and were far from reliant on torture for tactical success.

French doctrine and counterinsurgency theorists recognized at the time that the goal of the insurgents and the counterinsurgents, the center of gravity for both, was the support of the population. Despite this knowledge, many French commanders tolerated or encouraged widespread and often random torture. By one estimate, 40 percent of the adult male Muslim population of Algiers (approximately 55,000 individuals) were put through the French interrogation system and either tortured or threatened with torture between 1956 and 1957. This action likely irrevocably alienated the entire 600,000-strong Muslim population of the city from the French cause. The French did not understand the link between their tactical procedures and the strategic center of gravity.

Strategic versus Tactical Success

French military operations in the city of Algiers in 1957 were extremely successful. By the fall of 1957 they had completely demolished the FLN network in the city. The major leaders of the movement were dead or captured, and the ability of the FLN to execute bombings and assassinations in the city no longer existed. This was accomplished through a very effective two-fold process. First, an exceptional intelligence system which systematically identified known and suspected terrorists and their associates and supporters. Second, a very effective response system which was able to act immediately and decisively on intelligence information before the FLN was aware of the compromised information. French tactics were undeniably effective. One French leader, who opposed torture, nonetheless conceded that without the systematic use of torture by the paras the battle could not have been won. That may be true, but the larger point, generally ignored by the French army leadership, was that with the torture, the war could not be won. After success in Algiers, the French expanded many of the tactics of 10th Parachute Division throughout Algeria. The results were similar: effective combat operations against the FLN while at the same time alienating the bulk of the Muslim population because of the widespread use of torture. Thus, winning the battle meant losing the war.

In 1962, as a result of very complex political factors, many of which can be related to the questionable tactics employed by the French army, Algeria gained its independence through popular vote sanctioned by the government of France. The European population quickly quit the country and mostly migrated to France. Thus, in 1962, as Algeria became independent, much of the FLN's political success could be attributed to the French victory in the city of Algiers. As intended by the FLN, the battle focused the world's attention on the war in Algeria and highlighted the position of the FLN to communities beyond Algeria's borders. It also forced the FLN political leadership to abandon Algeria as unsafe. This move ultimately enabled them to wage their political campaign free from the threat of arrest or attack. Likewise, the battle of Algiers convinced the leadership of the FLN that a military solution in Algeria could not be won and this caused them to refocus and reprioritize their political efforts which were ultimately effective. Thus, though a decisive tactical defeat for the FLN, by winning the battle of Algiers, the French army set the conditions for the ultimate political victory of the FLN and the independence of Algeria from France.

CHAPTER 7
THE LONG URBAN WAR
Operation *Banner*, 1969–2007

The experience of the French in Algeria and the French and Americans in Vietnam indicated that following World War II a shift had occurred in warfare. Nuclear weapons made global war unthinkable. Instead two limited forms of warfare replaced the total war that typified global conflict. One was limited regional conventional war. This is the type of war fought by United Nations forces in Korea and on numerous occasions between various Arab nations and Israel. The other type of limited wars were wars of national liberation or revolution. This was the type of war that the French experienced in Algeria, and was also a component of the conflict in Vietnam. The French experience in Algeria, fighting the Algerian nationalist movement, the FLN, was very close to a pure Maoist revolutionary war. Beginning in 1969, the British Army, who had significant experience dealing with nationalist movements in the decades of imperial contraction after World War II, was faced with the challenge of a very unique urban enemy who was in many ways similar to the urban insurgents of Algeria. From 1969 to 2007 the British Army and other security forces were committed to a war with a variety of Irish paramilitary groups opposing British policy in Northern Ireland. The war was primarily fought in Northern Ireland, but occasionally spilled into England, and British military bases in Europe. The primary enemy was the Provisional Irish Republican Army, the PIRA, and affiliated or like-minded groups, operating with the goal of forcing the British Army out of Northern Ireland, and unifying Northern Ireland with the Republic of Ireland.

Ulster is the traditional northern province of Ireland. In 1922 six of Ulster's nine counties were separated from the Irish Free State and formed into Northern Ireland, a part of the United Kingdom. This shift was to protect the minority Irish Protestant community from Irish Catholic dominance. The majority of the population within the six northern counties were Protestants who emigrated to Ireland at the invitation of British government in the 17th century. The geography of Northern Ireland is classic green rolling countryside of farms interspersed with small villages and stands of forest. Several moderate-size cities are the focus of economic and political activity: the two largest being Londonderry, also known as Derry, and Belfast. The Atlantic Ocean marks the northern boundary while the Irish Sea does the same for the northeast and east. To the south and west, Northern Ireland shares a 220-mile border with the Republic of Ireland. To the west this border runs along the edge of County Londonderry and County Tyrone; to the south the border touches from west to east County Fermanagh, County Tyrone, and County Armagh.

The opponents of British policy used terrorist and guerrilla tactics and operated primarily in and amongst the civilian population of Northern Ireland. In 1969, when "The Troubles" began, that population was 1.5 million. At that time approximately 35 percent of the population was Roman Catholic while the balance was Protestant, primarily of the Presbyterian and Church of England denominations. By the end of the conflict the Roman Catholic population had increased to slightly over 40 percent of the total. The conflict was not about religion, but the religious affiliations of the population generally defined the opposing political views of the population, which were the source of conflict.

The Roman Catholic population was politically defined by two primary issues. The most important issue to the Catholic population was equal civil rights and opportunity. A secondary but also important issue was the unification of Northern Ireland's six counties with the predominantly Catholic Irish Republic, which bordered Northern Ireland to the south and west. However, republicanism, supporting the political unification of Ireland, did not automatically equate to unqualified support to violent paramilitary groups. The dominant political characteristic of the Protestant population of Northern Ireland was the desire to remain an independent country within the United Kingdom (UK). In this relationship, Northern Ireland's parliament was responsible for the internal affairs of Northern

Ireland, while the national government in London was responsible for the international policy of the UK. Thus the major political issue separating the two parts of the population was unification with the Republic, advocated by "Republicans," and loyalty to the United Kingdom, advocated by "Loyalists."

The bulk of Northern Ireland's population was located in the two major urban areas of Northern Ireland. Londonderry, the second largest city, had a population of about 60,000 in 1969, which had increased to about 85,000 by 2008, and was about 75 percent Catholic. Belfast, the largest city in Northern Ireland, had a population of 295,000 in 1969 and had decreased in population to 268,000 by 2008. The decrease in population was primarily due to flight of the middle class from the inner city to new suburban developments, and was not related directly to the violence. These two large urban areas represented about 20 percent of the country's population, but were the scene of the largest proportion of the violence and military operations.

A Complex Situation

Operations by the British Army and allied security forces in Northern Ireland were greatly complicated by the multiple groups opposing British policy. The obvious and the primary enemy of the British was the Provisional Irish Republican Army (PIRA). However, at various times other Irish republican groups were also active but not associated with the PIRA. These included the original Irish Republican Army (IRA), the Irish National Liberation Army (INLA), and the Real Irish Republican Army (RIRA). The PIRA was formed in 1970 when it broke away as an organization from the IRA. The split was due to strategy differences within the IRA. The original IRA wanted to pursue the goal of a united Ireland primarily through socialist political action. The IRA members who formed the PIRA favored a strategy based on violent action to drive the British government out of Northern Ireland and force the Protestant population to submit to reunification as the price of peace. The INLA was much smaller and less capable than the PIRA and were focused on a radical Marxist political agenda as well as violence. The RIRA broke from the PIRA over the 1998 Good Friday Agreement which ultimately led to the end of British military operations in Northern Ireland. The small band of die-hard fighters in the RIRA continued to prosecute violence

Map 7.1 British Army Deployment and Major Events, Northern Ireland, 1969–2007

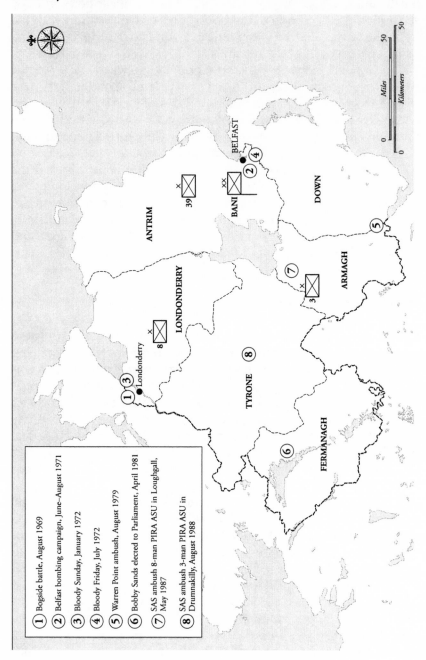

1 Bogside battle, August 1969
2 Belfast bombing campaign, June–August 1971
3 Bloody Sunday, January 1972
4 Bloody Friday, July 1972
5 Warren Point ambush, August 1979
6 Bobby Sands elected to Parliament, April 1981
7 SAS ambush 8-man PIRA ASU in Loughgall, May 1987
8 SAS ambush 3-man PIRA ASU in Drumnakilly, August 1988

with diminishing capability after the Good Friday agreement into the 21st century.

In addition to the PIRA and similar republican groups seeking reunification with Ireland, there were also paramilitary groups who used violence to preserve the status quo. These groups included the Ulster Freedom Fighters (UFF) and the Ulster Volunteer Force (UVF). The political objective of these groups was to preserve Protestant political dominance in Northern Ireland. They opposed any concessions or compromise with the Catholic community and the PIRA in particular, as a step toward ending Protestant political control and ultimately toward unification. In that their violence was not state-sanctioned and in many cases sought to thwart British policy, they were an enemy of the British security forces. However, because they did not generally target the army or security forces, and they were overall somewhat less violent than the PIRA, they were never the primary objective of military operations.

The British Army was the largest organization among several that the British government employed in its war with the PIRA. At its height in the 1970s the on-the-ground strength of the British military in Northern Ireland was approximately 28,000 troops. The army sustained a troop strength greater than 11,000 for most of the 38 years of the conflict. In the mid-1980s the army was organized into three brigades: the 8th Brigade was responsible for the western part of the country including the city of Londonderry; the 3rd Brigade was responsible for the rural area on the southern border in Armagh County; and the 39th Brigade was responsible for the northeast part of the country including the city of Belfast. The three brigades were commanded by Headquarters British Army Northern Ireland, located in the city of Lisburn, just outside of Belfast.

All units of the British Army were subject to operations in Northern Ireland, including heavy armored units and field artillery. The non-infantry units reorganized and retrained as infantry for duty in the country. Units that operated in Northern Ireland were deployed in the country in one of three statuses: roulement units which did short four-to six-month rotations into the country; deployed units which were stationed in the country for two year-long tours; and garrison units which were permanently stationed in the country. Roulement was the British Army term for short four- to six-month tours that allowed the army to quickly adjust the number of battalions in the country according to conditions. Units deployed in the country deployed with their entire compliment of soldiers as well as the soldiers' families. There were also battalions on alert who could reinforce the forces already in the country within hours if an emergency developed. An important unique army establishment was the Ulster Defence Regiment (UDR). This force consisted of regular army infantry battalions, commanded by regular British Army officers, but manned by part-time local Irish army reservists. The eight battalions of the UDR were distributed throughout the country and operated as battalions under the command of the regular British Army brigades.

In addition to the army, the other major security force in the country was the Royal Ulster Constabulary (RUC), the country's police force. When the conflict started, the force consisted of 7,000 personnel, which was a relatively small police force for the size of the population. Only about 3,000 members made up the full-time RUC, the rest being reservists. At the beginning of the conflict the RUC had three major components. The regular uniformed RUC did the bulk of the general policing and were the first responders to any type of riot, disturbance, or attack. The RUC Special Branch was the non-uniformed part of the force, responsible for investigations and police intelligence. Finally, in the early years of the conflict there existed a police reserve force known as the "B Specials." This force was on call to augment the uniformed RUC in emergency situations. The B Specials were disbanded early in the conflict because of their lack of discipline. By the mid-1980s the RUC's full-time strength was over 8,000 and it had another 2,000 officers in a reserve force.

Another important component of the army operating in Northern Ireland was the various special units which operated directly for army headquarters in Lisburn. The action component of this force was the Special Air Service (SAS), who were capable of conducting reconnaissance, surveillance, and combat operations against the paramilitaries. The British also formed special intelligence units in support of their operations. The first was the Mobile Reconnaissance Force. These forces were taken from the regular army battalions serving in Northern Ireland, but dressed in civilian clothes, and given some special training. They operated in support of the regular army battalions. Another special intelligence unit was 14 Intelligence Company. This company was formed by volunteers who received intense special training and worked undercover in Northern Ireland doing reconnaissance and surveillance. They operated only in civilian clothes and their operations were closely coordinated with the SAS.

Peacekeeping

"The Troubles" began in Northern Ireland in 1968 as a relatively benign peaceful movement led by the Northern Ireland Civil Rights Association (NICRA) advocating for civil rights for the Catholic minority. This movement was used as a vehicle by political activists including the IRA to promote their own broader agendas. However, in 1969 it remained a relatively peaceful protest movement that had, as its objective, fairly legitimate demands regarding Catholic suffrage and representation. A disproportionate response to the movement by Northern Ireland's Stormont government eventually escalated the political movement to an armed clash between the paramilitaries and the British security forces. In the early years of this clash, 1968 to 1971, the British government and military pursued a peacekeeping strategy with the objective being to calm the emotions of both the Catholic and Protestant communities and quickly return the country to normal non-violent political activity. This objective failed due to hesitant decision-making by the national leadership, intransigence on the part of the Northern Ireland government, and poor decisions by the British leadership.

The civil rights movement began in late 1968 with several peaceful marches. However, in October 1968 a civil rights march was staged in Londonderry without a permit from the government. The RUC was on hand and broke up the march with water cannons and police reservists. In January 1969 a more substantial march was organized by the People's Democracy group, a more radical student-based civil rights organization. That march was attacked by loyalist mobs while the RUC stood by and failed to intervene. Over 80 marchers were injured. Marches and violence continued through 1969. During that period, the non-violent civil rights movement was failing, the Stormont government appeared unable or unwilling to promote institutional reform, and the RUC were not acting to prevent violence, and in some cases instigated it, losing any legitimacy it had had with the Catholic community. Events culminated in the summer of 1969 with annual loyalist marches. In the summer of 1969 various officials warned that they would be provocative but they were nonetheless authorized by the government. The marches were seen as triumphal by the Catholic community. In August a march by loyalists in Londonderry was interrupted with rocks and bottles thrown by Catholic youths. The RUC intervened and pursued the Catholic mob into the Catholic

Bogside neighborhood of Londonderry where the police were met by rocks, petrol-bombs, and barricades. Over the course of three days, riots spread from Londonderry to Belfast and the RUC's resources were overwhelmed. The RUC responded to the riots with mobilized police reservists and all the weapons in their armory, including armored cars and machine guns. Loyalist mobs ransacked isolated Catholic communities, burning homes and forcing the residents to flee. As the violence escalated, the Stormont government was forced to call on London to authorize the British Army to support the police. On August 15, 1969, the army was ordered to Northern Ireland.

The British Army arrived in Northern Ireland with no strategy and little knowledge of the local situation. The Catholic community's perception of events in the summer of 1969 was that it was being attacked physically by the loyalist majority, that the Stormont government and RUC colluded in the attacks, and that the likelihood of political reform was remote. The Protestant community's perception of the situation was vastly different. Loyalists believed that the Catholic community and the IRA had embarked on the first step in a campaign to bring down the government, they also believed the Stormont government was ineffective, and local loyalist paramilitaries were the only alternative to stop the continued chaos perpetrated by the Catholics. The objective of British Army operations was to separate the two sides, to provide security, and allow local conditions to return to normal. The army was welcomed by the minority Catholic community and perceived as protectors of the minority from the large hostile Protestant mobs. The only problems with the British Army's plan was there was no political strategy designed to remove the grievances of the minority community, and they were not legally neutral in the conflict – ultimately the army was legally and politically allied with the Stormont government and the Protestant majority.

To this point in the conflict, the summer of 1969, the IRA had not taken an active role in the violence that had occurred. That violence resulted in seven deaths and was perpetrated mostly by unorganized Catholic youth on one side, and much better organized loyalists, including the RUC, and the notorious RUC reservists, the B Specials, on the other. For their lack of involvement, the IRA was chastised and ridiculed by both communities. The slogan "IRA – I ran away," was used to taunt the IRA. These events highlighted divisions within the IRA between those who saw the organization primarily as a political organization and those who saw it as an army. Ultimately, the latter group split from the original and formed the Provisional IRA, whose initial objective was to provide organized armed resistance on behalf of the Catholic community in response to the type of rioting that occurred in the summer of 1969.

For its part, the British Army was largely successful in bringing the violence under control through the remainder of 1969. Both sides respected the army's presence, and the army established informal relationships with leaders in both communities in order to limit misunderstandings and achieve some cooperation toward a peaceful common goal. Checkpoints and army barriers were established to keep the two communities separate. Army operations concentrated in the most potentially volatile areas: Londonderry and Belfast.

As 1969 rolled over into 1970 it seemed that the initial deployment of the army was successful. However, the army had no control over, and little influence on, national politics in London, or even more importantly, with the Northern Ireland Stormont government. Though the army perceived its mission as a neutral peacekeeper between the two sectarian communities, in reality the reason for the army's deployment was to support the police activities of the Stormont government. Thus, the army was legally not a neutral player but rather an extension of the British government, and, more important, also an extension of the sectarian Stormont government. This political situation quickly undermined the army's position relative to the Catholic community as a protector of the minority.

Through 1970 tensions increased between the two Northern Irish communities. The Northern Ireland government was not able to reform to meet the legitimate demands of the Catholic community. The Catholic community protested the lack of reform. Protestant agitators pressed the government to meet protests with force. The British government refused to intervene decisively and in 1970 the British national elections brought in a new governing party with a more conservative policy toward the situation in Northern Ireland. Finally, the PIRA became active and assumed the role of protector of the Catholic community. In June riots occurred in Belfast in which the British Army did not intervene. The PIRA and Protestant groups got into a gun battle in which six people were killed. In response to the rioting and violence in Belfast the British Army imposed a curfew on the Catholic Falls Road neighborhood of Belfast and conducted extensive house-to-house searches for PIRA members and weapons. The searches turned up numerous weapons but were conducted in a completely arbitrary manner, destroying property and belongings, and totally alienating the Catholic community. The curfew and search broke the trust between the army and the minority community. In 1970 the PIRA began its first bombing campaign using homemade bombs to intimidate the Protestant community and register its displeasure with government policy. Numerous bombers were killed in the act of making and in placing the bombs. The bombing campaign was not very effective and bombing had not yet become the main weapon of the PIRA.

Counterinsurgency

The sectarian violence escalated in 1971 as the PIRA took the offensive against the British Army and the Stormont government. The first British soldier killed in the conflict was shot by a PIRA sniper in February of that year. Through the year, the PIRA steadily stepped up attacks against the British Army and the Protestant community. Rioting broke out frequently in response to British Army searches for weapons and PIRA members. The confrontations between the British Army, the Catholic community and the PIRA became increasingly violent. Another deliberate bombing effort was made by the PIRA beginning in March 1971. This one was very effective. By August the PIRA had detonated over 300 explosive devices and injured over 100 individuals, most of them civilians. Over the course of 1971 the death toll steadily mounted: 88 civilians were killed; 98 suspected members of the IRA and associated republican groups died; 21 members of loyalist paramilitary groups were killed; and 45 members of the security forces (including the British Army and the RUC) were killed in operations.

PIRA operations began to take on a particularly brutal character in 1971. Catholic girlfriends of British soldiers were abducted and tarred and feathered. In March three young off-duty British soldiers were lured from a pub on the promise of attending a party and meeting girls. They were abducted, taken to a remote roadside, and executed by a pistol shot to the head. In December a prominent Protestant politician was assassinated in his home by the IRA. A concentrated PIRA bombing campaign in the summer of 1971 saw a series of 20 bombs detonated in heavily trafficked areas of Belfast over a 12-hour period. Not all of the violence, however, was waged by the republican paramilitaries. The loyalist paramilitaries were very active throughout 1971 as well, and on December 4 detonated a bomb in McGurk's Bar in Belfast killing 17, and injuring another

17. It was the worst single bombing attack of the entire conflict and the target was not affiliated with the IRA. The frequency and brutality of the violence of 1971 led to one of the most detrimental and controversial operational decisions of the conflict: the British government's decision to implement internment.

Political pressure from the Protestant civilian population on the Stormont government to take decisive action against the PIRA increased steadily and significantly throughout 1971. The options for the government were somewhat limited. The British Army and the RUC were already fully deployed and taking aggressive measures against the republican paramilitaries. The final option was the internment of suspected paramilitary members. This tactic – mass arrests and confinement of known or suspected PIRA members – had been used with great success against the IRA in the 1950s. The national government gave Stormont permission to use the British Army to execute internment over the objections of both the army and the RUC. The objections, however, were because of a lack of preparation rather than a policy disagreement. Thus, on August 9, 1971, the British Army and the RUC conducted raids all across Northern Ireland as part of Operation *Demetrius*, to arrest and detain without trial suspected members of paramilitary groups.

The internment policy failed both as a tactic and as a strategy for numerous reasons. Tactically the operation was largely a failure. The intelligence files outlining the organization of the republican paramilitaries were hopelessly out of date. Thus, very few of the 342 people arrested in the initial raids were actually active paramilitaries. The IRA claimed that virtually none of its people were arrested. Word of the impending raids had leaked and many paramilitary leaders went into hiding. Over 100 designated arrestees escaped the British net. No Protestant paramilitary members were targets, thus the raids appeared purely sectarian. The response of the Catholic community was completely unanticipated. All of Northern Ireland erupted in some of the most intense violence of the entire conflict: over 7,000 Catholics fled their homes; a few thousand Protestants did likewise, burning their homes to the ground as they fled; thousands of cars were looted and burned; hundreds of people were injured; and 24 people were killed. The death toll included two British Army soldiers, two IRA members, and 14 Catholic civilians and six Protestant civilians. A Catholic priest was shot and killed by the British Army as he was administering the last rites to a dying man in the street. Catholic relations with the British government and the Protestant community reached a new low. Over the remaining months of 1971 the violence continued unabated, and would increase in intensity into 1972.

The results of internment were even more devastating for British strategy in Northern Ireland. In addition to local conditions worsening, British policy was internationally condemned. Incarceration without trial, particularly erroneous incarceration, was offensive to Britain's European neighbors. International support for the Catholic cause increased tremendously. Harsh interrogation techniques also brought international condemnation and accusations of torture and human rights violations from the international community. The Republic of Ireland was brought firmly into the conflict on the side of the Catholic community as over 2,000 Northern Irish Catholics fled as refugees across the border, and mobs in Dublin burned the British embassy to the ground. The internment policy brought almost no tactical gains to the British but caused huge tactical and operational problems as violence escalated. It also focused international attention and condemnation on the internment policy specifically and Britain's overall policy in Ireland in general. Finally it became a rallying cry for the Catholic minority to further resist British and Protestant rule, and proved to be a huge boon to IRA recruiting and popularity among the Catholic population.

The conflict in Northern Ireland entered its fourth year in the midst of an accelerating cycle of attack and counterattack involving republican paramilitaries, loyalist paramilitaries, and the security forces, with the civilian population trapped between the combatants. While the violence accelerated, Catholic protest marches against the injustice of both Stormont and British policy continued unabated. These marches, however, had subtly changed in purpose. While in 1968 and 1969 their primary purpose was to highlight the legitimate grievances of the Catholic minority in a non-violent manner, they now became an important tool of the republican paramilitaries. The marches were designed to create confrontation with security forces. Under the cloak of these confrontations the PIRA could attack the security forces and provoke a violent response. This created the perception of a Catholic community closely tied to the IRA in common cause against the security forces, which gained for the PIRA the aura of defending the community against aggressors, and facilitated IRA recruiting.

The major confrontation between the British Army and the Catholic community over internment occurred in January 1972 and became known as "Bloody Sunday." The event began as a Catholic civil rights march in Londonderry on January 30, 1972. British troops deployed to control and contain the protests, PIRA members were present within the protest group, and as violence escalated to throwing rocks at the army the army responded by opening fire. Control of the British soldiers, mostly members of the British Army elite parachute regiment, broke down and they opened fire on the crowd and killed 14 civilian protestors, of whom seven were teenagers. In addition 13 others were wounded by army fire. Extensive investigation of the incident could not provide evidence that the IRA fired on the British troops first, or that the marchers were unusually provocative. The event provided increased impetus to the sectarian division of the population and the intransigence of both sides. It also further increased the attractiveness of the IRA among the general Catholic population and perpetuated the cycle of escalating violence that began in 1971. Also, prompted by "Bloody Sunday," the British government under Prime Minister Edward Heath lost confidence in the Stormont government to solve the security situation and reform the political situation. In March 1972 the British government dissolved the Northern Ireland parliament and installed direct rule of the country from London.

The IRA's response to "Bloody Sunday" was "Bloody Friday," on July 21, 1972. In an 80-minute period the PIRA exploded 22 bombs across Belfast, killing nine people and wounding 130. Most of the killed and injured were innocent civilians. The "Bloody Friday" bombings were part of an extensive bombing campaign that saw over 1,300 bombings over the course of the year. The response of the British government was Operation *Motorman*, designed to restore government control of and presence in Catholic neighborhoods which had been barricaded since 1970, and thus eliminate sanctuaries for the PIRA.

Operation *Motorman* was a massive military operation that involved 29 British Army battalions and over 25,000 troops. The army moved into Catholic neighborhoods in the early hours of July 31, 1972, against rock- and petrol-bomb throwing mobs. However, the size and speed of the operation rapidly intimidated the Catholic community and the British Army was firmly in control of the areas by nightfall. The IRA chose not to resist the operation and instead focused on ensuring that its leadership escaped capture. The British Army shot four people in the course of the operation, all in Londonderry, killing one known IRA member and one civilian, and wounding two civilians. During the course of the operation the army deployed several engineer combat vehicles to crush barricades. This was the only time during the conflict that the British deployed heavily armored combat vehicles to Northern Ireland. After opening up the Catholic neighborhoods, the army did not leave. Instead, it built protected patrol bases in the republican enclaves to ensure that the neighborhoods were firmly and permanently under government control. Operation *Motorman* was successful in permanently restricting the PIRA's freedom of movement in Northern Ireland, eliminating what were sanctuaries from police and army interference and observation, and increasing the army's and the police's ability to gather intelligence. Notwithstanding the success of Operation *Motorman*, 1972 was the most violent year of the entire campaign with a total of 479 people losing their lives.

The PIRA response to Operation *Motorman* was increased violence and attacks against Protestants, the RUC, and the British Army. In response, the British Army stepped up its efforts against the PIRA, completing the transition from peacekeeping operations to full counterinsurgency operations. These operations, however, were not very effective. Though Operation *Motorman* made it more difficult for the PIRA to operate, it did not stop them. British counterinsurgency strategy was not adequate to the conditions in Northern Ireland. The type of counterinsurgency strategy with which the British Army was familiar called for a significant use of force and dramatic constraints on the sympathetic civilian community. Neither course was available to the army in the context of British Northern Ireland within the European community. Thus, British force was not sufficient to even curtail the operations of the IRA, much less destroy the organization, and the British Army was virtually powerless to intervene with the Catholic civilian community. However, enough force and interference with the civilian community occurred to ensure that the IRA retained the sympathies and support of the bulk of Catholics despite the tremendous number of innocent deaths that resulted from IRA operations. The violence continued through 1973 and 1974 – death totals in those years were 255 and 294 respectively.

Despite direct rule from London, little changed on the political front. After imposing direct rule the British government attempted to build a nonsectarian Northern Irish government based on power sharing between the communities. This effort was defeated by a combination of loyalist politicians, loyalist paramilitaries, and the Protestant-dominated trade unions. The Sunnydale power-sharing arrangement failed in the summer of 1974. The British Army's failure to curb loyalist paramilitary violence, which claimed 209 lives in 1973 and 1974, as well as the army's failure to intervene in the trade union strike of 1974, continued to confirm to the PIRA and the Catholic community that the army was a sectarian tool. British military operations were, however somewhat effective at disrupting PIRA operations and organizations. Casualties in 1975 to 1976 among PIRA operatives were 41 killed and numerous arrested. Total casualties on all sides including noncombatants in 1975 and 1976 were 260 and 295, indicating that despite the disruption caused to the PIRA, the two sides were locked in a deadly stalemate.

Policing

In 1975, the PIRA changed their strategy and determined to pursue a long war, in which they would attrite their adversaries over time until public pressure forced the British Army to leave Northern Ireland, and forced the Protestants to acquiesce to unification. As part of this strategy the PIRA reorganized into a cell structure as advocated by classic Maoist revolutionary war doctrine. These small units of four to 10 members were called Active Service Units (ASUs).

The British, however, were also adjusting. In 1976 they introduced their elite special operations forces, the Special Air Service (SAS), into operations in Northern Ireland. They also made a key decision in 1976 to change the security force strategy. Since the end of the peacekeeping mission, the British had pursued a classic counterinsurgency strategy in Northern Ireland that was primarily focused on securing the population and destroying the PIRA. Beginning in 1975 the British changed their strategy to one of police primacy. This shift was more than just moving the RUC to the fore of operations; it also included the end of internment, the beginning of civil trials and conventional imprisonment, political engagement with the Irish Republic to seek a political solution, back-channel talks with the PIRA, and the implementation of political reform.

The switch to police primacy, along with an increase in the effectiveness of the RUC, had some immediate effects as the PIRA was put on the defensive and their ability to operate was curtailed. Deaths resulting from PIRA attacks dropped dramatically beginning in 1976. However, it was not a long-term solution. The PIRA was still able to execute operations. Also, no important progress was made to separate the Catholic community from its tacit support of the republican paramilitaries. This was largely because of the continued sectarian nature of the RUC and British operations. No serious efforts were made by the RUC or the army to act against loyalist paramilitaries. In the years 1972 to 1979 the loyalist paramilitaries accounted for the deaths of 609 persons (as compared to 1,067 deaths caused by republican paramilitaries). In addition, the RUC was notorious for abusing prisoners with suspected ties to the PIRA. The RUC was widely believed to routinely beat confessions from those it arrested. Those confessions were then used to achieve long prison terms in court. Thus, the Catholic community remained estranged from the British government and continued to provide sanctuary for the PIRA. The lack of progress in Northern Ireland was one of many issues that contributed to a change in the British government in 1979 as the Labour Party, in charge since 1974, was replaced by the Conservative Party led by Prime Minister Margaret Thatcher, marking the third change in government since the beginning of the conflict.

Margaret Thatcher's government's engagement with Northern Ireland began inauspiciously in May 1979. Even before the Conservative Party officially took over the reins of the British government, an INLA bomb killed the designated British Secretary of State for Northern Ireland, Airey Neave, in March. On August 27, the PIRA executed two of its most notoriously successful attacks of the conflict: a bomb assassinated Lord Louis Mountbatten, uncle of Queen Elizabeth II's husband Philip; and a multiple bomb ambush in Northern Ireland killed 18 members of the British Army. These attacks confirmed the new British government's commitment to a hard-line approach to Northern Ireland policy.

The inflexible approach of Margaret Thatcher's government toward Northern Ireland policy became evident in the handling of the IRA prisoner hunger strike. The Thatcher government refused to consider giving in to republican prisoner demands to be accorded non-criminal special status. Beginning in March 1981, prisoners began to go on hunger strikes. The first hunger-striker, Bobby Sands, died in May. By the end of August a total of 10 prisoners had died. The British government did not give the prisoners political status, though by the end of the strike in October 1981, they had conceded on a number of demands. Though the British government conceded on several demands, the government declared victory over the hunger strikers; however it was a pyrrhic victory at best. The hunger strikers once again focused critical Catholic and international attention on British operations and policy in Northern Ireland. The strikers galvanized the Catholic community in much the same way as internment and "Bloody Sunday" had. The PIRA had widespread Catholic community support, such that Bobby Sands was elected to a seat in the British House of Commons from the district of Fermanagh and South Tyrone during his hunger strike in prison. That victory inspired increased political participation by the PIRA's political branch, Sinn Fein. Sinn Fein's increased role gave the PIRA a political strategy to accompany their military strategy that ultimately was characterized by the slogan "armalite and ballot box."

The British political mishandling of the hunger strike strengthened the PIRA, however, in the Anglo-Irish Agreement of 1985, the British government somewhat redeemed its earlier policy misstep. The Anglo-Irish Agreement was an extremely important political milestone in the war between the Northern Irish republican paramilitaries and the British security forces. It established several important policy markers. First, it officially recognized a role of the Republic of Ireland in the future of Northern Ireland. Second, it firmly established that Northern Ireland was a part of the United Kingdom. Third, it recognized that the status of Northern Ireland would only change with majority consent. Finally, the agreement established a formal mechanism for joint Anglo-Irish government policy coordination on issues related to Northern Ireland. In the short term, none of these policy issues would make any real difference in the state of the war. They all would become important in the next decade.

In the short term the Anglo-Irish Agreement was important more for who opposed it than who championed it. It was vehemently opposed by the vast majority of Protestant residents of Northern Ireland. All the Protestant political parties opposed the agreement and widely condemned it to the public. Margaret Thatcher was condemned, and 200,000 Protestants rallied against the agreement in front of Belfast city hall. In addition, Protestant unions called a nationwide strike to protest the agreement, similar to the strike in 1975 that had doomed the Summerdale agreement. The PIRA, ironically, was also vehemently against the agreement. Their major objection was the fact that in the agreement the Irish Republic recognized British sovereignty over Northern Ireland. The objections of the Protestant majority and the PIRA to the agreement are important because they were ineffective. The RUC, backed up by the army, unlike in 1975, controlled the Protestant protest. The PIRA found itself isolated from the Catholic community in its opposition to the agreement. Catholics, both in Northern Ireland and in the Irish Republic supported the agreement as a major political step forward.

Though an important political achievement, there were no immediate changes in the tactical situation in Northern Ireland due to the Anglo-Irish Agreement. However, the effectiveness of security force operations increased dramatically through the 1980s. Though there were several attempts to resurrect army security primacy in the 1980s, the policy of the RUC leading security matters remained intact. This had two important results. It increased legitimacy of British security forces, at least in some important domestic and international audiences, if not among the Northern Irish Catholics. It also allowed the RUC to develop significant covert intelligence capability. This, combined with increased army covert capability, made it increasingly difficult for the PIRA to operate.

The British Army's elite SAS was the major military action component in Northern Ireland beginning in the 1980s. The SAS first deployed to Northern Ireland in 1976, mostly as a political statement to demonstrate the resolve of the British government. In the 1970s one of the four squadrons deployed into Northern Ireland for six-month long tours of duty. In the 1980s the presence of the SAS was reduced to a troop of approximately 20 operators and the length of the tour was increased to a year. At the time of their initial deployment the SAS had no particular training in urban warfare, or integration into urban police operations. Their capabilities over the next 20 years demonstrated increased refinement, capability, and also the inherent difficulty of urban special operations, particularly in a policing environment.

In the 1970s the SAS suffered from a lack of good intelligence, but as RUC and army intelligence capabilities increased in the 1980s, so did the abilities of the SAS to launch effective attacks. Though most of the SAS operations were passive surveillance or backup to RUC arrest operations, they launched a significant number of arrest operations on their own and also several spectacular ambushes. The number of arrests made by the SAS is unknown because in arrest operations the SAS quickly handed captured paramilitaries over to the RUC and thus their role went unrecorded. However, action operations in which the SAS engaged the PIRA could not remain covert. In the 1970s, in several encounters with the PIRA, the SAS killed six paramilitaries while losing none of its own. In the 1980s, with a much reduced presence in Northern Ireland, the SAS lost two of its own operators and killed 26 paramilitaries. Its most intense ambushes were in 1987 and 1988. In May 1987 a heavily armed eight-man PIRA ASU was ambushed in the process of bombing an RUC police station in the village of Loughgall. All eight paramilitaries were killed while several soldiers were injured as the bomb severely damaged the police station. In March 1988, an SAS unit killed all three members of a PIRA ASU as they were preparing to bomb British headquarters in Gibraltar – the only direct confrontation between security forces and the PIRA outside of Great Britain proper. Later that same year another three-person ASU was ambushed by the SAS near the town of Drumnakilly in Northern Ireland. The SAS remained active in Northern Ireland in the first part of the 1990s and accounted for 11 paramilitaries with no SAS casualties.

One of the reasons for the success of the SAS in the 1980s and 1990s was the creation of a specialized intelligence unit for Northern Ireland: 14 Intelligence Company. This unit was created specifically to operate in the urban environment in Northern Ireland, its members were highly trained special surveillance specialists carefully selected to blend into the urban population. The operatives of 14 Company included older individuals and women, to increase their ability to avoid suspicion. The activities of 14 Company were coordinated with the SAS under one command called Intelligence and Security Group Northern Ireland. The command operated directly for the British military command in Northern Ireland. Though the damage done to the paramilitaries by the SAS and 14 Company was significant in terms of members killed and captured, perhaps the greatest damage done was psychological. The SAS was a formidable foe and paramilitaries were increasingly aware that at any time and in any place they might be under surveillance and targeted by British military special operations capability. This inspired increased caution, and internal security measures which greatly inhibited the paramilitary's ability to conduct operations.

Though able to conduct some very significant operations in the 1980s and 1990s, including the highly disruptive bombing of the London financial district, the PIRA was increasingly on the defensive. Its ability to inflict casualties reflected this. Casualty rates steadily decreased in the 1980s and 1990s, particularly among security forces. There were two reasons for the decreasing PIRA effectiveness, particularly as the conflict entered the early 1990s. One reason was the effectiveness of the RUC and to a lesser extent, the British military and national intelligence services, to infiltrate informers into the republican paramilitary groups and to turn existing members of the group into informants. Such was the extent of security force penetration of paramilitaries that in the early 1990s the PIRA killed more of its own members as suspected informers, than it did members of the British military. Sophisticated electronic surveillance measures and effective army and police framework operations also contributed to the increasing quality of security force intelligence and decreasing freedom of action for the PIRA.

The other reason for reduced effectiveness of the PIRA was the increased activity of the loyalist paramilitaries against both the Catholic community in general and the PIRA in particular. The loyalist paramilitaries were not aggressively targeted by the security forces for the simple reason that in a resource-constrained environment they were considered the lesser of two evils. The loyalist paramilitaries, as a matter of policy and general practice, did not target security forces. That said, there is also no doubt that many in the RUC and in the major army reserve unit, the Ulster Defense Regiment (UDR), were at least sympathetic to the loyalist paramilitaries if not actual members of one of the various loyalist organizations. Much of the arms and intelligence that the Protestant paramilitaries had available came from these sympathetic sources – hundreds of weapons were stolen over the years from UDR armories. Thus, the loyalist paramilitaries were a significant and capable force and in the late 1980s and 1990s they began to hit Catholic and suspected PIRA targets with great effectiveness. In 1992 the loyalist paramilitaries killed 38 people compared to the republicans killing 40, however in 1993 they killed 49 compared to 38 killings by the republicans, and in 1994 it was 37 to 25. In many ways these statistics are indicative of even greater violence, since the population that the loyalists targeted was significantly smaller than the PIRA's target population.

Though the loyalist paramilitaries were not officially sanctioned by the British government, they operated outside of the law, and they often – like the PIRA – targeted innocent civilians, there is no denying that they were very effective in influencing events. The Catholic civilian population feared the loyalist paramilitaries because of their ruthlessness and because there was no protection against them. The PIRA also feared them because, unlike the security forces, they were not inhibited by any notions of due process and rule of law, and they were willing to attack the friends and relatives of the PIRA when the primary targets were not available. Both groups also feared the loyalists because they were very effective. The PIRA and the various loyalist paramilitaries frequently engaged in cycles of tit-for-tat violence that affected both sides. However, because of the loyalists' larger numbers and sympathizers within the security forces, the PIRA most often came out the worse from the exchange. These conditions made the Catholic community more sympathetic to a peace process which might halt the sectarian attacks, and it encouraged the Sinn Fein politicians within the PIRA to push the organization to accept a political solution given that the military strategy of bombings and sniping was becoming problematic.

Because of the increased military pressure from security forces and loyalist paramilitaries, and the decreasing support from the Catholic community in general, the PIRA declared its first extended cease-fire in August 1994. During that time it negotiated with the British government but, because of the dependence of the Conservative British government on Protestant votes in Northern Ireland, the negotiations made little progress. The major issue was the requirement to decommission PIRA weapons prior to substantive talks regarding a political settlement, a requirement to which the PIRA and Sinn Fein would not agree. In February 1996, the PIRA's cease-fire ended. In May 1997 the Conservative British government of John Major was replaced by the Labour government of Tony Blair. The Blair government continued the process begun by Major, but since it did not rely on Northern Irish votes, it compromised on the issue of decommissioning, permitting that issue to be discussed in parallel with political talks. In July 1997, the PIRA renewed its cease-fire. On April 10, 1998 – Good Friday – the governments of the Republic of Ireland and Great Britain, along with the representatives of most of the prominent political parties of Northern Ireland, agreed to a political solution to the sectarian Troubles of Northern Ireland. Sinn Fein represented the PIRA in the negotiations and signed the agreement. The only major party that did not agree was the loyalist Democratic Unionist Party (DUP). Among the important provisions of the agreement were: respect by all parties for human rights; respect for the desires of the majority regarding the issue of unification; understanding of the interest of the Republic of Ireland; rejection of violence as a means of settling political disagreements; and finally that both unification with Ireland and independent membership in the United Kingdom were legitimate political positions.

The Good Friday Agreement effectively ended the conflict in Northern Ireland, though much political negotiation, and police and military operations, remained. Republican opposition to the agreement continued to manifest itself through violence carried out by a splinter group of the PIRA – the Real Irish Republican Army (RIRA). They made their opposition known most violently in the

Omagh car bombing in August 1998 which killed 21 people of all affiliations and wounded over 100. However, groups like the RIRA and their loyalist equivalents did not have large followings and had decreasing political effects after 1998. Managing the efforts of such groups was well within the capabilities of the RUC (renamed the Police Service of Northern Ireland [PSNI] in 2001) without army support. After 1998, violence like the Omagh bombing and smaller-scale events tended to reinforce public support for the power-sharing formula that the Good Friday agreement put in place. The last British soldier killed in the Troubles died in Northern Ireland in 1997. The last member of the RUC killed as part of the Troubles died in 1998. In July 2007 the British Army formally ended Operation *Banner*, the British military operation in Northern Ireland, after 38 years.

Urban Counterinsurgency Tactics

Over the course of the 38-year war with the Irish paramilitaries in Northern Ireland the role of British conventional forces was substantial and important. The bulk of the army forces deployed to Northern Ireland were required to perform two different but related missions depending on the circumstances during their deployment. One mission was population control during marches and riots. The other was what came to be called framework operations. Framework operations were routine operations conducted regularly to keep continuous pressure on the paramilitaries and ensure that the security forces retained the tactical and operational initiative. There were three main types of tactical framework operations: patrolling, vehicle checkpoints, and observation posts.

Patrols were used to show the presence of the security forces, add protection to RUC patrols, discourage the movement of paramilitaries, and obtain both knowledge of local conditions at the tactical level, and intelligence. In the early years patrols routinely detained individuals for formal questioning but this was eventually found to alienate the civilian community and was replaced by patrol members – not necessarily the patrol leader – "chatting up" people encountered during the patrol. Patrols were vulnerable to both explosives and gun attacks. The key to the protection of the patrols was keeping the timing, area, and routes random and unpredictable. Also important was mutual protection. The typical attack occurred by a gunman who ambushed a patrol at short range and then made a quick escape. Single patrols were very vulnerable to this type of attack. Gun attacks were most easily discouraged by threatening the escape of the gunman. To do this the British Army first developed the technique of mutually supporting parallel patrols. An attack on one patrol quickly brought the other patrol in support. This idea was enhanced by eventually developing the multiple-patrol technique in which several small teams, typically three or four consisting of four men each, patrolled in a seemingly random pattern, frequently crossing tracks, but always within supporting distance. Explosives could not predict where or when the patrol would be and gunmen could not predict where the supporting patrols were located and thus could not be assured of an open escape route. The key to the success of patrolling was carefully planning the patrol routes. The paramilitaries were very careful to study patrol routes and if they discovered patterns in the activity they planned operations accordingly.

Vehicle checkpoints were another way to reassure the public and to limit the mobility of the paramilitaries. Checkpoints fell into two types: permanent, and unannounced temporary checkpoints, called "snap" checkpoints. The permanent checkpoints were necessary to ensure security-force control of major roadways, however they were vulnerable targets themselves and rarely disrupted paramilitary operations because of their overt nature. However, their role was denial of access to the major routes and forcing paramilitary movement onto the smaller and slower secondary road network. The army established snap checkpoints to ensure that the paramilitaries understood there were no safe movement routes and they occasionally did result in the identification and arrest of known paramilitaries.

Observation posts fell into two broad categories: covert and overt. Overt observation posts served the same purpose as permanent vehicle checkpoints: they denied freedom of movement to the paramilitaries in particularly important areas. Covert observation was much more difficult. Throughout the campaign, regular army units employed close observation platoons that operated covertly to observe and gather intelligence. They received specialized training and would typically occupy derelict buildings at night and remain hidden in position for days. Overt observation posts were heavily protected positions in important, heavily trafficked parts of cities or in neighborhoods known to be sympathetic to paramilitaries. They used a wide range of sophisticated listening and observation devices and again, the expectation was that these known positions would deny the use of the area to the paramilitaries.

Intelligence analysis and acquisition was probably the most important element in the success of the security forces at all levels of operations. By the end of the campaign one in eight British troops in Northern Ireland was directly involved in the intelligence process in some manner. In addition to the techniques contributed by the regular army infantry units and the special operations units mentioned above, as time went on the army developed a significant electronics intelligence capability which included cameras, signals intelligence, and airborne intelligence – both manned and unmanned. In addition the army intelligence capability was integrated into the local intelligence network run by the RUC Special Branch. This capability was relatively ineffective in the early years of the war, but by the 1980s it was a very sophisticated and effective operation. Also MI5, a British national intelligence agency, had a strong presence in Northern Ireland. However there were problems throughout the history of the conflict, with the various intelligence agencies not effectively sharing information. Still, in the last decade of the campaign the combined intelligence capability of the security forces severely constrained the paramilitaries and disrupted literally hundreds of operations before they could be executed.

The Military Role in Urban Insurgency

There are many strategic lessons that can be taken from the British experience fighting a determined and skilled insurgent in the urban areas of Northern Ireland. One of the most important, learned only over time by the British forces, was that the key to success was the allegiance of the civil population. In the case of Northern Ireland, the key factor was the attitudes of the Catholic and Protestant communities. The various paramilitaries were in a similar situation – needing to be perceived as legitimate by the civilian population. The strength of the PIRA came from its support in the Catholic community. That support was generated by the aggressive actions of the RUC and the sectarian policies of the Stormont government in the early years. That support hardened in the face of the relatively clumsy and unfocused army counterinsurgency efforts through the 1970s. Arguably, it took the entire decade of the 1980s and the first years of the 1990s for the British security forces to learn to apply more sophisticated tactics, tied into an integrated political and military strategy, and wean the Catholic community from its steadfast support of the PIRA.

One of the keys to the ultimate success of the British strategy in Northern Ireland was the army learning the counterintuitive effects of military actions. What the British security forces learned, over many years, was that when the PIRA indiscriminately attacked civilian targets, support for it among the general Catholic population decreased. However, as the security forces responded to the PIRA attack with searches, arrests, and raids, often poorly targeted and involving collateral damage to innocent civilians and their property, support for the PIRA increased. These phenomena perpetuated the cycle of violence in the war and in fact became part of the PIRA's long-war strategy. However, in the mid-1980s, the security forces began to discern that if the security forces responded to PIRA violence covertly, or with precisely targeted arrests, there was a net decrease in popular support for the PIRA. Thus, as the security forces took a lower profile in the late 1980s and early 1990s, the popular support for the PIRA slowly and steadily decreased. The PIRA's response to decreasing support was to lash out with even less discriminating attacks and thereby further delegitimize itself in the eyes of the Catholic population. Losing the confidence and support of the general Catholic population was not the only reason that the PIRA was at increasing variance with Sinn Fein's political strategy, but it was an important aspect in why the PIRA ultimately conceded to a political solution to the war.

The British Army's experience in Northern Ireland is an important demonstration of the increasingly sophisticated nature of urban warfare in the late 20th and early 21st centuries. Importantly, the British Army's operations in the Northern Ireland conflict required a much more complex understanding of the role of military forces and the definition of success and winning in war than was required to understand most previous conflicts. Northern Ireland demonstrated that winning an urban insurgency was as much about an integrated national counterinsurgency strategy as it was about military effectiveness. The British military was never seriously challenged directly by the military capabilities of the paramilitaries. However, effective paramilitary politics, information operations, combined with ineffectual British government political reforms and an abysmal economic environment, allowed the PIRA and other paramilitaries to be effective out of all proportion to their actual military capabilities. The British Army won its war with the paramilitaries in the urban environment of Northern Ireland not because it destroyed the paramilitaries, but rather because it created a secure enough environment such that political reform and compromise, and economic development could advance to the point that the information operations of the paramilitaries were ineffective. Thus, urban warfare had evolved to the point that it was not about destroying the enemy, instead military operations were about creating secure enough conditions that political success was possible.

CHAPTER 8
URBAN DEATH TRAP
The Russian Army in Grozny, 1995

After many years absent from major urban combat, the Russian army, the victors at Stalingrad and the largest, most lethal urban battlefields of World War II, found itself once again confronting urban combat, this time in the Russian province of Chechnya. In the early 1990s, separatist movements sprang up all over the former Soviet empire as people, long subjugated by Moscow, sought to take advantage of the end of the Cold War and win sovereignty for themselves. The traditional inhabitants of Russia's Chechen province were one of the ethnic groups who wanted self-determination, and in 1991 they declared their intent to become independent and took control of the province, and its capital city Grozny. It wasn't until 1994 that Russia tried to reassert its claim to dominion over Chechnya, and the Russian army invaded.

In the early 1990s Chechnya had a total population of about 1.2 million. The province is located in the north Caucus Mountains region of southern Russia. It is bordered on the west, north and east by the Russian Republic. In the south it shares a border with the country of Georgia. The terrain of the province is generally mountainous and covered with dense forests. The city of Grozny, in the center of the country, was the focus of most military operations during two separate wars between Chechen independence forces and the Russian army, in 1994 and 1999.

Grozny was a city that traced its roots to the early 19th century when Russia, at war with the Ottoman Turks, formally claimed the area. Terek Cossacks of the Russian army established a fort called

Fortress Groznaya (which means "Terrible" Fortress). Grozny was an important outpost from which Czarist Russia, through its Cossacks, controlled the Muslim mountain people indigenous to the northern Caucasus. Before World War I, oil was discovered in Grozny and the surrounding area and economic development transformed the military base into a city. During the Russian Revolution and the civil war which followed, the Cossacks, then the basis of the Russian ethnic population in Grozny, sided with the pro-Czarist White forces and lost control of Grozny to the Bolsheviks who were aided by the indigenous Muslim tribes. Over the next 70 years Grozny was the center of much anticommunist sentiment – stemming from both the anticommunist Cossacks and the Muslim mountain people. Both the Cossacks and the Muslims were subjected to forced migration by the Communists. Their places in Grozny were taken by non-Cossack Russians. By the time of the collapse of the Soviet Union in 1990, most of the Muslim population had returned and they made up about two-thirds of the population of the province, but only a small percentage of the urban population of Grozny, which remained largely ethnic Russian. Russians claim that prior to the first Chechnya war in 1994, most ethnic Russians were forced by the Chechen majority to flee Chechnya, thus in the first battle of Grozny most of the city's residents were Muslim. However, some international observers and the advocates of an independent Chechnya claim that the Russian population was never forced to leave by the Chechen government, and remained until forced to depart by the war conditions, when Russian bombing caused between 200,000 and 300,000 ethnic Russians to flee the province. In 1994, in the months before the first battle for Grozny, the city had a mixed Chechen-Russian population of approximately 490,000 – almost a third of the province's population. The city and its suburbs covered approximately 90 square miles. The city was a mixture of buildings ranging from one-story residences to massive 15-story housing structures. Almost all of the structures in the city were made of reinforced concrete. The Sunzha River was a major terrain feature within the city and flowed northeast to southwest dividing the city into a northern and southern sector.

The Road to Grozny

On December 11, 1994, the Russian Republic, under President Boris Yeltsin, launched its military into Chechnya to restore that province to the control of the Republic. The Russians were motivated by a number of factors, the two most important being access to, and control of oil; and ensuring that they stopped the dissolution of the former Soviet Union while the Russian Republic still had sufficient land and resources to be regarded as an international power. Chechnya had significant indigenous oil stocks, and its location, and particularly the location of the city of Grozny, made it a key distribution point for oil and oil products coming from neighboring provinces. By 1994 Chechnya had effectively been independent for almost three years – though its status was not legal according to the Russian constitution, and it was not recognized by the Russian government in Moscow. Other peripheral provinces were in danger of following the Chechen example. Thus the government in Moscow determined to demonstrate that it had the will and capability to preserve the integrity of what remained of the former Soviet Union, lest further disintegration occur. By December 21, Russian forces had advanced through Chechnya and closed in on Grozny from the north, southwest, and east. On December 26, the Russian government authorized the Russian army to advance into Grozny itself.

The Russian army that served the Russian Republic in 1994 appeared to be virtually identical to the formidable Soviet Red Army which had intimidated Europe for half a century and which had destroyed the vaunted German war machine in World War II. However, less than five short years after the end of the Cold War, the army was neither the mighty machine that fought on the Eastern Front in World War II, nor the menace that had threatened NATO since the 1950s.

The battle for Stalingrad during World War II had honed the Soviet army into an expert urban warfare force. Subsequent campaigns in World War II built on that expertise, which reached its peak in the battle for Berlin in 1945. However, after World War II, Soviet forces gradually lost that expertise. The Soviet army was not committed to any significant large-scale combat for almost 50 years – the one exception being Afghanistan where no major urban combat occurred. More importantly, Soviet doctrinal thinkers focused on operational maneuver warfare. The Soviet army believed that the major lesson learned in World War II was that victory was the result of flexible and rapid maneuver by massed mobile armies built around large armor and mechanized infantry formations. The prospect of lengthy and resource-consuming urban combat was anathema to the maneuver focus of the Red Army. Soviet army leaders believed

Map 8.1 The Initial Russian Attack into Grozny, December 1994

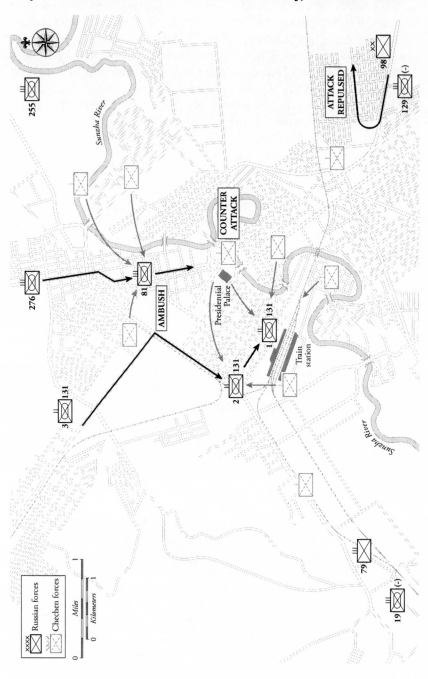

that in a confrontation with NATO, western armies would abandon western European cities rather than see them and their populations destroyed in street-by-street battles. They also believed that any city that might be decisively defended could be bypassed by mechanized spearheads, and then carefully reduced or induced to surrender once surrounded. Urban warfare, once a key competency of the Red Army, was absent from both Soviet doctrine and practice by the end of the Cold War.

The Red Army of the Cold War, despite its lack of expertise in urban fighting, was still a superbly equipped, well-led, and well-trained modern military force. However, the same could not be said for the army that entered Chechnya just four years after the end of the Cold War. The political collapse of the Soviet Union heralded an internal collapse inside the Red Army. Communism, and the discipline and authority built around the Soviet Communist Party, was one of the bedrocks of the Red Army. When Soviet Communism collapsed so did the Red Army. Externally, the army still appeared a formidable force. Though Soviet military forces had numbered over five million in the late 1980s, the rump of the forces still available to the Russian Republic in 1994 retained a formidable strength of over two million. However, the quality of the force was dubious.

The collapse of the Soviet Union was occasioned by the collapse of the Soviet economy. The economic collapse had significant effects on the army. Budgets were cut and training was cancelled; and more importantly, routine logistics functions came to a standstill. The army could barely feed itself, and getting access to necessary commodities such as fuel became problematic. As the country disintegrated politically, the population began to refuse to comply with conscription. As regions of the country declared their autonomy from Moscow, large elements of the military stationed in those regions, such as the Ukraine, broke away. The military high command was focused more on political survival and privileges than on its soldiers and units. Soldiers in garrisons began to desert. Other soldiers sold their personal, and even unit equipment, including weapons, in order to buy food and alcohol. Pay for the soldiers, never very much, failed to materialize for months. Regular army units, the motorized rifle regiments and divisions, were the hardest hit by these conditions. Elite units such as paratroopers and Spetsnaz special operations forces, nuclear forces, and the air force and navy were not as dramatically affected. The conditions within the regular army forces were disastrous. By 1994 most units were only shadows of their paper personnel strengths, they were receiving virtually no training, and much of their equipment was inoperable.

The Russian force assembled outside of Grozny in December 1994 numbered nearly 24,000 men: 19,000 from the Russian army and approximately 5,000 from Russia's internal security forces. The army forces consisted of five motorized rifle, two tank, and seven airborne battalions plus supporting artillery, engineers, aviation and other elements. The major army equipment included 80 tanks, over 200 infantry fighting vehicles, and over 180 artillery pieces. There were over 90 helicopters in the supporting aviation element. Despite these numbers, the force's combat power was modest by Cold War standards. Its combat elements resembled the combat power of a reinforced motorized rifle division. The seven airborne battalions were some of Russia's best elite troops, however the airborne battalions themselves were very small units and the total of the seven battalions was likely smaller than that of the five motorized rifle battalions. The concept of the Russian operation was for the army to lead the advance to Grozny. Then, on order, attack the city to seize important government, economic, and communications centers. The internal security units would advance behind the army and once the city was under army control the security forces would take over control from the army.

Chechnya, the breakaway province, did not have an army. The military forces of the province were built around a small cadre of former Soviet soldiers. They formed a small provincial guard that probably numbered fewer than a thousand. Another group of approximately 5,000 was made up of irregular volunteers with little formal military training. They were led by those volunteers who had experience in the Soviet army, of which there was no shortage. There was some Russian military equipment left in the province following the withdrawal of the Soviet Army in 1991, which included about 40 main battle tanks, 30 armored personal carriers and scout vehicles, and about 30 122mm medium artillery pieces. The Chechen fighters organized as squads of six to seven men. Each squad had at least one RPK medium machine gun, one RPG rocket-propelled grenade launcher, and one designated sniper. Three squads combined with a medium (82mm) mortar team made up the basic fighting unit. Three of these platoon equivalents were formed to make up a 75-man fighting group, the equivalent of a small company. They communicated with each other using commercial handheld radios. The Chechen forces' major advantage was that they were highly motivated, knew each other well, and had a thorough knowledge of the urban terrain over which they fought.

Street Ambush

By December 30, 1994, the Russian forces completely surrounded the city of Grozny. Though positioned on most of the major routes into the city, the Russians did not orient their force to isolate the city. For most of the battle the Chechen forces were able to bring supplies and reinforcements into the city from the southeast.

Four assault task forces were formed to attack into the city along four separate axes. From the southwest, General Major Petruk would attack with a regiment from 76th Airborne Division and two mechanized assault groups from the 19th Motorized Rifle Regiment. Their objective was the city railroad station, and to isolate the Presidential Palace from the south. A task force under General Major Pulikovsky was assigned to attack from the northwest with the 131st Motorized Rifle Brigade, and elements of the 276th and 81st motorized rifle regiments. The 255th Motorized Rifle Regiment under General Rokhlin was given the mission to attack the city from the northeast. Finally, General Staskov was to lead the southeastern task force consisting of elements of the 129th Motorized Rifle Regiment and part of the 98th Airborne Division. Their mission was to occupy the southeastern part of the city and seize a series of bridges over the Sunzha River. On paper this appeared to be a very formidable force and a solid plan, but only because it did not reflect the problems inherent throughout the Russian military in 1994. None of the units had trained in large-scale military operations, much less urban warfare. The motorized rifle units in particular were made up of hastily assembled units from all over Russia and many soldiers had only been together for a few weeks. Collective training as a unit was almost nonexistent and the individual training of many soldiers barely covered the use of their individual small arms. Commanders were not given time to conduct detailed planning for their missions, undertake reconnaissance, or rehearse with their troops.

The Russians were not expecting to fight a sustained battle for the city of Grozny, nor were they mentally or physically prepared for such a battle. Thus, as the battle developed, initial failings on the Russian side were as much due to lack of understanding of the situation as to professional incompetence, although there was an abundance of the latter. There were three phases of the battle. Phase one was the opening days of the attack. During this phase Russian commanders and soldiers were not fully aware of the combat environment in which they were engaged. In phase two of the battle, the Russian forces reorganized, developed tactics, and systematically wrestled the northern portion of the city from the Chechen defenders. In the final phase of the battle, Russian forces secured the city, eliminated the remaining Chechen forces in the northern part of the city, and pushed the Chechen forces out of southern Grozny.

The plan for the entry into the city was reasonably well conceived. However, its execution was extremely poor. Of the four major commands that were to enter the city, only one mounted a determined effort. In the west, the predominantly airborne forces of General Major Petruk encountered light resistance in the industrial areas just outside the city. However, the planned air support for the attack did not appear, and the units stopped their advance to await developments. In the east the airborne task force under General Major Staskov met heavier resistance on its assigned route of advance. The Russian forces, rather than fight through the resistance, turned north seeking an alternate route. They then ran into minefields and barricades. This force too, stopped its attack and awaited further orders. The northeastern force, under General Rokhlin, moved into the outskirts of the city and then considered its mission accomplished and switched to the defensive. The only force that made a determined effort to achieve its assigned objectives was the mechanized task force under General Major Pulikovsky approaching from the northeast – and they paid a great price for it.

General Pulikovsky's force began its movement at 6am on December 31. Though ostensibly attacking to seize the city, the command's understanding of the situation was completely unrealistic. Pulikovsky and his subordinates viewed the operation as a show of force to intimidate the Chechens into submitting to Moscow's governance. They did not expect any serious opposition and therefore the units moved forward in a column formation with no reconnaissance or security forces deployed. Some of the motorized infantry slept in the back of their armored carriers. By midday, Pulikovsky's force had entered the outskirts of the city. The 81st Motorized Rifle Regiment proceeded down Pervomayskaya Street moving directly south toward the Presidential Palace, while the 131st Motorized Rifle Brigade moved parallel to them to the west along Staropromyslovskoye Boulevard and then Mayakovskaya Street. Initially all went well and the tanks and armored personnel carriers rumbled slowly down the very quiet streets of the city in carefully organized and aligned columns – as if on parade. The movement was very slow and deliberate, partly because the Russians were in no hurry, and partly because the units were not well trained and commanders wanted to ensure they did not lose control.

In the early afternoon, the 81st MRR made contact with the Chechen defenders. Numerous Chechen battle groups, probably totaling more than a thousand fighters, ambushed the carefully spaced column of armored vehicles from buildings and alleys on both sides of the street. Squads of fighters engaged with the armored vehicles with machine guns and RPGs from the upper stories of buildings. The top armor of the tanks and armored vehicles was thin: the RPGs easily penetrated the armor and destroyed numerous vehicles. The leaders of the Chechen forces were veterans of the Soviet army and knew how to execute an ambush. The attacks focused first on the lead and trail vehicles in each march unit. Once they were destroyed, the other vehicles were trapped and exposed in the street, which quickly became congested. Then, at a more leisurely pace, the RPG fire systematically engaged the rest of the column. Russian officers tried to rally their men but the buildings made radio communications difficult and the individual Russian units were hastily put together, consisted of many new conscripts, and very poorly trained. They were not equipped to operate on their own and when isolated by the ambush and lack of communications, discipline quickly broke down. Russian troops abandoned their vehicles and fought their way to the rear. Many didn't make it to the hastily organized rally points. The Russians found that the ZSU-23-4 mobile antiaircraft vehicle, which was armed with four rapid-firing 23mm cannon, was one of the few weapons that could quickly and effectively suppress Chechen ambush positions. The rapid fire of the heavy cannon easily penetrated building walls, and the ability of the turret to traverse rapidly and elevate the guns to rooftops intimidated snipers and RPG gunners. The performance of the ZSUs was a small Russian success in an otherwise dismal battle performance. The crews of tanks and BMP mechanized fighting vehicles jumped from their vehicles, often while they were still operational, and made their way by foot to the rear. Other vehicles did not move, waiting in vain for orders, their engines idling until they were hit and set ablaze by Chechen RPGs. By afternoon the attack of the 81st MRR was completely defeated and the regiment was chased from the streets of Grozny, leaving behind dozens of abandoned and destroyed tanks and personnel carriers.

In contrast to the advance of the 81st MRR, the 131st Rifle Brigade's move into the city was unopposed. By 3pm the brigade had reached its initial objective and reported no opposition. It was ordered on to its final objective in the center of town: the main railway station and town square. The brigade was unaware of the fate of the 81st MMR. By late afternoon the brigade reported its arrival at the railway station without opposition. One battalion occupied the station; a second battalion occupied the freight station several blocks away. The third battalion remained in reserve on the outskirts of the city. The troops at the main station dismounted and many went into the station and generally took a break. No effort was made to establish a defensive position. The brigade assumed the other attacking units were having similar experiences and would soon be linking with them at the station.

Not long after arriving at the station, the 300 men of the 1st Battalion, 131st Brigade were engaged by Chechen small-arms fire. After destroying the 81st MRR, Chechen fighters roamed the city looking for additional Russian units to attack, and discovered the unprepared battalions of the 131st. The Chechen fighting groups communicated by radio and soon fighters from all over the city swarmed toward the railway station. Suddenly BMP infantry fighting vehicles and tanks in the city square were exploding from RPG hits. Many of the Russian troops were dismounted and not near their vehicles. Troops who were in the vehicles were caught unaware, had no idea what was happening or where the enemy was, and because of their poor training, were unable to respond effectively. The Russian soldiers found themselves surrounded and under attack from rockets and machine guns from all sides. Estimates are that over a thousand Chechen fighters surrounded the station. Officers who moved into the open to evaluate the situation and rally their men were quickly cut down. Due to poor communications, and poor coordination, radio calls for reinforcements and artillery support went unanswered. The troops at the railway station formed a perimeter in and around the railway station and waited for reinforcements.

The fight at the railway station quickly engulfed the battalion at the freight station and it too saw its stationary vehicles destroyed by rockets fired by quick-moving gunners popping out of alleys or firing from the upper stories and roofs of buildings. Machine-gun fire and snipers kept the battalion pinned down, and destroyed vehicles blocked many of the streets. As in the 81st MRR ambush, tank crews found that their main guns could not depress low enough to engage enemy in the basements of buildings, or elevate high enough to engage the upper stories and roofs of buildings. In some cases crews panicked, and were gunned down as they abandoned tanks and armored personnel vehicles that were still operational. The reserve battalion was ordered to move in and reinforce the engaged elements of the brigade, but they were ambushed on the same streets that had been clear and quiet that morning and were quickly pinned down and fighting for their own survival. As darkness fell, the battle at the railway station raged on.

The morning of January 1 began with groups of Russians, including the bulk of the 131st Brigade, pinned down in the city or on the routes leading into it. Russian operations focused on extracting their forces and suppressing the Chechen fighters. Weather grounded the Russian air force on January 1 and 2, but the Russians relied heavily on the one weapon that the Chechens and the weather had little ability to affect: artillery. Russian artillery began pounding the city on January 1, in what appeared to be an indiscriminate manner. In reality, the Russians were attempting to hit what they thought were Chechen defensive positions, not realizing that what they perceived as a deliberate Chechen defense of the city built around strong defensive points was in reality moving ambushes. Thus, Russian artillery ravaged blocks of apartments as well as obvious military targets such as the Presidential Palace. The main victims of the barrages were Chechen civilians. Russian units remained trapped in the city, most notably the battalions of the 131st Brigade, hunkered down in defensive positions under constant Chechen sniping. Units outside the city, in particular parachute infantry units that had not been prepared to attack the previous day, attempted to renew the attack but the Chechen fighters, buoyed by their success the previous day, stymied all Soviet attempts to resume the attack. The Russian units outside the city were still unclear of the situation inside the city and the position of the surrounded units. Some Spetsnaz Russian special forces and paratroopers penetrated into the city but had no real objective. They wandered the city trying to avoid being cut-off themselves and eventually fought their way back to their own lines.

On January 2, the remnants of the 131st, mounted in previously abandoned armored vehicles recovered from the battlefield, attempted to break out of the city. The brigade commander was killed as the survivors fought through Chechen ambushes to escape the city. By January 3, what remained of the brigade had either escaped the city, died, or been captured. The brigade had lost the entire

1st Battalion – approximately 300 men and 40 armored vehicles. In total the brigade lost 102 of 120 armored vehicles, and 20 of 26 tanks; almost all of the officers in the brigade had been killed; total casualties in the brigade were approximately 700–800 personnel. The 81st MRR lost approximately 60 armored vehicles and suffered several hundred casualties. In total the two brigades that attacked from the north lost over 200 armored vehicles of all types, and sustained approximately 1,500 casualties. The Chechen fighters tried to take advantage of their success and push the Russian forces completely out of Grozny on January 2 and 3, however the Russian forces were very formidable in defense and the Chechens suffered significant casualties without removing the Russians from the city approaches. The failed Chechen counterattacks ended the first and bloodiest phase of the battle for the city.

After the defeat of the New Year's Eve attack, the Russian army reorganized, reevaluated, and prepared to renew the offensive. The second phase of the assault to capture Grozny began on January 7, 1995. This time the Russians executed a systematic attack in which infantry platoons supported by tanks, infantry fighting vehicles, armored personnel carriers, artillery and mortar fire, and air strikes, systematically advanced through the city toward the Presidential Palace. The small Russian assault groups attacked each building, captured it, and used it as a base to assault the next position. Artillery fire advanced ahead of the infantry. Tank fire raked each building before the infantry attacked. In this manner the Russians advanced steadily, block by block, toward their objective. They also systematically destroyed the city as they moved, and undoubtedly killed countless civilians caught up in their advance.

As the Russians attempted to advance on January 7 they met renewed Chechen resistance. The Chechens used a variety of techniques to thwart the rapid Russian advance. Civilians were taken hostage, Chechen fighters blended in with the civil population wearing civilian clothing, buildings and derelict vehicles were booby-trapped, sewers and other subterranean tunnels were used to move unobserved behind advancing Russian forces, and minefields and barricades were used to channel Russian forces into prepared ambush sites. The Russians responded by increasing the use of artillery and dispatching small reconnaissance units. The reconnaissance units were also tasked with finding pockets of Russian survivors from the New Year's Eve attack and Russian soldiers being held prisoner in the city. Despite firing artillery into the city at a rate of 20–30 rounds a minute, the Russians were unable to make significant advances. Reports indicated that even Russian special operations units were captured by the Chechens. On January 9 the Russians paused and unilaterally declared a cease-fire to begin the next day and last until January 12. Both sides violated the cease-fire but no major offensive operations occurred.

On January 12, Russian forces resumed the attack, beginning with a three-hour artillery and rocket barrage aimed at the city center. Intense fighting occurred as reinforced Russian units fought building to building toward the city center aiming to capture their original objectives including the railway station and the Presidential Palace. Elite Russian naval infantry units were added to the mixture of Spetsnaz, paratroopers, motorized infantry, and tank units fighting into the city. Additional Russian troops moved south of the city to attempt to close routes that were being used to both resupply and reinforce the Chechen forces in the city, and evacuate key leaders and heavy equipment out of the city. For five days Russian forces systematically fought toward the city center. On January 19 the Russians secured the Presidential Palace and two days later the train station and the center of the city. The Russians then moved to the north bank of the Sunzha River and mopped up remaining pockets of Chechen fighters. On January 26, Russian military units turned over control of Grozny north of the river to internal security police forces. Chechen resistance in the center of the city had collapsed, but the battle was not over. The Chechen combat groups, estimated by the Russians to number about 3,500 fighters, withdrew over the Sunzha River, blowing up bridges as they withdrew, and established a new defense on the south side of the river.

While police security forces, reinforced by the army, battled isolated pockets of Chechen fighters left on the north bank of the river, Russian military forces crossed the river to drive the fighters from their remaining strongpoints in the final phase of the battle. The Russians made liberal use of air support, attack helicopters, artillery, and Shmel flamethrowers. The Shmel weapons were particularly effective at clearing snipers and RPG gunners from suspected ambush positions. The Chechens were fighting a rearguard action not so much to protect withdrawing forces but rather to draw out the battle. Every day of resistance and fighting in Grozny was a political and propaganda victory for the Chechens. On February 8, the Russians declared 80 percent of the city under their control. On February 16, a four-day cease-fire was called to exchange prisoners and wounded. On February 20, combat resumed and three days later the Russians surrounded the last significant Chechen forces in the city, ending major operations.

Varying Tactics

The battle for Grozny was an intense six-week urban combat experience. Total Russian losses during the battle are estimated to be approximately 1,700 killed, hundreds captured, and probably several thousand wounded. Chechen casualties are completely unknown due to the inability to distinguish fighters from civilians and the decentralized and informal structure of the Chechen forces. Most of what is known of the battle is the result of researchers putting together snippets from contemporary news reports, official Russian reports, and interviews with participants on both sides. Both the Chechen and Russian leadership had, and continue to have, a vested political interest in portraying the performance of their forces in the best possible manner and denying operational difficulties. On the Chechen side the defense of the city has to be considered a victory despite the loss of the city. The outnumbered and underequipped defenders of the city prevented a larger, lavishly equipped force from securing the city for almost fifty days. Simultaneously, they inflicted significant tactical losses on the attackers, waged an effective information campaign, and greatly strengthened the political strength and legitimacy of the Chechen independence movement. The best that can be said for the performance of the Russian forces is that they eventually achieved their objective. The battle revealed a surprisingly low level of capability within the military forces of Russia.

The actual operational details of the battle are sparse, but a great deal is known about the tactical techniques applied by both sides. On the defense, the Chechens fought what some have called a defenseless defense. They relied on the unusual urban tactic of mobile combat groups rather than strongpoints. This tactic was particularly effective in the early stages of fighting because the Russians attacked to penetrate the city along specific axes of advance rather than on a broad front. The Russian approach, lack of adequate command and control, as well as insufficient numbers and disregard for their flanks, allowed the Chechen mobile groups to maneuver throughout the city at will and control the initiative in the battle even though they were on the defensive. As the Russian force grew in size and the Russian attack became more systematic in the second and third phases of the battle, it became more difficult for the Chechen forces to maneuver.

A Russian response to the Chechen tactic was the development of "baiting." Small forces, such as a mechanized platoon or squad were sent forward to spring a Chechen ambush. Once exposed, a larger mobile force, supported by attack helicopters and artillery, used massed firepower to overwhelm the Chechen fighters. The Chechen response to the deliberate and expansive use of artillery and airpower by the Russians was "hugging." Once engaged, Chechen fighters moved as close as possible to the attacking Russians to make it impossible for the Russians to employ their massive advantages in artillery and airpower. The Russian goal in the streets of Grozny was to identify the Chechen defenders before becoming decisively engaged and then destroy them with long-range direct and indirect firepower. The Chechen approach was just the opposite: stay as closely engaged with the Russians as possible. The employment of these tactics resulted in massive amounts of damage and significant civilian casualties as neither side considered collateral damage an important tactical consideration.

The most effective tactical weapons employed in Grozny were a mixture of old and new technology. The sniper armed with his scoped rifle proved a very reliable and essential element of successful urban combat. The Chechen forces employed formally trained snipers as well as competent designated marksmen in the sniper role. The Russian army, once they reverted to systematic offensive operations, included snipers to cover the infantry as they assaulted buildings. A new weapon, employed by both sides but with particular effect by the Chechen forces, was the rocket-propelled grenade, the RPG-7. This weapon was incredibly easy to use and lethal to all armored vehicles, including tanks. It was lightweight and easily carried by one man and so could quickly be positioned in the upper stories of buildings and on rooftops. The Chechens demonstrated the versatility of the weapon as they used it against armored vehicles, in open areas against infantry, against low-flying helicopters, and even in an indirect fire mode by launching the rockets over the tops of buildings at Russian forces on the other side. The Russians had access to this weapon as well but limited its use primarily to the traditional anti-armor role. Chechens sometimes increased the lethality of their snipers by equipping them with an RPG as well.

Russian forces employed a new weapon, one that had not been seen in urban combat before but which was ideally suited to the environment: the RPO-A Sheml. The Sheml was called a "flamethrower" by Russian sources but in its operation bore little resemblance to the traditional flamethrower that literally projected burning fuel at the target from short range. The Sheml was a rocket-propelled thermobaric weapon. It launched a 90mm rocket from a lightweight launch tube at targets up to a thousand meters away. When it hit the target the warhead of the rocket dispersed a fuel igniter which exploded after mixing with oxygen from the surrounding air. The resulting explosion was extremely powerful and hot. Enclosed areas such as bunkers, caves, and buildings magnified the effect of the explosion. Typically, any flammable materials in the vicinity were ignited. The Sheml became a favorite weapon for dealing with suspected sniper and RPG positions. The devastating effects of the weapon had a psychological impact on Chechen fighters, who rapidly abandoned firing positions before the Russians could launch a Sheml in response.

Tanks were a critical component of the Russian army's success, as proven in other conventional urban combat experiences. However, the use of tanks evolved over the course of the month-long battle. At the beginning, Russian attacking forces relied extensively on tanks as the basis of operations: tanks led the attack and were supported by the other arms. Using these tactics Russian tank losses were extensive. The high losses among the tank forces caused the Russians to change their tactics by leading with dismounted motorized rifle troops and paratroopers. Dismounted forces were followed closely by infantry fighting vehicles and antiaircraft systems such as the ZSU 23-4. Tanks overwatched operations and added the weight of their main guns to the fight but were careful to always remain behind a screen of infantry.

From the very beginning of the battle, the Russians made frequent and liberal use of artillery. Artillery was a traditional weapon of the Russian army in battle but in Grozny it had only limited positive effects. The availability of supporting artillery in large numbers did much to reassure Russian troops of their firepower superiority over the Chechen forces. This was an important psychological effect given the shock to Russian morale caused by the New Year's Eve attack. However, Russian artillery was not particularly effective against the Chechen forces because of the fluid nature of their defensive tactics. The lavish use of artillery, however, had a large adverse effect on the civilian population and on Russian civilian support for the war. Most of the residents of the central part of the city were ethnic

Russians and they became the victims of Russian air and artillery bombardment. Estimates of civilian casualties in the six-week battle range from 27,000 to 35,000 killed. The number of wounded civilians was estimated to be close to 100,000. The Russian and international media reported negatively on the civilian loss of life and support for the Russian war effort suffered both within Russia and in the international community.

Controlling Information

The battle for Grozny demonstrated the importance and effects of information operations on urban combat in the digital communications age. The Russian government tried to prevent information leaving the battlefield rather than managing that information. Reporters were barred from moving with Russian troops and observing the battlefield freely from the Russian side. In contrast, the Chechen commanders encouraged the media to observe their operations and interview commanders and soldiers. The Chechens, using the media effectively, managed to portray the battle as sympathetic freedom fighters fighting against the oppressive army of a tyrannical regime. Despite the efforts of the Russian government, information reached the Russian population anyway, but that information often dramatically contradicted official Russian government statements and was sympathetic to the Chechen point of view. The Russian government quickly lost credibility with both the Russian people and the international community. Political opposition to Russian military operations consequently grew rapidly, both within and outside Russia.

The Russian military successfully seized the city of Grozny from the Chechen fighters in 1995. However, the methods they employed indicated the major characteristics of the Russian military. First, it was a blunt military instrument and incapable of precise operations. The Russian military did not outfight the Chechens, it overwhelmed them. Second, Grozny demonstrated that the Russian government did not understand the careful coordination between the instruments of national power necessary for success in urban operations in a digitally connected and global political environment. Russian disregard for information operations, collateral damage, and particularly civilian casualties gave the Chechens significant strategic advantages even as they lost the battle at the tactical level. Those advantages would build over time, and result in Chechen forces recapturing Grozny in the summer of 1996, and in the negotiated withdrawal of Russian forces from Chechnya that same year. A formal treaty between the Chechen government and the Russian government was signed in 1997 which stabilized the relationship between the two governments until the war began anew in 1999.

CHAPTER 9

INVADING THE URBAN SANCTUARY

Operation *Defensive Shield* and the Battle
for Jenin, 2002

In September 2000 the Palestinian people, represented by Yasser Arafat, his Fatah Party, and the Palestinian Authority (PA), began a low-intensity war against the state of Israel over a spectrum of grievances ranging from the original founding of Israel in 1948, to the failure of the Palestinian–Israeli peace talks brokered by US President Bill Clinton. That war was known as the Second Intifada, or the Al Aqsa Intifada. The Arabic word Intifada is translated as "uprising," and from 2000 to 2005 it manifested as strikes, protests, and a clandestine war of rocket and terror attacks against Israel by various Palestinian groups. The Intifada ended in 2005 when a series of events including the death of Yasser Arafat dramatically decreased the terrorist attacks from within the territory controlled by the Palestinian Authority.

The violence waged against Israel increased to unprecedented levels in 2002 and early 2003. Attacks were occurring inside Israel at a rate of one every three to four days. In March 2003 the violence reached a new level: nine attacks occurred between March 2 and 5. These were followed by suicide bomber attacks on March 9, 20, and 21, as well as numerous gun and grenade attacks. The attacks culminated with the suicide bomb attack on the Park Hotel in Netanya on March 27, which left 30 dead and 130 injured. March became one of the bloodiest months of the Intifada as 130 Israelis died in terrorist attacks. The Israeli government, under Prime Minister Ariel Sharon, responded by ordering the Israeli Defense Forces (IDF) to take action to prevent further attacks. The response from the IDF was Operation *Defensive Shield*.

Operation *Defensive Shield* was a large Israeli offensive military operation designed to significantly degrade the ability of a variety of Palestinian groups to attack Israel. The plan called for a massive movement of conventional Israeli military forces into the occupied West Bank territory to seize and destroy bomb factories and weapons caches, as well as kill or arrest Palestinian militant fighters, leaders, bomb-makers, and financiers. It was the largest military operation in the occupied West Bank area since Israel seized the territory from Jordan in 1967.

The concept of the operation was to rapidly, and in overwhelming force, occupy the Palestinian urban areas which were the bases from which various organizations staged terrorist operations into Israel. In phase one, the towns would be secured and access to the towns would become controlled. In phase two, the IDF would systematically raid known or suspected bomb-making facilities, and search residences suspected of harboring weapons or known members of terrorist groups. In the course of these operations the IDF planned to arrest and detain known or suspected members of a variety of terrorist groups. Specific raids were also planned to kill or arrest specific members of the terrorist leadership.

The Palestinian leadership did expect a response from the IDF, but they did not know exactly what form that response would take. The size and complexity of the operation came as a complete surprise to Yasser Arafat. The only Palestinian area that was prepared for the Israeli assault was the Palestinian refugee camp in Jenin. Under very able leaders, the Palestinian fighters in Jenin had some time to prepare a relatively sophisticated defense of the part of the city in which they were based. This was one of the reasons that Jenin became one of the centers of Palestinian resistance to the Israeli offensive.

The Dilemma of the West Bank

The total population of the area called the West Bank was about three million residents including over half a million Israeli settlers. Most of the people lived in the major urban centers of the area. The population was predominately of Arab descent and Muslim (75 percent). The Arab Muslim population divided into two major groups: the original inhabitants of the region, and refugees who had come to the West Bank from Israel, mostly during and following the Israeli War of Independence in 1948. The refugee population numbered approximately 800,000 individuals, living in 19 camps. Two significant minority communities lived in the region: Christian enclaves which had been integrated into the communities of the region for centuries made up approximately 8 percent of the population; and Jewish settlers, who had moved into the region and established highly segregated communities after the Israeli conquest of the area in 1967, made up about 17 percent.

The six objectives of Operation *Defensive Shield* were the six most populous cities in the West Bank: Jenin, with a population of approximately 50,000; Tulkkarm, approximately 55,000; Qalqiliya, approximately 40,000; Nablus, approximately 125,000; Ramallah, approximately 25,000; and Bethlehem, with a population of approximately 25,000. In total about 325,000 civilians lived in the urban areas subject to Israeli operations. Though most of the population was sympathetic to the attacks on Israel, only a small portion was actively engaged in supporting terrorist activity.

Large Palestinian refugee camps were located adjacent or near five of the six urban areas targeted by the Israelis (the exception being Qalqiliya). The United Nations Relief and Works Agency (UNRWA) established the refugee camps in 1948, but they were camps in name only. More than 60 years after they were established, the camps resembled typical poor Middle Eastern neighborhoods. In many ways they were similar to the type of complex casbah building configuration that the French army had faced in Algiers. The buildings were low two- to three-storied flat-roofed buildings, made of concrete and brick, built around courtyards and narrow alleys. Most housed multiple families, and often a small group of buildings housed members of an extended family. The streets were typically wide enough for a small car, but many were pedestrian access only and just a few feet wide. The camps were integrated into the local communities economically, though they maintained a strong self-identity. The camps were largely self-administering, and had all of the amenities of the surrounding community including power and water. In some camps, such as the one in Jenin, local militant groups dominated the population, despite the presence of PA police and administrators. In total, approximately 180,000 refugees resided in the 10 camps associated with the cities targeted by the IDF.

The Israeli army was divided into an active force and a large reserve force. For Operation *Defensive Shield*, 30,000 reservists were called to active duty, allowing the IDF to mobilize several reserve brigades and division headquarters. The IDF ground forces were organized into three commands: Southern, Central, and Northern. The Central Command commanded Operation *Defensive Shield* while Southern Command monitored the Gaza Strip and the Northern Command remained focused on Syria. Each command had two to three active divisions, each commanded by a brigadier general; each active division had one to three brigades. The primary combat formation of the IDF ground forces was the brigade, which was assigned to a division but which, for operations, could be assigned to any division headquarters depending on the needs of the mission. IDF brigades were of three types: armor, mechanized infantry, and paratrooper. The brigades participating in *Defensive Shield* were either mechanized infantry, or paratrooper. Elements of the armored corps, as well as special forces, engineers, and air force attack helicopters, supported the infantry brigades. Each of the major objectives (cities) of the operation was assigned to an active division headquarters, and that division commanded the various brigades and supporting units attacking that particular city.

The IDF operations in the West Bank were aimed at disrupting three terrorist organizations, and by implication they also had to deal with a fourth organization that was armed and a potential adversary. The latter was the PA police forces. These forces were responsible for law and order in the West Bank, and were loyal to the PA led by Yasser Arafat. Thus, although they were not actively attacking Israel, they were expected to oppose the IDF incursion into the West Bank. There were three primary militant groups in the West Bank. The Al Aqsa Martyrs' Brigade specialized in suicide bombings as well as gun attacks. In 2002 they were covertly sponsored by the Fatah party, a relationship that was only admitted to after Operation *Defensive Shield*. The Palestinian Islamic Jihad was a small but deadly group that originated in Egypt and after several migrations was based out of Damascus, Syria. They had a close association with the Hezbollah terrorist group in Lebanon and through them with Iran. The last important active terrorist group opposing the Israelis in 2002 was Hamas. Hamas was the political rival of Fatah and had its strongest support in Gaza. However, like the other groups, it had a strong presence in the West Bank. Hamas was responsible for the very deadly Park Hotel attack just prior to the Israeli offensive. All three groups used the urban centers of the West Bank as bases for operations in and against Israel. They also used those bases to manufacture weapons, as recruiting and training stations, and to plan and conduct propaganda campaigns.

Map 9.1 Operation *Defensive Shield*, March–April 2002

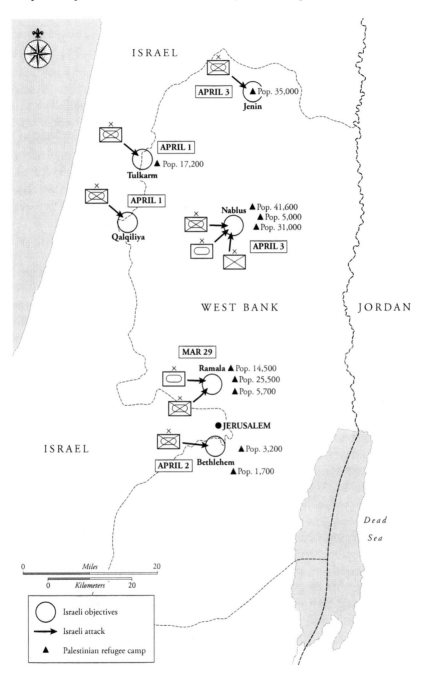

ISRAEL

APRIL 3 ▲ Pop. 35,000
Jenin

APRIL 1
▲ Pop. 17,200
Tulkarm

APRIL 1

Qalqiliya

Nablus ▲ Pop. 41,600
▲ Pop. 5,000
▲ Pop. 31,000
APRIL 3

WEST BANK

JORDAN

MAR 29
Ramala ▲ Pop. 14,500
▲ Pop. 25,500
▲ Pop. 5,700

● JERUSALEM

ISRAEL

▲ Pop. 3,200

APRIL 2 Bethlehem
▲ Pop. 1,700

Dead
Sea

0   Miles   20
0   Kilometers   20

◯ Israeli objectives

→ Israeli attack

▲ Palestinian refugee camp

The IDF Responds to the Terrorist Attacks

Operation *Defensive Shield* began on March 29 as Israeli military forces launched into the West Bank to seize control of the city of Ramallah. The major objective in Ramallah was the headquarters of the PA and Fatah, and its leader Yasser Arafat. The IDF attacked Ramallah with a combined infantry and armor force supported by attack helicopters. IDF forces quickly penetrated into Arafat's Tegart Fort compound and surrounded him in the offices of one building. By the end of the day the IDF had secured the city with no losses to the attacking forces. A curfew was imposed and the IDF then began to systematically seek and arrest known and suspected terrorists. Over 700 individual arrests were made. Thirty defending Palestinian militants and PA police were killed. Arafat remained in his headquarters, with all communications cut off, under house arrest, until May.

Two days after the seizure of Ramallah, April 1, the IDF seized the two border towns of Tulkarm and Qalqiliya. The IDF operations were not seriously resisted in either town. In Tulkarm nine militants were killed and the Tegart Fort used as the headquarters for the PA in the city was destroyed by an air strike. The next day IDF forces moved across the border into Bethlehem. That operation, thought to be relatively simple, turned into an international incident as the IDF surrounded and laid siege to 32 militants and over 200 hostages in the Christian Church of Saint Mary, thought to be the birthplace of Jesus Christ.

No substantial fighting units were thought to be in Bethlehem and the city itself borders on Israel proper, so staging and moving into the city were not considered major problems. For this reason, the mission was assigned to the IDF Reserve Jerusalemite Brigade, an IDF reserve unit. There was a high-value person list for Bethlehem whose arrests were a priority task of the operation. The IDF knew, from previous experience, that one course of action the militants could pursue, if given the opportunity, was flee to the Church of Saint Mary. This had happened on at least one previous occasion. For this reason the Jerusalemite Brigade was supported in its mission by the elite Air Force Shaldag commando unit (also known as Unit 5101). One of the commando's missions was to secure the church to prevent its use as a sanctuary.

The operation was executed against sporadic and ineffective resistance and the town quickly came under IDF control. However, the Shaldag unit was delivered by Israeli Air Force helicopters to its positions a half hour late. That was sufficient time for armed militants to escape capture and find sanctuary in the Catholic church, and to take hostages. The church was quickly surrounded by IDF infantry and tanks and a 39-day siege began. Over the course of the next five weeks, the siege and IDF tactics and actions were subjected to the scrutiny of the international media and the subject of much diplomacy. During the siege, eight militants were shot and killed by IDF snipers stationed around the building. Two Israeli border police were wounded in one of the several small firefights that occurred. In the end, however, the siege was ended diplomatically with all the hostages released unharmed, and 39 militants going into exile in Sicily and Europe.

The major focus of Operation *Defensive Shield* was the two urban areas attacked on April 2 and 3, Nablus and Jenin. Nablus was considered the most difficult mission for several reasons: it was located deepest in the West Bank, it was the largest in total population, and it had the most refugee camps and the largest refugee population at over 70,000. Because of this the mission of seizing the city was assigned to the active army West Bank Division under Brigadier General Yitzhak Gershon. For the mission the division had two veteran Israeli brigades: the Northern Command's Golani Infantry Brigade and the Paratrooper Brigade. The IDF activated a reserve armor brigade and assigned it to the division to provide support for the infantry.

Operations in Nablus began on April 3 and took about five days to complete. By April 8 the last militant fighters holding out in the old city casbah decided to surrender. The Israeli plan to capture the city was relatively simple. The Paratrooper brigade was responsible for clearing the Balata Refugee Camp, the largest in the West Bank with over 20,000 residents packed into a maze of buildings in .25km². The brigade would then move west and enter the casbah, the old city quarter. The Golani Brigade moved through the city and attacked the old city quarter directly. Both brigades were extremely successful in accomplishing their mission of killing or capturing militants while at the same time minimizing civilian casualties, collateral damage, and most importantly, minimizing Israeli casualties, but they took dramatically different tactical approaches to achieving their aim.

The Golani Brigade, as mechanized infantry, took an equipment-centric approach to attacking Nablus. The general tactic was to work as an engineer, infantry, armor team. Tanks overwatched the tactics and suppressed enemy fire or potential enemy positions with machine-gun and tank fire. If the building being assaulted was occupied, the tank softened it up with fire from its main gun. The infantry assault was led by an engineer D9 bulldozer. The armored bulldozer was impervious to all Palestinian fire and it cleared the approach to the building of booby-traps, mines, and in many cases widened the alley or street so that it was large enough for the infantry carriers and tanks to follow. Once at the building, the D9 used its blade to collapse a wall and then withdrew. The dozer was followed by an Achzarit heavy armored personnel carrier. The carrier brought the infantry right to the building where they dismounted and attacked into the building through the breach created by the dozer. This method was a slow, firepower-intensive method that did a lot of damage to buildings but kept the advancing IDF force under armor protection most of the time. Special forces snipers also worked with the advancing mechanized force, picking off Palestinian fighters at long range as they attempted to flee, or maneuvered against the flanks of the advancing vehicles and infantry.

A different, but no less effective approach was used by the paratroopers. Though they had access to attached mechanized infantry, tanks and dozers, the paratroopers as a standard did not have the firepower or armored protection of the mechanized infantry so they could not use the same tactics. The paratroopers advanced using tried and true urban fighting techniques. As a tactical standard they refused to recognize and use windows and doors, and instead advanced primarily through the interior spaces of adjoining buildings. The paratrooper technique was to create mouse holes between buildings using explosives or pick axes, and move by squads along multiple planned routes, each route planned through a series of adjoining buildings. Stairs were also avoided and the troops moved between floors by blasting holes through floors and ceilings. The goal of the paratrooper advance was to reach their objective without ever appearing on the open street or alley. The paratroopers also employed their snipers to great effect. The snipers, firing from concealed positions and great distances, picked off targets as the advancing infantry forced the defending Palestinians to retreat or reposition.

As the Palestinian militants lost men and were gradually forced back they were equally frustrated by their losses and their inability to inflict any significant damage on the attacking IDF forces. Finally, in the face of dwindling resources, lack of success, and mounting casualties, the Palestinian groups in the casbah surrendered. The IDF suffered only one casualty in the battle and that was due to friendly fire. The Palestinian defenders lost approximately 70 fighters. Most surprising, given that intense combat in the midst of a large civilian population continued for five days, was the lack of significant collateral damage. Only eight civilians were killed in the fighting in Nablus, and despite employing bulldozers, tanks, and demolitions, only four buildings were completely destroyed, though hundreds were significantly damaged. The IDF took several hundred prisoners in the battle and killed or arrested numerous top-level experienced militant leaders.

Operation against militants in Jenin began on April 2, the day before the attack at Nablus, with IDF forces moving into the city and sealing it off from outside communications and support. Of the two cities, the IDF analysis was the Jenin operation would be the easier to accomplish: the city was not nearly as big as Nablus, it was very close to the Israeli border, the refugee population was less than half the size of that in Nablus, and all the refugees were located in a single camp. Because of these considerations, the forces assigned to Jenin were not as robust: the mission was assigned to a reserve division commanding the 5th Reserve Infantry Brigade, reinforced by a battalion from the Golani Brigade as well as special forces, armor, and engineers.

The IDF forces operating in Jenin were organized under Reserve Division No. 340 under the command of Brigadier General Eyal Shlein. The 5th Reserve Infantry Brigade and a battalion of the Golani Brigade occupied the city of Jenin on April 2, 2002, and by the end of the first day they had the bulk of the city under control. That was the prelude to the major part of the operation which was to move into and establish control of the Jenin Refugee Camp. The Jenin Refugee Camp was located in the southwest portion of the city; it was only about 0.5km² (one-fifth square mile). Access into the refugee camp was carefully controlled by a consortium of Palestinian militant groups who had erected barricades and checkpoints on every avenue into the camp. On April 2, using loudspeakers, the IDF broadcast its intention to occupy the camp and requested all civilians leave the area of military operations. Most of the camp's 16,000 residents chose to evacuate the camp, however many did not leave until the lead army units began to move into the area. Still, 1,000–4,000 civilians remained in the camp throughout the fighting, alongside several hundred dedicated militant fighters.

The several hundred fighters in the city of Jenin were different from any other group of fighters yet met by the Israelis during Operation *Defensive Shield*. Though, like the militants in the other cities, they comprised members of Al Aqsa Martyrs' Brigade, Islamic Jihad, Hamas, and the Palestinian Authority security forces, this group within Jenin decided to subordinate themselves to a unified command inside the camp. This unusual situation was due to the presence of Abu Jandal, who was a uniquely capable and charismatic leader. He was a veteran of the Iraqi army, had fought in Southern Lebanon, and was the leader of the coalition of the various militant groups in Jenin. He understood that though it was impossible to beat the Israelis militarily, it was very possible to achieve a strategic political victory in Jenin, while losing the tactical battle in the camp. To do this they needed to make the taking of the camp a lengthy, and most importantly, casualty-producing battle for the IDF.

On April 3, after completely isolating the city from all outside communications and access, including ensuring that no media organizations had access to the operation, the IDF entered the camp. The 5th Brigade moved into the camp slowly and methodically from the northeast. They were very wary of exposing themselves to casualties. Many of the reservists were less than enthusiastic about being called to active service with no notice, and some disagreed with the political policy behind the operation. They were also nervous because they had almost no training in urban warfare techniques. At Nablus a reserve tank crew had refused to obey orders to attack into the city because they felt unprepared for urban battle. A brigade commander eventually convinced the soldiers to go into battle. At Jenin there were no combat refusals, but the 5th Brigade's officers were very conscious of the soldiers' lack of training in urban combat. The brigade also had leadership challenges. The brigade commander had only taken command of the brigade a few days before the operation began. On the first day of operations in the city a very experienced company commander was killed by a militant. This resulted in the officers approaching the battle with even more caution than usual, and the 5th Brigade advanced slowly and methodically throughout the battle.

As the 5th Brigade moved slowly and steadily to breach the perimeter of the camp, the IDF complicated the defenders' problems by launching another attack from the southwest. This attack was conducted by Battalion 51 of the Golani Brigade. In addition, a company from the Nahal Brigade attacked the camp from the

9.2 The IDF Attacks Nablus, April 2002

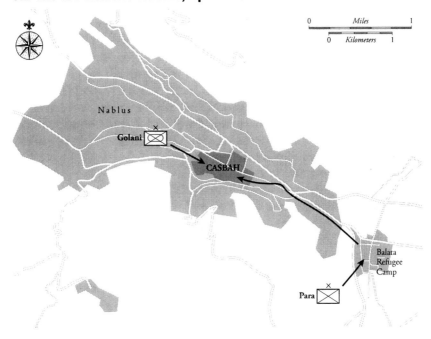

southeast. Both of the main attacks, the 5th Brigade and the attack of Battalion 51, were supported by special forces and air force Apache attack helicopter. Elements of the elite Shayetet 13 (naval commandos) and Duvdevan (counterterrorist commandos) special forces units were operating in the city as well. However, jet aircraft support and artillery support, as in Nablus, were prohibited.

IDF special forces conducted two broad types of missions in the urban fight. One type of mission was in direct support of the attacking conventional infantry brigade. In that role the special forces would overwatch the regular infantry and armor movement with snipers. Typically, snipers were deployed in a good vantage point 500 meters (1,640ft) or more to the rear of the conventional troops moving forward. From their position they were able to engage any opposing snipers or gunmen firing at the conventional force. They were also in an ideal position to engage any militants attempting to flee in front of the conventional infantry attack. This type of mission was conducted by either an elite army-level special forces unit or, more typically, the brigade reconnaissance company which was an elite unit in all Israeli brigades and had special forces training and capabilities.

The other type of missions conducted by special forces as part of the urban battle were much more specialized, and generally limited to the elite national-level special forces units. These types of missions could include assaults to capture or kill major militant leaders, or to rescue hostages. Israeli special forces also conducted covert missions. In these missions they drove specially outfitted civilian cars, wore civilian clothes, and blended in with the Palestinian civilian population. Usually, but not always, in this covert role the missions were limited to reconnaissance and information gathering.

Two other important units employed as part of the Jenin operation were army engineers equipped with Caterpillar-built D9 armored bulldozers, and Merkava tanks of the armored corps. These heavy armored elements were employed in a manner similar to their use in Nablus. The D9R dozer made by the US Caterpillar Corporation was not a purpose-built military vehicle but rather a very powerful civilian construction bulldozer. The vehicle was 13 feet tall, and 14.7 feet wide with its standard blade; it weighed 54 tons, and was powered by a 405hp engine. The D9's first major military use was during the Vietnam War when the US Army used them to clear jungle. The Israeli military added massive armored plating to the machines to give them the capability to work while under fire. Israeli soldiers nicknamed the giant bulldozers "doobi," which translates to "teddy bear." Its armor protection could deflect all small-arms fire and even rocket-propelled grenades. There are reports that D9R dozers survived improvised explosive device (IED) attacks by bombs weighing as much as 440lb and 1,100lb. The initial advance into the refugee camp began with an armored bulldozer clearing the three-quarter mile approach to the camp. During that operation an engineer officer noted that the dozer set off over 120 IEDs without sustaining significant damage.

The 5th Brigade entered the camp dismounted. The Palestinian militants were surprised, and pleased, that the Israelis did not lead with armored vehicles. The decision to begin the attack on foot was to minimize civilian casualties. For three days the Israeli infantry slowly and methodically advanced. Their movement was greatly hampered by the extensive mining that the Palestinians did on all approaches into the camp. Militant fighters reported that they deployed 1,000–2,000 IEDs. Some were large antivehicle devices but most were small, about the size of a water bottle, designed to kill infantry. The militants' objective was to inflict as many casualties as possible on the IDF, and their main method of doing that was by setting up booby-traps throughout the camps. In particular the Palestinians booby-trapped the major alleyways, doors and windows to houses, cars, and the interior of houses. Inside houses IEDs were placed in doorways, cabinets, closets, under and inside furniture. They concentrated their booby-traps in abandoned houses, or in the homes of prominent militants that they were sure the Israelis would search. In the first three days of the battle little progress was made into the camp, seven IDF soldiers were killed, and in some cases units only advanced at a rate of 50 yards a day.

The IDF estimated that the Jenin operation would take 48–72 hours to complete. By April 6 they were four days into the operation, units were still only advancing very slowly against very stiff opposition, and casualty rates were much higher than expected. Israeli army headquarters began to put pressure on the division commander to pick up the pace of operations. The IDF had a long history of rapid, decisive operations. Speed was a highly valued quality because with it came surprise and the shock effect. The IDF was also concerned with speed for strategic reasons. The history of the wars between Israel and its Arab neighbors indicated that in any major military operation, especially if it was successful, international and United States diplomatic pressure would be put on the Israeli government to end the operation. This pressure would steadily mount until invariably the Israeli prime minister halted the operations. Thus, the Israeli senior commanders understood that the IDF had an unknown but finite amount of time to clear and seize Jenin. If that did not occur before the diplomats halted operations then the operation would fail.

While the 5th Brigade slowly moved ahead, in the southwest Battalion 51 was making better progress. This difference was because the Battalion 51 commander determined to use the same tactics that the Golani Brigade had used in Nablus: leading with D9 dozers, then mechanized infantry in their carriers, and finally, tanks firing in support. However, the slow progress of the 5th Brigade allowed the Palestinians to focus on Battalion 51, and thus, despite the battalion's aggressive tactics, it was fighting fiercely for every building. On April 8, as fighting ended in Nablus, the Golani Brigade commander, Colonel Moshe Tamir, visited and assessed the situation in Jenin. He recommended that more aggressive tactics, similar to those of Battalion 51, be adopted. Division headquarters continued to emphasize speed to the commanders in Jenin, and set the next day, April 9, as the date the mission had to be completed.

Early on the morning of April 9, a 5th Brigade Infantry Company from Reserve Battalion 7020 moved forward to occupy a building to serve as the base for the day's operations. As they moved forward, wearing their night-vision devices in the early morning darkness, they diverted from their planned route. As they moved down a 3ft-wide alley between buildings they were suddenly attacked by bombs thrown at them, and small-arms fire. Within seconds, a half dozen soldiers were hit and down, including the company commander. The ambushed element of the 5th Brigade found itself cut off, surrounded, and under intense fire from militant gunmen shooting from upper-story windows. All but three men in the unit were killed or wounded as they sought cover in a small open courtyard. An initial effort to rescue the element inadvertently stumbled into a booby-trapped room and set off an IED that killed two more men and wounded several others.

Unmanned aerial reconnaissance loitered over the firefight and sent real-time images of the plight of the troops to IDF headquarters but the close range of the engagement – the combatants were within 30 feet – prevented the Israeli command from supporting their troops with heavy weapons. In the midst of the fight the Palestinians dashed forward and dragged off the bodies of three Israeli soldiers killed in the fight, with the intent of using the bodies as a negotiating lever at a later date. After several hours of frustrating combat, Shayetet 13 entered the battle and counterattacked to retrieve the bodies. The naval commandos quickly overran the Palestinian militants, retrieved the bodies of the fallen soldiers, and relieved the surrounded force. In total, 13 Israeli soldiers were killed and many more were wounded. It was the largest loss of life in a single day for the IDF in 20 years.

The ambush of April 9 consumed the energy of the Israeli command on that day, and put it further behind its timetable for securing the camp. It also demonstrated that careful, dismounted work in the tight confines of the camp could lead to unacceptable casualties. Thus, when the command renewed the attack the next day the 5th Brigade adopted a much more aggressive approach. On April 10 the Israeli attack was led by D9 bulldozers, followed by infantry mounted in the heavily armored Achzarit personnel carriers. Tanks and attack helicopters fired into buildings ahead of the dozers and infantry to force militants out. The dozers were extremely effective and literally buried any militants who tried to stay and fight in the rubble of their building. Several civilians who were unable to evacuate the area also became victims of the relentless destructive power of the armored bulldozers. When the Israelis estimated that they had arrived at the center of the Palestinian defensive network, they unleashed the full capabilities of the dozers which, under the covering fire of infantry and tanks, systematically eradicated a 200m by 200m (650ft by 650ft) square of two- and three-story buildings that formed the heart of the refugee camp. By the end of April 10 the central urban complex of the refugee camp, the center of the militants' defensive scheme, was reduced to a flat, featureless open area devoid of any structures or cover. The Palestinian fighters had no choice but to retreat in front of the Israeli attack into the last remaining unoccupied neighborhood of the camp.

On April 11 the Israeli forces in Jenin prepared to continue the ruthless onslaught which had carried them into the heart of the camp the previous day. However, as the Israel armored vehicles and infantry prepared to attack, the Palestinian militants in the camp began to surrender. During the day approximately 200 fighters gave themselves up to the Israeli forces. A small number managed to flee though the surrounding Israeli security ring and a few die-hards continued to fight on in isolated pockets, until they were crushed in their buildings by bulldozers. By the end of April 11 the battle for Jenin was over.

In the eight-day battle for the control of the Jenin Refugee Camp the Israeli forces lost 23 soldiers killed and 52 wounded. From a casualty point of view it was the most significant combat action of IDF since the 1982 invasion of Lebanon. Detailed analysis by non-Israeli investigators determined that the defending Palestinian militants lost 27 fighters killed, hundreds wounded, and over 200 were taken prisoner by the IDF. The civilians who remained in the city suffered as well: 23 civilians were killed in the battle, unknown hundreds were wounded, well over 100 buildings were completely destroyed and another 200 rendered uninhabitable, and over a quarter of the camp's population, over 4,000 people, was made homeless. Still, the IDF was satisfied with the results of the operation. They had killed or captured several key militant leaders, taken into custody hundreds of fighters, and destroyed several bomb and rocket factories. They had also gleaned a wealth of intelligence from interrogations, and captured documents and equipment. Despite their success, however, the IDF made a critical mistake in the operation which would have effects well beyond the immediate objectives of *Defensive Shield*.

Map 9.3 The IDF Attacks Jenin, April 2002

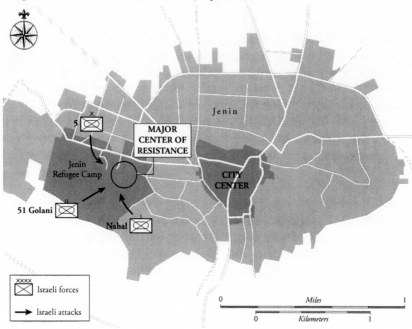

The Massacre and Information Operations

Before the battle of Jenin was over, the international press began reporting allegations of a major massacre of civilians in the city. As the battle raged, Palestinian officials, citing reports from civilians who evacuated the camp, claimed that the IDF was executing civilians, burying families in their homes, burying bodies in mass graves, summarily executing fighters and civilians alike, and firing rockets into homes. The accusations were widely reported in the international press and though it was reported that the accounts were not verified, they were widely accepted as being at least based on truth. Lending credibility to the accusations was the IDF's complete exclusion of the media from the battlefield. Several early inaccurate statements by Israeli officials alluding to significant civilian casualties fueled media speculation and Palestinian accusations. Vague official statements from the IDF did nothing to put down the rumors. Several international organizations including Human Rights Watch (HRW) and Amnesty International (AI) began to collect witness statements from civilians before the battle was over and had teams prepared to enter the camp as soon as the IDF permitted. On April 18, the first team from AI entered the camp and made an initial assessment that there was a strong possibility that the accusations were true. Over the two months following the battle, AI, HRW, the UN, and several news services including CNN and the BBC all did detailed investigations. The systematic and thorough investigations revealed that rather than a massacre, the IDF description of events as a battle between the IDF and Palestinian militants was substantially true. The independent organizations all confirmed that the casualties, of all types, reported by the IDF were generally accurate.

Though the investigations eventually confirmed the IDF version of events, the fact that the investigations were necessary was a result of the IDF policy of isolating the battlefield from media coverage. Denied the ability to cover the battle, the media reported the only information it had available, which was the sensational and ultimately highly inaccurate accounts of a massacre presented by the Palestinians. Once the story made headlines around the world, the damage was done. International pressure on the Israeli government increased dramatically and the legitimacy of the mission was questioned by many countries, including Israel's chief ally, the United States. Once the massacre stories were published they became the accepted narrative of the battle for many audiences, despite the findings of subsequent investigations. For the Palestinians the massacre story was generally accepted as true and Jenin became a rallying cry for the Palestinian cause, a source of endless propaganda, and a major recruiting tool for the ranks of militant fighters.

Battle Tactics in the Casbah

In the battles of Operation *Defensive Shield*, the Israeli Defense Forces demonstrated a solid basic capability to conduct operations within the extremely dense urban environment of West Bank cities and refugee camps. Many tried and true urban combat techniques continued to be effective and necessary to success. The battles in the refugee camps also demonstrated new capabilities and threats in the urban environment. Finally, they reflected the continued importance and growing necessity of urban combat.

The Israeli military had very powerful and professional armored forces, as necessary to fight the conventional threats presented by the Arab countries on its borders. The traditions of armored combat influenced the Israeli tendency to prefer armored forces in the urban environment. The successes of Israeli armor and mechanized forces in 2002 demonstrated that the protection, firepower, and psychological effect of armor in a city remained a great advantage. Using armor also mitigated the number of casualties suffered by the attacking forces, a critical consideration for a small force like the IDF. Unlike the Russian initial deployment in Grozny, however, Israeli tanks operated in close coordination with a screen of protective infantry. Operation *Defensive Shield* also demonstrated one particularly important disadvantage of armor in a world dominated by global news coverage: the amount of collateral damage, including civilian casualties, that results whenever armor is operated aggressively in a city where a civilian population is still present.

The extensive use of D9 bulldozers by the Israeli military was a unique characteristic of Israeli urban warfare. The IDF used the dozers to somewhat compensate for the lack of available artillery and airpower. The dozers gave the Israelis the ability to precisely destroy enemy positions which, in a less constrained combat environment, would have routinely been subject to artillery and air attack. The D9s proved, however, to be highly controversial. Many civilian casualties were attributed to the bulldozers and they also destroyed a large number of buildings during the campaign leaving thousands of civilians homeless. The use of the D9 dozers meant that the IDF incurred the animosity of the Palestinian population for many years to come.

The Israelis also made extensive use of Apache attack helicopters in support of their ground troops. In the IDF, helicopters are operated by the Israeli air force. There were no reports of helicopters being lost to ground fire which implies that the aircraft were employed very carefully, and fired from positions already secured by IDF ground forces. American experiences with helicopters in urban operations – Mogadishu, Somalia (1993), and Panama City, Panama (1989) – indicated the significant vulnerability of helicopters to ground fire when operating over cities. This different experience was likely because the Americans, whose helicopters are part of the army maneuver forces, integrate helicopter operations very closely into ground maneuver operations as both an attack platform and as transport, and thus expose the aircraft to greater risks.

As in all previous urban operations, intelligence was a key to success. The battle for Jenin demonstrated how difficult it is, for even an excellent intelligence service like that of the IDF, to penetrate into a hostile urban environment and accurately determine important tactical details. Remote sensors in the form of unmanned aerial vehicles (UAVs) greatly increased the tactical situational awareness of IDF commanders and allowed them to shift forces to meet threats. As the battle progressed, intelligence support to the attacking Israeli ground forces improved. This was because the IDF created tactical interrogation units that questioned captured militants and civilians as soon as they came under IDF control. These intelligence units were organized to both send the acquired information up the chain of command, and – importantly – quickly send new and important information directly back to the units in combat.

A final important aspect of the Israeli success in the urban battle of Operation *Defensive Shield* was the use of special forces. The Israelis employed relatively large numbers of special forces to the urban battles of March and April 2002, particularly the operations in Nablus and Jenin. These included the reconnaissance companies of each brigade which were trained in special forces tactics such as sniping and covert reconnaissance. Thus, the defending Palestinians had to not only contend with brute force conventional threats like the D9 bulldozers and Merkava tanks, but also the equally deadly special forces snipers and raiders.

The D9 dozer was a new urban weapon employed by the IDF. On the Palestinian side they employed an old weapon, the booby-trapped IED, but they did so in unprecedented numbers. With just a little time to prepare, the militants were able to distribute thousands of devices, and in doing so they significantly slowed the advance of the IDF infantry. IDF engineers, both dozer operators and explosive ordnance disposal (EOD) specialists, were critical to maintaining the momentum of the attack. The IDF learned that they did not have enough specialist EOD personnel, and thus after the battle they increased the emphasis on EOD training among their infantry.

IDF Security Operations

Though the IDF was sensitive to civilian casualties, and no massacre occurred in Jenin, it is important to understand the type of military operation that the IDF was tasked to accomplish during Operation *Defensive Shield*. By going into the urban areas of the West Bank, the IDF was invading the urban centers of a foreign, and generally hostile, population. The West Bank was not part of Israel, and at the time of the operation it was under the political control of the Palestinian Authority. Thus, the operational context was more like the Russian army in Grozny than the British in Northern Ireland or even the French in Algeria. In both the latter cases, the military had the objective of eliminating the urban enemy while at the same time not alienating the urban population, who were citizens of the United Kingdom and France respectively. The IDF's operational concern with civilian casualties was more out of respect for the law of war and international opinion, than the military and political objectives of the campaign. Thus, they were comfortable emphasizing speed, firepower, and armored forces, and destroying as many buildings as necessary to achieve the military objective, as long as the laws of war were observed. Thus, the IDF perspective of the battle was as a battle against a security threat to Israel. The enemy was a guerrilla force hiding among a sympathetic enemy population in a foreign city.

For their part, the Palestinian defenders, though hopelessly overmatched by Israeli military power, demonstrated – as the Chechen fighters had – that adroit manipulation of the information spectrum could yield some positive strategic results even when the outcome of the conventional military battle was a foregone conclusion. The Palestinians were aided in this by the Israeli forces, who demonstrated no understanding of the vital importance of engaging the enemy in the information spectrum of war.

The Palestinian capacity for attacking Israel was significantly diminished by the urban battles of 2002, but not eliminated. The battles were not meant to, and the IDF was not capable of, eliminating the reasons behind the Intifada. Therefore, as soon as the IDF withdrew, and the militants acquired and trained new recruits, the Intifada continued. The Israeli–Palestinian war would not end until 2005. The best that Operation *Defensive Shield* could accomplish was reducing the Palestinian militants' capability to conduct terrorist attacks inside Israel. It accomplished that goal and therefore was a successful operation.

CHAPTER 10

SYSTEMATIC URBAN WARFARE

"Ready First" in Ramadi, 2006–07

When the 1st Brigade Combat Team (1BCT) of the US Army's 1st Armored Division (AD) received its orders sending it into western Iraq in June 2006, it was one of a long list of army and US Marine combat units assigned to operations in Iraq's Al-Anbar Province since the US invasion of Iraq in March 2003. There was no reason to believe at the time that the operations of the "Ready First" Brigade in the provincial capital of Ramadi would be any more decisive or exceptional than the operations of previous units. What happened in the next nine months, however, became the greatest success story of US arms to come out of Operation *Iraqi Freedom*. Between the summer of 2006 and the spring of 2007, the deadliest city in the most dangerous anti-US province in Iraq was not just pacified, but became the model for successful urban counterinsurgency for the rest of the war in Iraq, as well as for operations in Afghanistan.

A Hotbed of Anti-Americanism

The US military came to Al-Anbar province in the last days of the initial invasion of Iraq, known as Operation *Iraqi Freedom One* (OIF1). Al-Anbar was far from what the US command viewed as the decisive point of the operation, the city of Baghdad, and so it was not critical to the invasion. The only decisive combat action that took place in the province in the initial weeks of the war was the seizure of the Hadithah Dam by the US Army's 3rd Battalion, 75th Ranger

Regiment. It took the Americans several months to realize the unique significance of Al-Anbar Province.

Al-Anbar Province, with a population of 1.23 million people, was the largest province geographically in Iraq, and was the only province dominated by Sunni Muslims, who comprised 95 percent of the population. Because it was dominated by Sunni Arabs, the province was favored by Saddam Hussein, and was a bastion of Ba'ath party support. It was also home to a large percentage of the Iraqi army's leadership. Because of its close affiliation with the Ba'ath Party and the army, and also because it was relatively untouched by the initial invasion and thus not exposed to the capabilities of the US military, it became the natural refuge of those fleeing Baghdad and bent on resisting the American occupation of Iraq.

Al-Anbar Province was the largest in Iraq, at 53,370 square miles, about the size of the American state of North Carolina, and it was located in the southwest corner of Iraq. The vast majority of the southern portion of the province was part of the Syrian Desert, which extended across the province's borders westward into Syria and south into Jordan and Saudi Arabia. The northern fifth of the province was a strip of land to the north and south of the Euphrates River. This strip includes the major cities of the province, the agricultural areas, the history, and the bulk of the population. The two largest cities of the province, Fallujah and Ramadi, were located in this area.

The largest city in the province was the provincial capital, Ramadi. Ramadi was a relatively new city in the region, established by the Ottoman Turks in 1869 to control the Iraqi Dulaim tribe. The city and its major suburbs were relatively large, about 15km (11 miles) east to west and 12km (9 miles) north to south. It had a population of between 400,000 and 450,000 at the time of the battle (it was about four times the size of Fallujah). The bulk of the city's population remained in the city throughout the fighting. The city was divided into a dense central city area and numerous suburban residential areas. The central city was bounded on the north by the Euphrates River, on the west by the Habbaniyah Canal, on the south by the railway line, and on the east by suburbs. Major suburbs, in addition to those to the east of the city, were also located west and northwest of the Habbaniyah Canal, and north of the Euphrates River. Two main bridges connected the central city with the suburbs: one crossing the Euphrates River to the northern suburbs; and one crossing the Habbaniyah Canal to the western suburbs. In addition, a major highway bridge crossed the Euphrates north of the city and connected the western and northern suburbs. The suburbs themselves were mainly residential areas, and they were divided into distinct districts, each aligned with a particular tribal group.

Before the US invasion of Iraq the city of Ramadi was a fairly modern Iraqi city. Because of its relatively recent history, Ramadi did not have a casbah as found in traditional old cities of the region. Buildings were predominantly built of concrete and in the central part of the city, they were very modern. The city's hospital had been built by a Japanese company in 1986 and at seven stories tall was the tallest building in the city. There were several five- and six-story tall buildings in the downtown area. Most of the buildings in the city and in the suburbs were traditional flat-roofed two- and three-story cement buildings. By the time the 1BCT arrived at the city, considerable fighting had occurred in the years since the invasion of Iraq in 2003. The central part of the city had been subjected to numerous artillery and air attacks, and improvised explosive device (IED) explosions were a regular occurrence on all of the city's main streets. For example, the city hospital had been regularly attacked by US Army multiple-launched rocket systems (MLRS). There was significant damage to the city center, many buildings were destroyed, and many more were damaged and uninhabitable. There were few undamaged buildings.

The roads of Ramadi were paved, but over the years debris, dirt, and garbage had accumulated on top of the paving. When the 1BCT arrived in the city they were covered with inches of grime. In addition, most of the city's infrastructure no longer existed. There was no power in the city, there was no garbage removal, many areas did not have running water, there was no telephone service (including no cell-phone service), and no operating newspapers. There was also no mayor or city council. The police force of the city consisted of 100 policemen, who never left their stations and often did not report for work. Essentially there was no functioning government.

The area of operations (AO) assigned to the 1BCT, AO Topeka, was slightly larger than the city and included another 150,000 civilians in addition to the population of Ramadi itself. This rural population was scattered among numerous small villages on the north and south banks of the Euphrates River. The vast majority of the people in and around Ramadi were from the Dulaim tribe confederation. The Dulaim, its subordinate sub-tribes and clans, made up 10–20 percent of the Iraqi army and were particularly prominent in the elite Republican Guard units. There were over a thousand clans within the Dulaim, and the tribes' membership extended over the

Map 10.1 Al-Anbar Province, Iraq, 2006

international borders into Syria and Jordan. Each tribe within the Dulaim confederation was headed by a sheik. The sheiks were secular leaders, usually selected by the tribal elders through a process that was unstructured, but based on heredity, competence, and democracy. The sheik's responsibility, in return for the loyalty of the tribe, was to ensure the security and well-being of the tribe, while also administering tribal justice. Seniority among sheiks was based on tribal wealth, measured in actual wealth, political influence, and the size of the tribe. Dozens of sheiks oversaw the tribes living in Ramadi and the surrounding area. Many of the most important sheiks oversaw their tribes from self-imposed exile – for reasons of safety – in places like Jordan.

In Al-Anbar Province the US forces and the security forces of the new government of Iraq (GOI) faced at least three different types of opponents. The first was Al Qaeda of Iraq (AQI), which was the most dangerous and ideological of the groups. The second were the Sunni nationalists who had been favored under Saddam Hussein and who had lost political power with the invasion. Finally, there was an unorganized criminal element that was bent on profiting from the general violence and lawlessness. The prime objective of coalition forces in 2006 was AQI, and those Sunni nationalist groups and criminal elements that supported AQI.

Al Qaeda in Iraq was organized in 2003 as part of the reaction to the US invasion. It was nominally a division of the larger Islamist Al Qaeda organization led by Osama Bin Laden and based in Pakistan. The leader of AQI was Abu Musab al-Zarqawi, who was a Jordanian. The size of the organization was unknown, but estimates ranged from 800 to several thousand fighters. Many of the group's members were foreigners who infiltrated into Iraq from Syria, but it also contained many radical Iraqi Islamists. Its leadership, however, was dominated by non-Iraqis. The goals of AQI were to force the US forces to leave Iraq, defeat the Iraqi security forces, overthrow the Iraqi government, and establish an Iraqi Islamist state. In October 2006, in the midst of the battle for Ramadi, AQI declared the Islamic State of Iraq with Ramadi as its capital. AQI employed a variety of hit-and-run guerrilla tactics against coalition forces, but uniquely favored the vehicle-borne improvised explosive device (VBIED), and the suicide bomber.

The other major group of insurgents were the Sunni nationalists. These fighters' loyalties were first to their sheiks and tribe, and second to the former Ba'athist government of Iraq. Many of them had had high rank and extensive military experience in the former Iraqi army or in other aspects of Saddam Hussein's intelligence and security apparatus. They considered themselves legitimate resisters of the foreign occupation and the Shi'ite-led Iraqi government. Through their tribal affiliations they had widespread popular support.

Both the Islamists and the nationalists were supported by criminals who hired out their services for pay. These criminals typically operated in small independent groups and were willing to snipe, emplace IEDs, and even attack Coalition Forces (CF) positions for predetermined payments. Bonuses were paid to these groups for the success of their operations and often they were required to show video evidence in order to be paid. In the first years of the Iraqi insurgency, 2003–05, the two major factions of the insurgency, Islamists and nationalists, worked together against the Coalition Forces. However, in areas where they had dominance, the Islamists, primarily AQI, began to enforce strict Sharia law. They arbitrarily killed or mutilated violators of strict Islamic law, and also began to demand both material and monetary support from the local populations. Anyone who protested against, or resisted, AQI demands was summarily executed. By the end of 2005 the nationalist Sunni resistance leaders realized that AQI were potentially a larger threat than CF. However, it was difficult for the nationalists to resist AQI's dominance because the nationalist sheiks were not unified, and AQI used highly visible executions to intimidate large portions of the population.

In the spring and summer of 2006, Iraqi nationalist insurgents and AQI controlled virtually all of the city of Ramadi. Insurgents could openly travel almost anywhere in the city, in groups, and carrying their weapons, without fear of CF or police notice, attack, or reprisals. CF estimated that in the summer of 2006 there were a total of about 5,000 insurgents active in Ramadi.

The 1BCT relieved the 2BCT, 28th Infantry Division, a brigade from the Pennsylvania National Guard. The 2BCT, over its year-long deployment, 2005–06, kept the two major supply routes (MSRs) – Route Michigan and Route Mobile – through the Ramadi area open, and protected itself and the main government complex in the center of the city. However, it had done little else to improve the US position in Ramadi. As the BCT redeployed, two regular battalions working in the city remained in the area and came under 1BCT control. The first of these was the 3rd Battalion, 8th Marines, whose major job was protecting the government building in the city center. The Marines operated out of Hurricane Point, on the northwest side of central Ramadi. The other was the 1st Battalion, 506th Infantry, who had responsibility for the east side of Ramadi and access from that direction. They operated out of Camp Corregidor just south of Route Michigan on the east side of the city.

The 1BCT, under the command of Colonel Sean MacFarland, arrived in Iraq in January 2006 configured as a typical cold war US armored brigade. It contained two tank battalions and a mechanized infantry battalion, with supporting elements that included a combat engineer battalion, an artillery battalion, a support battalion (medical, maintenance, and supply), a reconnaissance troop, an intelligence company, and a signals company among others. Immediately after arriving in theater the BCT lost its mechanized infantry battalion on a separate mission. It then proceeded to relieve the 3rd Cavalry Regiment in Tal Afar. For five months it operated in Tal Afar under the operational control of the 101st Airborne Division. In May it was ordered to Ramadi to relieve the national guard and took control of AO Topeka in June. It left one armored battalion in Tal Afar to provide heavy armor to the Stryker brigade that assumed control of that city.

Operations in Al-Anbar Province were under the command of Major General Richard Zilmer, US Marine Corps, and the 1st Marine Division. The 1st Marine Division, acting as a joint (multiservice) and combined (multinational) command – Multinational Forces West (MNFW) – commanded all ground military forces in the province. As the 1BCT moved from its positions in Tal Afar to Ramadi it moved from under the command of the 101st Airborne Division to MNFW. The BCT arrived in Ramadi in late May with only one of its original three combat battalions. It was then augmented by battalions remaining in Ramadi as well as the Central Command operational reserve so that when it began operations it had five combat battalions under its command.

The 1BCT's initial deployment committed all five of its combat battalions to operations. The 1st Battalion, 6th Infantry (TF 1/6), operated out of Camp Diamond and was responsible for Ramadi north of the Euphrates River. The 1st Battalion, 35th Armor (TF 1/35) operated out of Camp Ramadi, a Saddam Hussein palace compound on the west side of the Habbaniyah Canal, just northwest of the central city. It was responsible for Ramadi west of the canal. The 1st Battalion, 37th Armor (TF 1/37) also operated out of Camp Ramadi, but was responsible for southern Ramadi east of the canal. The 3rd Battalion, 8th Marines (3/8 Marines) operated out of a combat outpost (COP), Hurricane Point in the northwest corner of the central city, and had a company permanently stationed at the central government complex in the center of downtown. The 1st Battalion, 506th (1/506) Infantry was stationed at Camp Corregidor on the east side of the central city and was responsible for the eastern portion of the city and area of operations. In total the BCT had over 5,000 personnel, 84 Bradley Fighting Vehicles, and 77 M-1 Abrams tanks under its operational control in AO Topeka.

In addition to the ground-combat battalions at its disposal, the 1BCT included the 2nd Battalion, 3rd Field Artillery. That battalion was given two tasks: develop and supervise a close-combat training program for the Iraqi army (and later police), and provide indirect fire support to the maneuver battalions in the city. The 16th Engineer battalion was designated to provide combat engineer support to the maneuver battalions, including the building of COPs. Two additional attachments to the BCT gave the brigade unusual capabilities. One of those detachments was two platoons of US Navy Sea, Air, and Land (SEAL) teams. These two SEAL platoons gave the BCT its own special operations capability. The other attachment was a section of Small

Unit Riverine Craft (SURCs) which belonged to the navy but were operated by the Marine battalion. The SURCs were used to patrol the Euphrates River and Habbaniyah Canal, they were able to search watercraft, look for swimmers, and also to insert and support patrols and snipers. This capability facilitated the BCT's ability to maneuver by water around Ramadi, avoid IEDs, and denied the waterways to the insurgents.

A New Plan

Though, geographically the US forces were well positioned to surround the city, in May 2006 operations were limited to securing the bases, and the central government complex downtown. The forces in and around Ramadi did not have the combat power to seize the city from AQI control. In the spring of 2006 the MNFW asked for a considerable additional number of troops to replace the 2BCT, 28th Infantry Division. They got 1/1 BCT. They wanted light infantry, they got a heavy armored BCT. They were told by their higher headquarters that commanders would get what they asked for, but they didn't. The 1BCT had five maneuver battalions available for operations in and around Ramadi. Ramadi was four times the size of Fallujah, yet in comparison, during the second battle for Fallujah, in November and December 2004, the US Marines employed eight battalions, of which two were mechanized and the other six were large Marine light infantry battalions.

However, comparisons with Fallujah were not important because the 1BCT's specific guidance from the MNFW was to "Fix Ramadi but don't do a Fallujah." The spectacular destruction, civilian casualties, and high allied casualties that characterized the battle for Fallujah were not acceptable in the battle for Ramadi. The 1BCT was prohibited from executing a street-by-street, block-by-block, conventional approach to securing Ramadi, even if they had had the combat power to do so. Another approach was called for.

Overall the US and theater strategy in early 2006 was to turn the war over to Iraqi security forces so that US forces could begin to disengage and return to the US. Tactically, this translated into hunkering down on the forward operating bases, taking as few casualties as possible, and giving responsibility to Iraqi forces as they reached appropriate levels of training and readiness. Sometimes, areas were turned over to Iraqi forces regardless of their ability to accept that responsibility.

The problem in Ramadi, however, was that the strategy required that an area be under US control before it was turned over to the Iraqi army (IA) or Iraqi police (IP), and Ramadi was not under US control. AQI had control over all areas of the city where US forces were not physically stationed. The 1BCT had to alter these conditions before the area could be turned over to the Iraqi army and Iraqi police.

The 1BCT was assigned two Iraqi army brigades to work with. One brigade was newly formed and proved not to be too valuable in combat. The other brigade had a good deal of experience. Both brigades were very understrength, and the soldiers of both were primarily Shi'ite Muslims – a problem because of the traditional distrust and animosity between the Iraqi Shi'ite and Sunni Muslim populations. The 1BCT assigned the entire newly formed Iraqi army brigade to partner with the US battalion at Camp Corregidor in eastern Ramadi. The more experienced Iraqi army brigade had each of its three battalions partnered with an American battalion: one with 1/6 Infantry north of the river; one with 1/35 at Camp Ramadi; and one with 3/8 Marines in Ramadi. Members of these Iraqi army units participated in all operations conducted by the BCT. Initially there were only approximately 100 ineffective Iraqi police in Ramadi. As more police became available they were also integrated into operations. The Iraqi forces, though not that important militarily, were important politically to the American objective of turning control of Ramadi over to the government.

The 1BCT did not have the combat power to seize a city the size of Ramadi quickly in a single operation. Additionally, the BCT's guidance was to not conduct a conventional urban attack as had been undertaken in Fallujah. Therefore the BCT determined to seize control of Ramadi using the technique developed by the 3rd Armored Cavalry Regiment a year previously in the city of Tal Afar. This technique was a phased operation built around several premises. First, the BCT had to disregard the forward operating base (FOB) approach to urban warfare. This approach, conceptually developed before the invasion of Iraq, envisioned basing combat units outside of the urban area and then projecting combat power into the city to achieve very specific effects. It was designed to minimize the amount of urban combat, and the amount of contact between military forces and the civilian population. The FOB approach worked when the combat units were working in support of friendly indigenous forces already inside the city, or when the city was under the control of a conventional opponent who had identifiable critical vulnerabilities that could be attacked. Neither condition existed in Tal Afar in 2005 or in Ramadi in 2006.

The approach to seizing Ramadi determined by the 1BCT was described as "clear, build, and hold." This later became the central concept of the US surge offensive throughout Iraq in 2007–08. The first step was for US forces to clear a particular discrete subsection of the city. This was accomplished by establishing a combat outpost in the midst of that section of the city. The US forces, supported by the Iraqi army, would then hold that section of the city against counterattacks or infiltration by AQI. As the US forces cleared and held their assigned part of the city, they and their Iraqi partners would simultaneously build institutions and infrastructure in that subsection to win the loyalty of that portion of the city's population. In this manner, sections of the city would gradually and systematically be brought under US control and then turned over to the government of Iraq and the Iraqi army. This operational technique was time consuming, but it allowed the attacking force to ensure dominant combat power at the point of attack and thereby minimize friendly casualties. The 1BCT determined to conduct one major operation a week to keep the initiative and maintain the momentum of the attack. The pace of the operation was also designed to keep AQI reacting to events, off-balance, and surprised. The goal of the clear, hold, and build strategy was to systematically eliminate AQI and nationalist insurgency dominance of the city and replace their presence with the dominance of Iraqi army and police forces.

A Slow but Systematic Battle

The first step in the 1BCT plan was to isolate the city from external support. The concept was not to stop traffic from entering the city, but rather to control traffic coming into the city. This was done by establishing outposts on the major avenues into the city central from the north, west, and east. The SURCs interdicted any waterborne traffic. These operations were to prevent the free flow of supplies and reinforcements into the city and thus prevent large-scale reinforcement of the approximately 5,000 combatants operating in the city. To this end TF 1/35 Armor was assigned the mission of controlling access from the west into the city; TF 1/6 Infantry was given the mission of controlling access to the city from the north; and 1/506 Infantry was assigned to control entry from the east. The 3/8

Marines, inside Ramadi, would continue the mission of securing the government center.

Controlling access into the city was a difficult mission just because of the size of the city and its suburbs and the huge volume of people and goods moving in and out. An example of the size of this task was the area of TF 1/35 Armor, covering the western approaches to the city. The battalion had a total of four combined arms teams (companies) to accomplish its mission. With these small units, it was tasked with securing the suburb of Tameen on the west bank of the Habbaniyah Canal and its population of 40,000, as well as the 20,000 people living north of Camp Ramadi in the Zangora district. To accomplish this mission the TF used a team consisting of a tank platoon, scout platoon, and mortar platoon to operate static vehicle observation posts securing routes Mobile and Michigan in their sector as well as the rural Zangora region north of Camp Ramadi. Two teams – one of mechanized infantry and one tank team – operated in central Tameen. These two units conducted a combination of mounted and dismounted patrols and static mounted observation posts to control the area. They were subject to daily sniping, IED attacks, VBEID attacks, and small-arms fire. Over a six-month period (TF 1/35 redeployed in October 2006), the infantry team took 25 percent casualties during operations in Tameen. However, the teams greatly restricted the ability of AQI to transit and influence their area of operations. Because of the size of the area, the fact that it was a supporting effort to the main operations in the central city, and the low density of troops available, a permanent COP in Tameen was not established until October 2006. Tameen was not completely pacified before the TF redeployed.

On June 7, 2006, a coalition airstrike near Baghdad killed Abu Musab al-Zarqawi, the leader of AQI. The 1BCT determined to take advantage of the degradation of the AQI leadership to accelerate the start of operations into the center of Ramadi. On June 14, the BCT ordered TF 1/37 Armor to move across the Habbaniyah Canal and establish COP Falcon in the southwest section of the central city. The was the beginning of the systematic clearing of Ramadi. The operation began with the night infiltration of a US Navy SEAL team into preselected buildings that would be the center of the COP. Seven buildings in total were occupied. Each family was paid $2,500 a month by the US military for the use of the building. The SEALs entered the building, evicted the Iraqis living there, and secured it. As the SEALs secured the building, a route clearance team moved rapidly from Camp Ramadi down the route to the COP, clearing IEDs as it moved. It was closely followed by a tank team. The tank team then linked up with the SEALs and relieved them of responsibility for the COP. The SEAL team then moved out several hundred yards from the COP and set up sniping positions along likely avenues that AQI would use to counterattack against the COP. Meanwhile combat engineers, escorted by mechanized infantry and tanks, moved to the COP with flatbed trucks carrying concrete barriers, generators, building material, sandbags and concertina wire. Power was established, antennae put up, and towers and heavy weapons installed. Within hours the COP was secure, and over the subsequent days the engineers continued to improve the position with more barriers, wire, and other defensive support. Two weeks later the COP was complete with over a hundred sections of concrete wall and 50,000 sandbags. It was invulnerable to machine-gun fire.

An entire US company made COP Falcon its permanent home. In addition, an IA company moved into the COP with the Americans. Eventually the SEALs set up a forward base at the COP. The COP was the base for CF operations in southwestern Ramadi, the purposes of which were to protect the civil population from AQI and its supporters, and to establish control of the area by the government. The COP also became the base for patrolling and intelligence gathering. Both conventional and special operations snipers also operated out from the COP. From the COP the BCT could exert effective control several hundred yards in all directions in the city. In normal operations a span of control of a few hundred yards is not tactically decisive, however, in urban warfare, and in particular in a densely populated city like Ramadi, controlling several hundred yards of terrain brought thousands of civilians and dozens of businesses under the shadow of the BCT's security. It also subjected all traffic transiting the COP's area of influence to COP stop and search capability. Thus, the COP Falcon became the first crack in AQI's control of the Ramadi population.

Over the course of the next nine months the BCT would establish 18 new COPs in Ramadi and through them extend its influence and control, and that of the government of Iraq, into every neighborhood in the city. COP construction became a standard operating procedure (SOP) for the BCT and they became adapt at attacking, seizing, occupying, and reinforcing a COP position in 24 hours. Tens of thousands of sandbags were needed to reinforce the COPs when established. On Camp Ramadi no-one was allowed to eat in the dining facility until they had filled two sandbags and placed them on a pallet before each meal. This policy produced thousands of sandbags a day and when a new COP was established, trucks arrived with pallets carrying tens of thousands of sandbags ready to fortify the position.

The AQI leadership quickly became aware of the threat that the COPs represented, and responded to it. In the case of COP Falcon, the response came quickly as AQI militants moved in small groups to attack the COP. Though quick to respond, the AQI attacks were inept. Most of the attacks never got past the screen of snipers whose purpose was to identify and break up attacks before they got close to the COP. One SEAL sniper team killed 25 insurgents moving toward COP Falcon in the first 24 hours after the army occupied it. Snipers not only alerted the COP of incoming enemy attacks, but also overwatched patrols operating out of the COP.

Intelligence was the key to successful operations and when the 1BCT arrived at Ramadi they had little to no reliable intelligence about central Ramadi. One of the purposes of the COP was to increase the intelligence available to the BCT. This was done through patrolling, and primarily through census patrolling. Census patrols were targeted at a specific neighborhood and their task was to identify all the persons living in that neighborhood, much like a typical government census would do. Knowing the people, where they lived, and who they were associated with in terms of family and tribe was absolutely critical information and could only be gleaned through door-to-door operations. These type of operations also made the CF visible to the population, reassured them of their intentions, and provided the opportunity for the population to provide additional information if they were inclined, without their cooperation being exposed to the insurgents. The BCT used this information to build a human terrain database of the urban battle space which guided subsequent operations and decisions.

Operations to establish the COPs began as soon as the BCT arrived in Ramadi in June, and continued apace throughout the summer at the rate of one new COP about every 10–14 days. It was a slow and systematic pace with the BCT under constant attack from AQI throughout its operations. The COPs were standalone installations, totally capable of defending themselves from attack from any direction, but they needed daily resupply. Much of the BCT's energy was devoted to protecting logistics convoys moving into Ramadi from IED, grenade, and gunfire attacks. Although these attacks were usually not successful, there were literally dozens a day and they caused all elements of the brigade to operate with patience and caution. The brigade did not have the manpower to operate at a faster pace. This began to change in September 2006.

By September 2006, 1BCT had made significant progress pacifying Ramadi north of the Euphrates and north of Camp Ramadi itself. It had also established a strong presence in Tameen and in the western and southern portions of central Ramadi. But the clear, hold, build strategy was beginning to falter because there were insufficient resources to both clear and hold simultaneously.

An Iraqi government presence was needed to hold territory cleared by CF as they systematically pacified Ramadi through the steady construction and occupation of COPs. Iraqi police were the ideal force to replace the COP once the area was pacified because IP had a legitimate presence in the COP neighborhoods even in peacetime, they had the combat capability to deal with inevitable small-scale insurgent activity, and most importantly, they could be organized and recruited locally. Unlike the Iraqi army forces, which were a national asset and subject to service anywhere in Iraq, the policy of the government of Iraq was to employ police in the area from which they were recruited. Thus, local Iraqi leaders, and CF, could recruit for the Iraqi police and be guaranteed that that manpower would, after individual training, report back to Ramadi for duty. The problem with recruitment, however, was that a recent effort to recruit police had been attacked by an AQI suicide bomber who managed to kill dozens of recruits. In addition, a sheik who supported police recruiting was murdered by AQI. So despite CF efforts to recruit police to back up the operations of 1BCT, the size and effectiveness of the Iraqi police in Ramadi did not change significantly through the summer of 2006.

The Awakening

The police situation, and really, the entire operational situation in Ramadi, changed dramatically in September 2006. The leadership of the Sunni population, 95 percent of the total population of Al-Anbar Province, were the tribal sheiks. Tribal sheiks were the leaders of their tribes and extended families. They were not elected but rather chosen to lead by the tribal elders based on their competence. They had no formal title or position sanctioned by either the new Iraqi government or the regime of Saddam Hussein. Most had had a close relationship with some branch of the former Ba'athist government, and like the general population in Al-Anbar, many had followers who had been important leaders in Saddam Hussein's military and intelligence apparatus. Many were also involved in low-level illegal activity such as smuggling. These sheiks, whose responsibility was the health and welfare of their tribe, had no great love for the government of Iraq or for CF, but in 2006 they were becoming increasingly estranged from AQI.

Relations between the Sunni sheiks and AQI came to a head in August 2006 when Sheik Abu Ali Jassim encouraged members of his tribe to support the 1BCT in northern Ramadi. Tribe members joined the Iraqi police and manned a police station along MSR Mobile just east of where the main highway bridge crossed the Euphrates River. AQI responded with a coordinated complex attack. They attacked the police station with a massive VBIED at the same time as kidnapping Sheik Jassim, whom they then murdered. Possibly worst of all, they did not return the sheik's body, thus denying his family the timely burial required by Islam. These attacks were the culmination of a brutal policy of murder and intimidation practiced by AQI against the mostly secular sheiks and their tribes for over a year. They, combined with the operations of 1BCT, drove the sheiks to reconsider their alliances.

One of the reasons that the Sunnis allied with AQI instead of the CF was that in their view, the long-term interests of their tribes lay with AQI. The CF's consistent message was that they were a temporary presence in Iraq. In contrast, the AQI message was that they were a force in Iraq for good. The sheiks' interpretation of those messages was that they had to have an accommodation with AQI. The 1BCT brought a different message to their operations in Ramadi. The brigade's message was that they were in Ramadi to stay until AQI was defeated. Their message to the sheiks was that if they remained loyal to AQI then they would also suffer the consequences. This new message from the CF, combined with the brutality of AQI, convinced one sheik in particular, Abdul Sattar Eftikhan Abu Risha, that the best interests of his tribe lay with the 1BCT. Sheik Sattar came to this conclusion sometime over the summer and began reaching out to the commander of the US forces in his area, Lieutenant Colonel Tony Deane, the commander of TF 1/35 Armor.

The conversations between Sattar and Deane began with the issue of recruiting local police to protect the neighborhoods north of Camp

Ramadi. Sattar, who was a minor sheik of a relatively small tribe, understood that by himself he would not be able to alter the balance of power in the city, so he worked behind the scenes with the other sheiks, convincing them that their long-term interest lay with the coalition and cooperation with US forces. His force of personality, despite his minor status, was sufficient that on September 9, 2006 he met with Colonel MacFarland, commander of the 1BCT and presented him with a written pledge declaring the Al-Anbar Awakening. That document, signed by 11 sheiks, pledged loyalty and cooperation to the CF and opposition to AQI. There was some vagueness regarding the government of Iraq in Baghdad, but Colonel MacFarland ignored that and welcomed his new allies.

The Al-Anbar Awakening was a turning point in the battle. The sheiks made hundreds of fighters available as recruits for the IP. More importantly, their tribal neighborhoods immediately became coalition-friendly and IEDs and sniping in those areas ceased immediately. The sheiks contributed a wealth of intelligence on AQI that included safe houses, names of leaders and fighters, supply routes, and weapons caches. They also began an active recruiting campaign to bring more sheiks into the alliance against AQI.

With the support of the sheiks, the 1BCT's offensive of establishing COPs could continue with new momentum. Though the hundreds of Iraqi police recruits would not be available until they completed weeks of training, the sheiks' loyal followers instantly became a militia of auxiliary fighters that could control terrain in their own neighborhoods, facilitate the establishment of COPs and take over COPs in the neighborhoods that were now friendly to the coalition. This "flip" by the sheiks took away AQI safe havens, intelligence sources, and manpower. It essentially made AQI militants fugitives in much of Ramadi. In return for the sheiks' support the 1BCT shared intelligence with them, provided protection and support when necessary, and steered millions of dollars in contracts and business to members of the allied tribes.

The Al-Anbar Awakening was the second disaster for AQI in Iraq, the first being the aggressive determined COP strategy of the 1BCT. AQI recognized the magnitude of the strategic change represented by the Sunni shift in allegiance and attempted to stop it. They attacked the new allies of the coalition to attempt to coerce them back into supporting their ideal of an Islamic State of Iraq. They also stepped up coercive pressure on sheiks who were neutral, or who may have been contemplating switching sides. The battle of the Shark Fin in

10.2 Deployment of 1BCT in Ramadi, Iraq, 2006–07

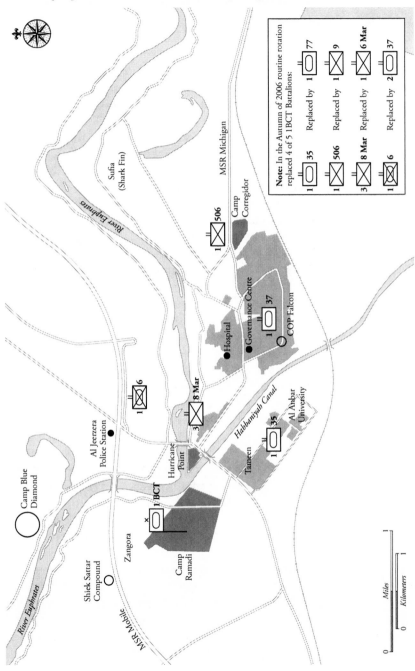

Note: In the Autumn of 2006 routine rotation replaced 4 of 5 1BCT Battalions:

1	35	Replaced by	1	77
1	506	Replaced by	1	9
3	8 Mar	Replaced by	1	6 Mar
1	6	Replaced by	2	37

November 2006 was an example of AQI's unsuccessful bid to keep the Sunni sheiks loyal.

Around 3pm on November 25, Lieutenant Colonel Chuck Ferry, commanding 1st Battalion, 9th (TF 1/9) Infantry at Camp Corregidor (TF 1/9 Infantry replaced 1/506 Infantry in October), received a call from Sheik Jassim Muhammad Saleh al-Suwadawi. The sheik was not a participant in the Awakening, but was one of the group of sheiks who had moved from being an active supporter of AQI to neutral. The sheik was the leader of the Albu Soda tribe, a small group located in an area east of Ramadi and just south of the Euphrates River called the Sufia, known as the Shark Fin by the Americans because of the shape of the bend in the river course. Jassim had been in secret discussions with both the Americans and Sheik Sattar as he contemplated joining the Awakening. He purchased a satellite cell phone so that he could stay in contact with Sheik Sattar. On November 25 he was using that cell phone to report that AQI fighters were attacking his people and he requested the help of the TF 1/9 Infantry to defend the homes of his tribe.

Colonel Ferry did not know Sheik Jassim, and he was in the midst of preparing for an operation to push in the opposite direction, into central Ramadi from the east, but he understood the concept and intent of the 1BCT plan, and thus he made a quick decision to reorient his task force and dispatch a tank and infantry team to support the sheik. At the Shark Fin, more than 50 AQI fighters arrived in several cars and trucks, armed with RPGs and AK-47 assault rifles. They immediately engaged a small contingent of the Albu Soda tribe who were armed but outnumbered. As this was occurring 1BCT moved unmanned aerial vehicles (UAV) over the scene and commanders were able to observe by video the firefight going on at the Shark Fin between the followers of Sheik Jassim and AQI. The 1BCT requested air support and quickly two US Marine F-18 fighters and a Predator drone aircraft were above the fight ready to support. The TF reaction force of Bradley fighting vehicles and Abrams tanks proceeded toward the area.

Colonel Ferry could see the sheik's men and AQI engaging on the video and he was able to talk to the sheik on the cell phone (through his translator). The F-18s were in position but the fighters were too closely engaged for the fast-attack aircraft to safely engage, so instead they made high-speed low-level passes and mock attack runs over the fight to let AQI know they were there in position and prepared to participate. The 1BCT was also in contact with the sheik, and they had his men wave towels and scarves so they could be identified on video. The AQI fighters, unnerved by the jets overhead, decided to break off the attack but as a final act of intimidation they tied the body of a tribal fighter to the bumper of their vehicle and dragged it behind their convoy of four vehicles as they loaded up and departed the Shark Fin. This was a mistake.

The cars dragging the body down the road were clearly visible to both the UAVs and the F-18s. As the cars left the neighborhood and they could be safely engaged they were attacked by the F-18s and the Predator-firing Hellfire missiles. Three of the four vehicles were destroyed. Other AQI fighters leaving the scene were intercepted by TF 1/9 who, using the night-vision devices on their vehicles, ambushed the fleeing AQI vehicles with tank and Bradley fire. By dawn the task force's quick reaction force was linked up with Sheik Jassim's fighters at the Shark Fin, the area was secure, and another sheik had joined the Awakening. Jassim's forces lost seven fighters while over a dozen AQI fighters were killed. The Shark Fin, one of the most important AQI support areas in eastern Ramadi, quickly became another bastion of support for the coalition and the Awakening movement, and a source of police recruits.

The Shark Fin fight was typical of the synergistic effects of the aggressive 1BCT tactics and the Awakening movement. The BCT inspired the sheiks to resist AQI, and the resistance of the sheiks enabled the aggressive tactics of the 1BCT. By November 2006, the operations of the 1BCT were hitting their stride. The brigade had control of over 70 percent of Ramadi, more sheiks were joining the Awakening movement, and both the coalition high command and the Iraqi government were becoming aware of and supporting the effort to pacify Ramadi. Hard fighting remained however. In December TF 1/37 began pushing east into some of the last AQI strongholds to establish police stations in preparation for the growing operational Iraqi police force. When the operation ended in January 2007 they had killed 14 AQI fighters, captured 72, and most importantly, established three police stations. By the end of January 2007 over half the tribes, 450,000 of the citizens of Ramadi were part of the Awakening movement. Most of the rest of the sheiks had openly declared their neutrality and had ceased resisting 1BCT and its Iraqi army and police allies. Only a handful of tribes were still in the AQI camp and they were mostly located in east Ramadi.

By the beginning of February the results of the combined 1BCT operations and the Al-Anbar Awakening were clearly evident and decisive. As the "Ready First" brigade began planning the end of its 15-month deployment in Iraq there had been no losses to IED attacks in a month. Operations by 1BCT, supported by the enthusiastic and effective efforts of the Iraqi army, police, and local militias, resulted in a casualty exchange rate of 55 killed AQI fighters for each loss to the 1BCT.

On February 18, 2007, the 1BCT, of the 1st Armored Division, relinquished control of Area of Operation Topeka, and prepared to redeploy from Iraq to its home bases in Germany. The 1BCT of the 3rd Infantry Division from Fort Stewart, Georgia took over the battle. When the "Ready First" left Ramadi the battle was not over, but the end was in sight. Large portions of the city were completely clear of AQI influence and openly supportive of coalition forces. Soldiers could walk the streets without their combat equipment. The 3rd Infantry Division continued the fight, building on the strong relations and the tactics established by the "Ready First." The coalition forces took additional losses, had more sharp firefights, but by the summer of 2007 the city was not only secured, but was one of the safest large metropolitan areas in Iraq. AQI gave up its plans for Al-Anbar to be the center of an Iraq caliphate and retreated to safer areas outside of the province.

The Example of Ramadi

The battle for Ramadi was not a quick or an easy victory. The 1BCT lost 83 soldiers killed and hundreds wounded during the battle. Equipment losses were also heavy: Task Force 1/37 alone lost a total of 25 tanks, infantry fighting vehicles and trucks during the battle. Iraqi army and police forces suffered similar casualties, but AQI's losses were many multiples more. The 1BCT estimated that in nine months of operations in the city approximately 1,500 AQI fighters were killed and another 1,500 were captured.

The Ramadi battle demonstrated the tactical and operational approach necessary to achieve success in the urban counterinsurgency environment in Iraq. The approach required three key elements. First, it required aggressive offensive action to clear insurgents from a selected neighborhood and to establish a permanent military presence in the midst of the urban civilian population. Second, it required that a competent and capable Iraqi army and police force be able to hold that area against insurgent counterattacks after it was initially cleared. Finally, it required a combined coalition and Iraq effort to build a working urban infrastructure in the cleared area to win and maintain the loyalty of the civil population by demonstrating the clear benefits of peace, stability, and the rule of law under the government of Iraq.

The battle of Ramadi also validated many of the fundamentals of urban combat proven in previous urban warfare experiences. Huge numbers of infantry were not required for the fight. However, well-trained infantry targeted very precisely at specific objectives linked logically to a comprehensive plan were important. Snipers and special operations forces were disproportionally important to the success of the battle. Those specialized forces, however, could not operate independently but had to be tied closely to the operations and objectives of the larger conventional force. Armor and mechanized infantry made important and vital contributions to the battle and gave the coalition forces multiple asymmetric advantages in all the firefights with AQI. Finally, the urban battle requires tactical patience if large-scale military and civilian casualties are to be avoided. The battle of Ramadi took a year to win. However, the city was not destroyed in the process, and given that the population of almost half a million people were present throughout the battle, civilian casualties were relatively light.

The approach of the 1BCT to operations in Ramadi was the three-step "clear, hold, build" tactical approach. But that three-step approach had two major lines of effort which supported each other. One was the security and combat operations conducted by the 1BCT and its allies. The other, equally important, was the political engagement of the population through the civilian leadership, the sheiks, which the military leadership actively pursued. These two lines of effort, one military and the other political, reinforced each other and led to the success. Without political engagement with the sheiks and the Awakening movement 1BCT's tactical operations would likely have still been successful, but they would have been much more costly, time-consuming and ultimately would have resulted in a city that was pacified but not cooperative. Likewise, without the support of the coalition forces, the sheiks' revolt against AQI would have been bloodier, taken longer, and probably would have resulted in an incomplete success.

The three-step, military-political, operational model clearly worked in Ramadi. It became the template for the tactical operations that characterized the surge of American forces into Iraq under

General David Petraeus in 2007 and into 2008. The surge offensive applied the tactics and operational approach used in Ramadi to all of the major urban areas in Iraq including Baghdad. Ultimately, the Ramadi operational approach, combining aggressive military action and political engagement with the urban population, was successful throughout the country. It brought sufficient security on a large scale to enable coalition forces to turn all major security operations over to the Iraqi army and police forces. Ultimately the urban operations techniques pioneered in Ramadi facilitated the withdrawal of all coalition military forces from Iraq in 2011.

CHAPTER 11

URBAN COMBAT IN THE 21ST CENTURY

A major task of modern militaries is predicting and preparing for the next war. Historically, those armies that accurately envision the future combat environment win the first battle of the next war – and often, the first battle is the last battle. An examination of the trends in ground warfare since World War II indicates that it is highly likely that most decisive combat in the 21st century will occur in cities. This vision of future war is supported by the historical trends of the last fifty years, global population trends, current events, and the nature of war itself. Preparing for future war in cities should therefore be the main concern of modern armies. History, as outlined in the previous chapters, provides some important hints to what type of battle that preparation should emphasize.

The history of urban combat since World War II demonstrates that urban battles have increasingly become common and, importantly, have been decisive. Stalingrad was not the largest battle fought on the Eastern Front nor were the losses suffered by the Germans at Stalingrad catastrophic. Thus, for purely material reasons, there was no reason at the time to think that Stalingrad was anything but a temporary setback. In fact, many World War II scholars believe that the German defeat on the Eastern Front was due to decisions made during Operation *Barbarossa*. Still, to the Germans of the World War II generation, Stalingrad was the beginning of the end. This is because of the immense psychological impact that the defeat at Stalingrad had on Germany. Because armies fight for cities not just for purely military gain, but also for political, cultural, and economic gain, the results of urban combat can have far-reaching effects well beyond the immediate change in the balance of the military situation. Stalingrad was a decisive turning point in World War II not so much for the loss of the German Sixth Army, but because Hitler had declared it an important and necessary objective, yet despite his declaration the Red Army denied him. Stalingrad dispelled the myths of the invincibility of Germany, and Hitler. The effect of that evidence on the psyche of opposing sides on the Eastern Front was immense but cannot be measured in numbers of divisions.

The history of modern urban battles demonstrated the vast variety of scenarios in which decisive urban operations may occur. At one extreme is full conventional global war. Stalingrad and the battle of Aachen represent urban combat at that extreme of the conflict spectrum. The battles of Hue and Seoul demonstrate that similar decisive conventional urban combat is also likely to occur in smaller-scale conventional regional conflict. At the opposite end of the spectrum from global and regional conventional war is urban combat prosecuted by modern armies operating in an internal security role. In this role, fighting against terrorists and revolutionaries, urban combat more closely resembles police work than conventional military combat. The French experience in Algiers and the British experience in Belfast and Londonderry represent this part of the spectrum of urban warfare. The late 20th century and first decade of the 21st century highlighted a hybrid type of urban warfare that lies somewhere between intense conventional combat and low-intensity internal security operations. This is the type of combat prosecuted by the Israelis in Operation *Defensive Shield* and by US military forces in Iraq. In hybrid urban warfare, many aspects of conventional combat are present such as the requirements for artillery, air, and armor support. Hybrid urban combat, however, requires much more than sophisticated conventional military capability. Hybrid combat also requires military capabilities not normally necessary for conventional combat. These include special operations capability, civil affairs expertise, sophisticated intelligence gathering focused on the human terrain of the urban environment, and close coordination between military and political policy. To be effective, it also requires combined operations and common policy with the government and military forces representing the urban population. In the hybrid urban combat environment, military forces must be able to operate simultaneously across the entire spectrum of urban combat intensity.

In the late 1990s the US Marine Corps famously described this hybrid urban combat as the "Three Block War." The Three Block War envisions that on one block tanks and airpower will support conventional attacks to destroy enemy combatants or capture a geographic feature. On the next block a robust military presence guards vital infrastructure and the civilian population against guerrilla and terrorist attacks. On a third block, a military unit focuses on training and working with police, rebuilding infrastructure, and establishing civilian governance institutions in close cooperation with the host government and the civilian population. This is the essence of contemporary and future urban combat. Success in the Three Block War requires ground forces organized, trained, and equipped for urban warfare in the 21st century.

The trends of military history support the idea that warfare in the 21st century will be dominated by operations in the urban environment. But it is not just military history that supports the idea of the increasing decisiveness of urban combat. The importance of urban combat is also supported by population demographics. Since World War II, increased access to modern medicine has led to a global population explosion. Between 1990 and 2009 the global population increased 28 percent. It has increased even more dramatically in developing parts of the world, areas that are the most likely setting for warfare in the 21st century: Africa's population has increased by 58 percent while the population of the Middle East has grown by 54 percent.

That dramatic increase in global population has been accompanied by a vast global rural to urban migration. In 1800, only 3 percent of the world's population lived in cities, but by 2000 almost one half of the global population lived in cities. By the year 2030 the UN projects that 60 percent of the world population will live in cities. This shift from rural to urban population will be most dramatic in those developing nations where simultaneously the population growth is most dramatic: in Africa, the Middle East, and Asia. An important subset of this move by people to the urban environment is the accompanying growth of urban ghettos and shantytowns. One-third of the global urban population lives in poverty and disease-ridden urban ghettos. This environment is characterized by crime, disease, and political unrest. Warfare is conducted in response to politics; politics is the interaction of citizens in society; and increasingly in the 21st century those citizens will interact in, and be citizens of, cities. Urban combat will be the most likely type of combat, regardless of the specific political circumstances prompting war in the 21st century, simply because the urban environment will be the dominant residential environment across the globe.

The most recent important military activities support the trend that urban operations will dominate warfare in the 21st century. The US military operations in Iraq from 2003 to 2011 were conducted almost entirely within Iraq's large cities. The 2011 Libyan civil war that resulted in the overthrow of the dictator Colonel Muammar Gaddafi was primarily a conflict fought in Libya's urban centers. The war began in the city of Benghazi in February 2011 and was characterized by government and rebel forces fighting for possession of Libya's important coastal cities. The rebels won the war and successfully ousted the dictator when they successfully captured Gaddafi's capital city, Tripoli, in August 2011. The same type of popular urban discontent that swept through Libya affected other Middle Eastern dictatorships in 2011 and 2012. In all cases, that discontent was centered among the large urban populations. In some cases, such as Egypt, major military operations were avoided as the government addressed the discontent by responding to the demands for reform.

In other countries, such as Syria, the disaffected urban population rose up, resulting in brutal urban combat involving revolting citizens and dissident military units on one side and the army loyal to the government on the other. Thousands of civilian casualties and millions of dollars of infrastructure damage resulted. The historical trends represented by the case studies in this book, combined with global demographic trends, and validation from the most recent significant military actions resulting from the "Arab Spring" of 2011 indicate that future ground warfare will undoubtedly focus on operations in and around the world's cities. Also, it is unlikely that future urban combat will be conducted on a small scale. In 2007 there were 468 cities with populations over one million. Modern militaries must be prepared to enter these large cities and conduct effective operations, and this will require the military capability to be effective in an environment of over a million potentially hostile civilians.

Preparing for war in the future means preparing to fight in the world's large cities. History illustrates many of the capabilities that the ground forces will need in future urban combat. The forces must be well trained and technically competent. The Russian experience in Grozny demonstrated that conscripted forces are likely to suffer grievously in urban combat and, as importantly, are likely to respond to the challenges of intense urban combat with indiscriminate or poorly coordinated violence resulting in inordinate civilian casualties. Success in the urban environment without extensive civilian casualties requires professional military forces. The force, however, does not have to be large. If the battle space is properly structured and sufficient time is allowed for operations, even relatively small combat forces can be very successful. The battles in Aachen, Seoul, Hue, and Ramadi all demonstrate that small but well-trained forces can be successful, even in intense urban combat, if well led.

Future urban military operations, as the historical record supports, will not just be about urban combat. Because the civilian population is integral to the urban environment, urban combat must be closely and effectively coordinated and synchronized with political policy. It will not be possible to execute truly successful urban combat operations unless those operations account for the welfare of the civilian population, and political policy ensures that the needs and grievances of urban residents are adequately satisfied. To help accomplish this, military leaders must carefully plan urban combat operations in conjunction with political guidance so that, unlike the French in Algiers, military victory does not contribute to political defeat.

One of the keys to the success of urban combat is to ensure that military forces conducting urban combat represent the urban population. This may be impossible for a foreign military force to achieve, therefore it is imperative that any military operations in urban areas are conducted by combined forces that include representatives of the urban population. General MacArthur understood that the politics of urban combat are as important as the tactics, and he therefore ensured that the X Corps included a small but very politically important South Korean military component. Similarly, 1BCT of 1st Armored Division ensured that all of its operations in Ramadi included elements of the Iraqi army and if possible the Iraqi police; not for their military capability but for the legitimizing influence they had with the civilian population; and for the political effects that Iraqi army success had on the stability of the Iraqi government. Commanders in urban combat must always remember that war is for political purposes, and in urban combat political purposes often are more important than tactical military requirements.

Urban combat has been a critical facet of warfare since the beginning of recorded military history. It dominated warfare for most of history. As modern militaries enter the 21st century they should understand that urban combat is again the dominant characteristic of war. This change is, however, not a sudden development. The trend of military history since World War II clearly shows the increasing frequency and decisiveness of urban combat. Similarly, military history also contains many of the secrets for understanding and operating in the complex urban environment of the future.

BIBLIOGRAPHY

Alexander, Joseph H. *Battle of the Barricades. US Marines in the Recapture of Seoul*. Marines in the Korean War Commemorative Series. Washington DC: US Marine Corps Historical Center, 2000.

Arnold, James R. *Tet Offensive 1968: Turning Point in Vietnam*. Oxford: Osprey Publishing, 1990.

Aussaresses, Paul. *The Battle of the Casbah. Terrorism and Counter-Terrorism in Algeria, 1955–1957*. New York: Enigma Books, 2002.

Beevor, Antony. *Stalingrad. Fateful Siege: 1942–1943*. New York: Penguin Putnam Inc., 1998.

Campbell, Duncan B. *Besieged. Siege Warfare in the Ancient World*. Oxford: Osprey Publishing Ltd., 2006.

Campell, Duncan. *Siege Warfare in the Roman World, 146 BC–AD 378*. Oxford: Osprey Publishing Ltd., 2005.

Condon, John P. and Mersky Peter B. *Corsairs to Panthers. US Marine Aviation in Korea*. Marines in the Korean War Commemorative Series. Washington DC: US Marine Corps Historical Center, 2002.

Cordesman, Anthony H. *Arab-Israeli Military Forces in an Era of Asymmetric Wars*. Stanford, CA: Stanford University Press, 2008.

Couch, Dick. *The Sheriff of Ramadi. Navy Seals and the Winning of al-Anbar*. Annapolis, MD: Naval Institute Press, 2008.

Craig, William. *Enemy at the Gates: The Battle for Stalingrad*. Old Saybrook, CT: Konecky and Konecky, 1973.

Davis, Paul K. *Besieged: 100 Great Sieges From Jericho to Sarajevo*. Oxford: Oxford University Press, 2003.

Deane, Tony. "An Interview with COL Tony Deane, Part I" and "An Interview with COL Tony Deane, Part II." Interviewed by Laurence Lessard (Fort Leavenworth, Kansas, September 3, 2008). Operational Leadership Experiences in the Global War on Terror, http://cgsc.contentdm.oclc.org/cdm/search/collection/p4013coll13 (accessed June 11, 2012).

Dewar, Michael. *The British Army in Northern Ireland*. London: Guild Publishing, 1985.

Duffy, Christopher. *Fire & Stone. The Science of Fortress Warfare, 1660–1860*. Mechanicsburg, PA: Stackpole Books, 1996.

Duffy, Christopher. *Siege Warfare. The Fortress in the Early Modern World, 1494–1660*. London: Routledge, 1979.

Edwards, Aaron. *The Northern Ireland Troubles. Operation* Banner, *1969–2007*. Oxford: Osprey Publishing, 2011.

Folkestad, William B. *The View from the Turret: The 743rd Tank Battalion in World War II*. Shippensburg, PA: Burd Street Press, 2000.

Geraghty, Tony. *The Irish War: The Hidden Conflict between the IRA and British Intelligence*. Baltimore, MD: John Hopkins University Press, 1998.

Glantz, David M. and House, Jonathan M. *The Gates of Stalingrad. Soviet-German Combat Operations, April–August 1942*. The Stalingrad Trilogy, Volume I. Lawrence: University Press of Kansas, 2009.

Gravett, Christopher. *Medieval Siege Warfare*. Oxford: Osprey Publishing Ltd., 1990.

Hammel, Eric. *Fire in the Streets. The Battle for Hue, Tet, 1968*. New York: Dell Publishing, 1991.

Holl, Adelbert. *An Infantryman in Stalingrad, from 24 September 1942 to 2 February 1943* (Trans. Jason D. Mark and Neil Page). Sydney: Leaping Horseman Books, 2005.

Horne, Alistair. *A Savage War of Peace: Algeria, 1954*. New York: Penguin Books, 1977.

Human Rights Watch. *Jenin: IDF Military Operations* (Vol. 14, No. 3 [E]). 2002.

Israel Ministry of Foreign Affairs. *IDF Operations Overnight (3–4 April) in Judea and Samaria*. April 4, 2002. http://www.mfa.gov.il/MFA/Government/Communiques/2002/IDF+operations+overnight+-2-3+April-+in+Jenin+and.htm (accessed November 5, 2011).

Israel Ministry of Foreign Affairs. *Jenin's Terrorist Infrastructure*. April 4, 2002. http://www.mfa.gov.il/MFA/MFAArchive/2000_2009/2002/4/Jenin-s%20Terrorist%20Infrastructure%20-%204-Apr-2002 (accessed November 5, 2011).

Kyle, Chris, with McEwen, Scott and DeFelice, Jim. *American Sniper. The Autobiography of the Most Lethal Sniper in US Military History.* New York: Harper Collins, 2012.

MacDonald, Charles B. *United States Army in World War II, The European Theater of Operations: The Siegfried Line Campaign.* Washington, DC: Center of Military History, 1984.

MacFarland, Sean. "An Interview with Colonel Sean MacFarland." Interview by Steven Clay (Fort Leavenworth Kansas, January 17, 2008). Contemporary Operations Study Team, On Point III.

Malkasian, Carter and Marston, Daniel (eds.). *Counterinsurgency in Modern Warfare.* Oxford: Osprey Publishing, 2008.

Matt, Rees. "Untangling Jenin's Tale," in *Time* (May 13, 2002). http://www.time.com/time/magazine/article/0,9171,1002406,00.html (accessed 5 November, 2011).

Michaels, Jim. *A Chance in Hell: The Men Who Triumphed Over Iraq's Deadliest City and Turned the Tide of War.* New York: St Martin's Press, 2010.

Ministry of Defense. *Operation* Banner. *An Analysis of Military Operations in Northern Ireland.* UK: Ministry of Defense, 2006.

Newsinger, John. *British Counterinsurgency, From Palestine to Northern Ireland.* New York: Palgrave, 2002.

Nolan, Keith William. *Battle for Hue, Tet, 1968.* Novato, CA: Presidio Press, 1983.

Oliker, Olga. *Russia's Chechen Wars 1994–2000: Lessons From Urban Combat.* Santa Monica, CA: Rand, 2001.

Pegler, Martin. *The Military Sniper since 1914.* Oxford: Osprey Publishing, 2001.

Ready First Combat Team, 1st Brigade, 1st Armored Division. *Operation Iraqi Freedom After Action Report, January 2006–February 2007.* Undated.

Rennie, James. *The Operators: Inside 14 Intelligence Company–The Army's Top Secret Elite.* London: Century, 1996.

Robertson, William G. (ed.) *Block by Block. The Challenges of Urban Operations.* Fort Leavenworth, Kansas: Command and General Staff College Press, 2003.

Sheldon, Walt. *Hell or High Water: MacArthur's Landing at Inchon.* New York: Ballantine Books, Inc., 1968.

Silverman, Michael E. *Awakening Victory. How Iraqi Tribes and American Troops Reclaimed al Anbar Province and Defeated al Qaeda in Iraq*. Havertown, PA: Casemate Publishers, 2011.

Taylor, Peter. *Brits: The War Against the IRA*. London: Bloomsbury Publishing, 2001.

Taylor, Peter. *Provos: The IRA and Sinn Fein*. London: Bloomsbury Publishing, 1997.

Thomas, Timothy. "The Battle of Grozny: Deady Classroom for Urban Combat." *Parameters* (Summer 1999), pp. 87–102.

Trinquier, Roger. *Modern Warfare: A French View of Counterinsurgency*. London: Pall Mall Press, 1964.

Tse-tung, Mao. *On Guerrilla Warfare* (Trans. Samuel B. Griffith). Chicago: University of Illinois Press, 1961.

United Nations. *Report of the Secretary-General prepared pursuant to General Assembly Resolution ES-10/10*. July 2002.

Van der Bijl, Nick. *Operation* Banner. *The British Army in Northern Ireland, 1969–2007*. South Yorkshire, UK: Pen & Sword Books, 2009.

Viollet-Le-Duc, E. *Annals of A Fortress. Twenty-Two Centuries of Siege Warfare* (Trans. Benjamin Bucknall). Barton-under-Needwood, UK: Wren's Park Publishing, 2000.

Weigley, Russell F. *Eisenhower's Lieutenants. The Campaigns of France and Germany, 1944–1945*. Bloomington: Indiana University Press, 1981.

Whiting, Charles. *Bloody Aachen*. Briarcliff Manor, NY: Stein and Day, 1976.

Wieder, Joachim, and von Einsiedel, Heinrich Graf. *Stalingrad: Memories and Reassessments* (Trans. Helmut Bogler). London: Arms and Armor Press, 1993.

Zhukov, Georgi K. *Marshal Zhukov's Greatest Battles* (Ed. Harrison E. Salisbury). New York: Cooper Square Press, 2002.

GLOSSARY

AD	Armored Division
AI	Amnesty International
AO	Area of Operations
AQI	Al Qaeda of Iraq
ARVN	Army of the Republic of Vietnam
ASU	Active Service Unit
BCT	Brigade Combat Team
BPC	Bataillon de parachutistes coloniaux (colonial parachute battalion)
CF	Coalition Forces
COP	Combat Outpost
DMZ	Demilitarized Zone
DRV	Democratic Republic of Vietnam
EOD	Explosive Ordnance Disposal
FOB	Forward Operating Base
HRW	Human Rights Watch
HUMINT	Human Intelligence
IDF	Israeli Defense Force
IED	Improvised Explosive Device
INLA	Irish National Liberation Army
IRA	Irish Republican Army
KPA	North Korean People's Army
LAW	Light Antitank Weapon
LVT	Landing Vehicle Tracked
MACV	Military Assistance Command Vietnam
MLRS	Multiple-Launch Rocket System
MNFW	Multinational Forces West
MSR	Main Supply Route
NICRA	Northern Ireland Civil Rights Assocation
OIF	Operation *Iraqi Freedom*
PA	Palestinian Authority
PAVN	People's Army of Vietnam
PIRA	Provisional Irish Republican Army
RCT	Regimental Combat Team

REP   Régiment Étranger de Parachutistes (Foreign Legion parachute regiment)

RIRA   Real Irish Republican Army

ROKA   Republic of Korea Army

RPC   Régiments de Parachutistes Coloniaux (colonial parachute regiment)

RUC   Royal Ulster Constabulary

RVN   Republic of Vietnam

SAS   Special Air Service

SEAL   Sea Air Land Team

SURC   Small Unit Riverine Craft

TACP   Tactical Air Control Party

TF   Task Force

UAV   Unmanned Aerial Vehicle

UDR   Ulster Defence Regiment

UFF   Ulster Freedom Fighters

UK   United Kingdom

UN   United Nations

UNRWA   United Nations Relief and Works Agency

US   United States

UVF   Ulster Volunteer Force

VBIED   Vehicle Borne Improvised Explosive Device

VNMC   Vietnamese Marine Corps

ABOUT THE AUTHOR

Louis DiMarco retired as a Lieutenant Colonel in the US Army in 2005 after more than 24 years of active service. His civilian education includes a Bachelor of Science Degree from the US Military Academy, a Masters in Military Art and Science from the US Army Command and Staff College, a Masters of Arts Degree in International Relations, and a PhD in History. Currently LTC DiMarco works on the faculty of the Army Command and Staff College, where he teaches military history and elective courses on the history of modern urban warfare and modern warfare in the Middle East. LTC DiMarco has authored several key Army doctrinal manuals including *FM 3-06, Urban Operations* (2002). He was a contributing author to the US Army's *Counterinsurgency Manual, FM 3-24* (2006). Other written projects include the *Army's Scout Platoon Field Manual* (1994), the first work in the Combat Studies Institute's Global War on Terror series entitled *Traditions, Changes, and Challenges: Military Operations and the Middle Eastern City* (2004); and the book War Horse: *A History of the Military Horse and Rider* (2008). LTC DiMarco has written and lectured on a variety of military topics including urban warfare and counterinsurgency.

INDEX

Reference to maps are in **bold type**.

14 Intelligence Company 130, 143

Aachen, battle for (1944) 47, 50–2, 53–62,
      103, 212, 215
   lessons of 101
   and Stalingrad 64–5
   tactics 62–4
abductions 134
Active Service Units (ASUs) 139, 142–3
Afghanistan 153, 189
air attacks 34, 39, 40, 41, 53, 56, 64, 68, 76,
      78, 92, 162, 163, 174, 206–7
aircraft 25, 41, 56, 58, 78, 206, 207; *see also*
      helicopters
Alexander the Great 20
Algeria 26, 103, 105–6, 122, 125, 188
Algiers, battle of (1956–7) 103, 106, 107,
      109–12, 116–17, 116–20, 122, 212, 215
   map **108**, **115**
Ali la Pointe 120
Allied forces 36, 47, 49, 51
Almond, Major General Edward 71
Alsdorf 54, 55, 56, 57
ambushes 142–3, 158–9, 161, 165, 182
American Civil War (1861–65) 17
Amherst, General Jeffrey 17
ammunition 35, 53, 56, 59, 64, 90
Amnesty International (AI) 184–5
amphibious operations 69, 71, 73, 76
Al-Anbar Awakening 204, 206, 207–8
Al-Anbar Province 189–90, **192**, 195, 202,
      203, 208
Anglo-Irish Agreement (1985) 141–2
antiaircraft systems 88, 159, 166
AQI *see* Al Qaeda of Iraq 192
Al-Aqsa Intifada 169
Al-Aqsa Martyrs' Brigade 172, 178
"Arab Spring" 214
Arafat, Yasser 169, 170, 172, 174
Ardennes forest 50, 52
area of operations (AO) 191
arrests 116, 117, 135, 139, 142, 149, 174
artillery 22, 23, 24, 61, 156
   American 53, 55, 56, 58, 59, 63, 64, 68,
      77, 92, 98
   Russian 34, 37, 39, 40, 161, 162–3, 165,
      166
ARVN *see* Republic of Vietnam Army
assassinations 109, 114, 134

Athens 16, 17
Aussaresses, Major Paul 111, 113, 118

Ba'ath Party 190, 193, 203
Baghdad 189, 190, 204
baiting 165
barbed wire 34, 200
Bardenberg 57
barricades 74, 76–7, 158, 162, 177
barriers 133, 200
battering rams 20
Battle of the Bulge (1944) 52, 62
beachheads 47, 49
Belfast 126, 127, 129, 132, 133, 134–5,
      137, 212
Belgium 49, 51
Ben M'Hidi, Larbi 107, 109, 114, 116, 118
Bethlehem 171, 174–5
Bigeard, Colonel Marcel 111
Bin Laden, Osama 193
Blair, Tony 145
blitzkrieg 25, 29
"Bloody Friday" 137
"Bloody Sunday" 136–7, 141
Bock, Field Marshal Fedor von 28, 29, 45
bombardments 22, 37, 41, 53, 72, 85
bombings 107, 109, 117, 118–19, 120, 140,
      145
   Northern Irish 134–5, 137, 142–3
booby traps 162, 176, 181
bridges 73, 81–2, 88
British Army 19, 125, 127, 129, 132, 133,
      134, 135, 137, 138, 147, 149
   21st Division 49, 50
   Special Air Service (SAS) 130, 139, 142,
      143
British government 131, 133, 137, 138,
      140, 145
British security forces 129, 131, 136, 141,
      142, 143, 148
buildings 25, 34, 61, 63, 74, 87, 89, 92, 93,
      97, 98, 159, 161, 163, 176, 191
bulldozers 176, 180, 181, 182, 183, 186, 187
bunkers 34, 44, 53, 55, 61, 63, 86, 166
Byzantine Empire 16

Camp Corregidor (Ramadi) 194, 195, 197,
      206
Camp Diamond 195
Camp Ramadi 195, 197, 199, 200, 202
cannons 22, 95, 159

Casbah (Algiers) 106, 107, 109, 114, 119
castles 22
casualties 39–40, 62, 69, 80, 109, 120
    Algerian 107, 118–19
    American 62, 82, 88, 89, 97
    Chechen 164
    civilian 60, 64, 134, 161, 165, 167, 180,
        184, 187, 188, 209, 214, 215
    French 107, 109, 117, 119–20
    friendly 23, 177, 196, 198
    Iraqi 196, 208
    Irish 133, 134, 135, 137, 138, 139, 140,
        142, 143, 146
    Israeli 169, 177, 181, 182, 183
    Palestinian 175, 177, 183
    Russian 162, 164
    Vietnamese 82, 92
Catholic community 81, 126, 129, 131,
    132, 133, 134, 135–7, 138, 140, 144, 145,
    148, 149
Caucasus Mountains 151, 152
Caucasus oil fields 28, 32, 33, 45, 153
cease-fires 145, 163
censuses 113, 114, 116, 201
Cheatham, Lieutenant Colonel Ernie C.
    90, 93
Chechen fighters 156–7, 158, 159, 160, 161,
    162, 163, 166, 188
    tactics 164–5
Chechnya 151, 152–3, 155, 156, 168; see also
    Grozny
checkpoints 114, 117, 133, 147, 177
Chiang Kia-shek 103
China 19, 79, 103, 104, 110
Christianity 112, 171; see also Catholic
    community; Protestant community
Chuikov, General Vasily 34, 37, 41, 43
Church of Saint Mary (Bethlehem) 174–5
Citadel (Hue) 85, 89, 94, 95, 96, 97, 98,
    100, 102
cities 16, 17, 18, 79, 82
    bypassing of 19, 25, 155
    defenses 20, 21, 22
    isolation of 65, 114, 198
civil rights 131, 136–7
civilians 26, 44, 63, 64, 92, 135, 213, 215
    in Aachen 59–60
    Chechen 161, 162, 164, 166–7
    French 107
    Irish 136, 138
    Korean 71, 78
    Palestinian 177, 180, 184–5
    in Stalingrad 30
    Vietnamese 93
    see also casualties: civilian
Clausewitz, General Carl von 16
clear, hold, build tactic 209
Clinton, Bill 169
close air support 78, 98, 101, 158, 179

clothing 83, 109, 119, 130, 162
Coalition Forces (CF) 193, 194, 201, 202,
    203, 204, 209, 210
Cold War 26, 151, 153, 155
collateral damage 60, 149, 165, 167, 177, 186
colonialism 105, 120
Colons 105, 106, 107, 109, 117, 119, 120
combat outposts (COPs) 195, 199, 200–2,
    204
combined forces 63, 79–80, 215
command and control 59
Communism 67, 68, 83, 103–4, 120, 121, 152
concrete 34, 40, 91, 98, 106, 152, 171, 191,
    200
conscripts 95, 98, 155, 159, 214–15
Constantinople 16
conventional war 10, 26, 104, 121, 125, 212,
    213
Corlett, General Charles H. 58
Cossacks 151–2
counterinsurgency 110, 112–14, 121, 122,
    138, 139, 189, 208
criminals, Iraqi 193, 203
CS gas 90, 91, 92, 94, 98
curfews 133–4, 174
Cushman, Lieutenant General Robert, III
    86

Daniel, Lieutenant Colonel Derrill 60
De Gaulle, Charles 120
Deane, Lieutenant Colonel Tony 203–4
Demilitarized Zone (DMZ) 82
Democratic People's Republic of Korea
    (DPRK) see North Korea
Democratic Republic of Vietnam (DRV)
    82, 83
Democratic Unionist Party (DUP) 145
Derry see Londonderry
destroyers 55, 60
Dien Bien Phu 105, 111
Don River 29, 37, 39
DPRK see North Korea
Dulaim tribe 191–2

Eastern Front 63, 64, 153, 211, 212
economics 17, 68
Egypt 19, 110, 172, 214
Eisenhower, General Dwight D. 50, 51
embankments 22
engineers 20, 22–3, 42, 77, 172, 177, 180,
    200
entrapment 29, 32, 39
Euphrates River 190, 195, 196, 202, 203, 206
evacuations 64, 88
explosive ordnance disposal (EOD) 187
extortion 193–4

factories 30, 34, 35, 170
Fallujah 190, 196, 197

false walls 107, 119–20
Fatah Party 169, 172, 174
Ferry, Lieutenant Colonel Chuck 206
FLN *see* National Liberation Movement
fortified cities 22, 23, 24
forward operating base (FOB) approach
  197–8
Fossey-Francois, Colonel Albert 111
foxholes 56
framework operations 146
France 21, 22–3, 24, 26, 47, 49, 103, 105,
  106, 107, 116
  intelligence 111, 113, 118, 119
  see also Algiers, battle of
Franco-Prussian War (1870–01) 18, 24
Frederick the Great 24
French Army 19, 106, 117, 119, 120
  10th Parachute Division 109–10, 111,
    112, 114, 122
French Foreign Legion 110, 111
French North Africa *see* Algeria
French Resistance 110
fuel shortages 36, 49
Fuhrer Directive No. 45 28–9, 33

Gaddafi, Colonel Muammar 214
Gaza Strip 172
Geneva Agreement (1954) 105
geography 50, 69, 74, 76, 106, 126
geopolitics 17
Georgia 151
German Air Force *see* Luftwaffe
German Army 40
  1st SS Panzer Division 58, 59
  3rd Panzer Grenadier Division 52, 54,
    56, 61
  4th Panzer Division 28, 29, 32
  6th Panzer Division 28, 29, 32, 33, 39,
    45, 212
  7th Division 49, 52
  12th Division 52
  14th Panzer Division 33, 34, 35
  22nd Panzer Division 36
  24th Panzer Division 29, 35
  28th Panzer Division 29, 33, 34, 45
  49th Division 52
  60th Panzergrenadier Regiment 58
  108th Panzer Brigade 54, 57
  116th Panzer Division 52–3, 54, 56, 57–8
  183rd Division 52
  246th Volksgrenadier Division 52, 58
  506th Heavy Tank Battalion 52, 54, 57,
    58, 62
  Group A 28, 29, 33
  Group B 28, 29, 33, 36, 37, 45
  I SS Panzer Corps 52, 54, 58, 62
  LI Corps 33, 34, 35
  LXXXI Corps 52, 54, 55, 57, 58, 62
  paratroopers 59

Germany 25, 27–8, 36, 37, 50, 51, 211
  inadequacies of 32, 35, 45
  tactics of 40–1
Gershon, Brigadier General Yitzhak 175
Giap, General Vo Nguyen 83
global warfare 25, 125, 212
Godard, Colonel Yves 110, 113, 116, 120
Good Friday Agreement (1998) 127, 129,
  145–6
GOI *see* Iraqi government
Grant, Ulysses 17
Gravel, Lieutenant Colonel Marcus J. 88,
  89–90, 92
Great Britain *see* United Kingdom
Greek city-states 16
ground forces 67, 78, 171–2, 186, 187, 213,
  214
Grozny 151–2, 153, **154**, 186, 188, 214
  battle of (1994) 156–64
guerilla warfare 104, 112, 126, 193, 213
guerre revolutionnaire doctrine 110, 112–13
gunpowder 21, 22
guns 25, 68, 77
  antitank 37, 44, 54, 60, 61, 63, 74
  assault 53, 54, 206
  machine 25, 42, 44, 60, 61, 63, 88, 92, 95,
    132, 156, 159, 160
  rifles 43, 90, 92, 94, 97, 98
  self-propelled 63, 74, 77, 88

Habbaniyah Canal 190, 195, 196, 199
Hadithah Dam 189
Halder, General Franz 45
Hamas 172, 178
Han River 72, 73, 74, 77, 78
Headquarters British Army Northern
  Ireland 129
Heath, Edward 137
helicopters 88, 99, 100, 156, 163, 165, 172,
  174, 175, 179, 182, 186
Henry V, King of England 21
Hezbollah 172
hiding places 107, 118
Highway One (Hue) 82, 87, 88, 99
Hitler, Adolf 32, 33, 36, 45, 49, 50, 52, 61,
  212
Ho Chi Minh 105
Hobbs, General Leland S. 58
Hodges, General Courtney 51
Holland 49, 50, 51
Holy Roman Empire 18
hostages 162, 175, 180
Hoth, General Hermann 28
house-to-house searches 61, 133–4, 201
Hue (1968) 81–2, **84**, **87**, **91**, 101, 103,
  212, 215
  battle for the north side 86–100
  North Vietnamese capture of 83–6
Huebner, General Clarence 59

hugging 165
Hughes, Colonel Stan 90
human intelligence (HUMINT) systems 113, 121, 122
human rights 136, 145
Human Rights Watch (HRW) 184–5
Hungarian Army 36, 39
hunger strikes 140–1
Hurricane Point (Ramadi) 194, 195
Hussein, Saddam 190, 192, 193, 195, 203

identification cards 113
ideologies 112–13, 120–1
IDF see Israeli Defense Forces
Imperial Palace (Hue) 81, 85, 95, 96–7, 98
imprisonment 139
improvised explosive devices (IEDs) 180, 181, 182, 187, 191, 193, 199, 200, 201, 204, 208
Inchon (1950) 69, 71, **70**, 72, 73, 74, 76, 77, 78, 79
indirect fire 101, 165
Indochina War (1946–54) 105, 110, 111, 112
infrastructure 191, 209, 213
insurgency 26, 105, 106–7, 112, 121, 122, 193, 194, 198, 201
intelligence 100, 118, 119, 121, 130, 204, 212
  Israeli 183, 187
  Northern Irish 142, 143, 144, 148
international attention 106, 107, 109, 120, 136, 140–1, 167, 174, 175, 181, 184, 185, 188; see also media
internments 135–6, 139, 141
interrogations 111, 113, 114, 117–18, 122, 136
Intifada 169, 188
Iraq 15, 189, 190, 212, 214; see also "Ready First" campaign
Iraqi Army 178, 191, 197, 198, 202, 208, 215
Iraqi government (GOI) 192, 193, 198, 202, 204, 209, 215
Iraqi police 197, 202, 203, 204, 207, 208, 215
Iraqi security forces 193, 196
Irish Army 130
Irish Free State 126
Irish National Liberation Army (INLA) 127, 140
Irish Republican Army (IRA) 127, 131, 132, 134, 135, 136, 138, 140
Islamists 193–4, 204
isolation tactics 101, 114, 198
Israel 113, 125, 169, 170, 212
  tactics 175–6, 181, 185–7
  see also West Bank
Israeli Air Force 174, 186
Israeli Defense Forces (IDF) 169, 170, 171–2, 174, 175, 176, 181, 185
  5th Reserve Infantry Brigade 177, 178, 179, 180–1, 182
  Golani Infantry Brigade 175–6, 177, 178, 181
  Nahal Brigade 178–9
  Paratrooper Brigade 175
  Reserve Battalion 7020 182
  Reserve Division No. 340 177
  Reserve Jerusalem Brigade 174
Israeli government 181
Israeli Navy 179, 182
Israeli Special Forces 179–80, 187
Italian Army 36, 39

Jandal, Abu 178
Japan 68, 73, 104
Jassim, Sheik Abu Ali 203
Jassim, Sheik Muhammad Saleh al-Suwadawi 206, 207
Jeanpierre, Lieutenant Colonel Pierre 111–12, 119–20
Jenin, battle for (2002) 170, 171, 175, 177–83, **184**, 186–7
Jerusalem 21
Jews 171
Johnson, Lyndon B. 82
Jordan 170, 190, 192
jungle warfare 90

Kadesh 19
Kalach 39
Kimpo Airfield 72, 78
Köchling, General Friedrich 52, 54
Korean Army see ROK Army
Korean War (1950–53) 26, 68, 103, 125, 215; see also Inchon; Seoul
KPA see North Korea People's Army 68
Kuomintang 103–4

Lacoste, Robert 109
LaHue, Brigadier General Foster 86–7
Lebanon 172, 178, 183
Leger, Captain 119
Libya 214
Lisburn 129, 130
logistics 17, 33, 49, 50, 51
Londonderry 126, 127, 129, 131–2, 133, 137, 212
Loyalists 127, 131, 132, 134, 138, 140, 144–5
Luftwaffe 40, 41

MacArthur, General Douglas 68, 69, 71, 76, 79, 215
MacFarland, Colonel Sean 194, 204
MACV see Military Assistance Command Vietnam
Major, John 145
major supply route (MSRs) 194, 199, 203
maneuverability 40–1, 47, 64–5, 76, 97, 100, 164–5
Manstein, Field Marshal Erich von 45

Mao Tse Tung 103–4, 105
Maoist strategy 104, 106, 112–13, 125, 139
marches 131–2, 136–7, 146
massacres 184–5, 187
Massu, General Jacques 109, 110, 111, 112, 114, 116
Mayer, Colonel Georges 111
Meadows, Captain Chuck 89
media, the 26, 109, 167, 175, 184, 185, 186
medical services 88, 93
Mexico 17, 18
MI5 148
Middle Ages 21, 24
Middle East, the 16, 214
Military Assistance Command Vietnam (MACV) 85, 86, 87, 88, 89, 90
Milk-Bar bombings 107, 109, 114, 117
mines 34, 77, 158, 162, 176, 180
missiles 207
mob action 119, 131–2
Mobile Group von Fritzschen 57
Mobile Reconnaissance Force 130
mobile units 50, 52, 113, 164–5
Model, Field Marshal Walter 52, 54
Mongols 19
Montgomery, Field Marshal Bernard 50, 51
morale 44, 71, 79
Morocco 105
Moscow 17, 18, 29, 153
Mountbatten, Lord Louis 140
Multinational Forces West (MNFW) 195, 196
Muslims 152, 170
    Algerian 105, 106, 107, 109, 112, 116, 117, 119, 122
    Shi'ite 193, 197
    Sunni 190, 192–3, 197, 202–3, 204, 206

Nablus 171, 175–7, 178, **179**, 181, 187
Napoleon Bonaparte 17, 24, 25
nation-states 24
National Liberation Movement (FLN) 103, 106–7, 109, 110, 112, 113, 114, 116, 117, 118–19, 120, 122, 125
nationalism 105, 120, 125
Neave, Airey 140
Netanya 169
neutrality 132, 133
night-time combat 55, 57, 72, 182
Normandy landings 47, 49
North Atlantic Treaty Organization (NATO) 153, 155
North Korea 67, 69, 71, 72
North Korea People's Army (KPA) 68, 73, 74, 76, 79, 80
    105th Tank Division 71, 77
North Vietnam 81, 82, 101, 105
North Vietnamese Army see People's Army of Vietnam (PAVN)

Northern Ireland 26, 125, 126, 127, 129–50, 188, 212
    lessons of 148–50
Northern Ireland Civil Rights Association (NICRA) 131
Northern Ireland Stormont government 131, 132, 133, 134, 135, 136, 137, 148
nuclear weapons 125

oil resources 28, 32, 33, 45, 153
Omagh bombing 146
open battlefield warfare 16, 24, 25, 40–1
Operation Banner (1969–2007) 125–46, 148–50
    map **128**
Operation Barbarossa (1941) 27, 29, 32, 211
Operation Blue (1942) 28–9, **31**, 33, 45
Operation Cobra (1944) 47, **48**
Operation Defensive Shield (2003) 169–70, 171–2, **173**, 174–88, 212
Operation Demetrius (1971) 135–6
Operation Market Garden (1944) 51, 53
Operation Motorman (1972) 137–8
Operation Uranus (1942) 37, **38**, **43**, 45
Operation Wacht am Rhine (1944) 52
Ottoman Empire 18, 151

Pacific Ocean 68, 69
Palestine 169, 170, 172, 178
Palestinian Authority (PA) 169, 174, 188
Palestinian fighters 176–7, 178, 180, 182, 183, 188
paramilitary operations 129, 131, 134, 136, 140, 141, 144, 147
paratroopers 59, 110, 113, 114, 116, 118, 161, 163, 176
Paris 16, 18, 110
patience 100, 101, 202
patrol bases 138, 146–7, 199, 201
Patton, General George S. 47
Paulus, General Friedrich 28, 29
peacekeeping 131–4, 138, 139
People's Army of Vietnam (PAVN) 82, 88–9, 92, 101
    4th Regiment 83, 85–6, 93, 94
    5th Regiment 83, 85, 86, 99–100
    6th Regiment 83, 85, 86, 90, 94, 95, 96, 97, 98, 100
People's Democracy (Northern Ireland) 131
Perfume River 81–2, 88, 96, 98
Persian Empire 16, 17
Petraeus, General David 210
Petruk, General Major 157, 158
Phu Bai 86, 88
Phu Cam Canal 87
pillboxes 53, 55
police 59, 67, 112, 117, 130, 139, 163, 175, 213

Iraqi 197, 202, 203
see also Royal Ulster Constabulary (RUC)
Police Service of Northern Ireland (PSNI)
  146
political strategies 101–2, 104, 132, 139,
  141, 145, 164, 178
politics 16, 71, 79, 126–7, 129, 133, 213, 215
population 71, 81, 148, 175, 212, 213–14
  ethnic 152, 166–7
  Iraqi 190, 191, 199, 201, 209
  Irish 126, 127, 146
  rises in 24, 25
    support of 104, 112
  tracking of 113, 114
ports 17, 68, 82
Presidential Palace (Grozny) 157, 158, 161,
  162, 163
propaganda 44, 50, 52, 163, 167, 172
Protestant community 126, 127, 129, 131,
  132, 133, 134, 135, 138, 141, 145, 148
Provisional Irish Republican Army (PIRA)
  125, 127, 129, 132–3, 134, 135, 136, 137,
  138, 139, 140, 141, 142, 143, 144–5, 148,
  149
psychology 41, 44, 61, 63, 65, 69, 79, 80,
  143, 166, 186, 211, 212
Pulikovsky, General Major 157, 158
Pusan 68, 69, 71, 72, 76

Al Qaeda of Iraq (AQI) 192, 193, 194, 196,
  197, 198, 199, 200, 202, 203, 204, 206, 207,
  209
Qalqiliya 171, 174
quadrillage system 114
Quebec 18–19

radio communications 156, 159, 160
raids 35, 106, 114, 117, 118, 135, 149
railroads 49
railway stations 160–1, 163
Ramadi 189, 190–1, 193, 194–210, 195,
  196–8, **205**, 215
Ramallah 171, 174
RCTs *see* regimental combat teams
"Ready First" campaign (2006–07) 189–210
Real Irish Republican Army (RIRA) 127–8,
  145–6
Red Army 29, 29–30, 32, 153, 155, 212
  5th Tank 37
  62nd division 33–4, 35, 39, 41, 42, 44
  64th division 33–4
  Stafka high command 30, 36
  veterans 159
refugee camps 171, 175, 177; *see also* Jenin,
  Nablus
refugees 30, 40, 170–1
regimental combat teams (RCTs) 72–4, 78
Renaissance, the 21–2
Republic of Ireland 125, 136, 141, 145

Republic of Korea (ROK) 67
Republic of Vietnam (RVN) 81, 82
Republic of Vietnam Army (ARVN) 98,
  101, 102
  1st Airborne 95, 96, 97
  1st Infantry Division 85, 86, 94, 96
  3rd Regiment 95, 96
  7th Armored Cavalry 88, 95, 96
  I Corps 95, 96
Republican Guard 191
Republicans 127, 139
reservists 130, 132, 171, 174, 178
revolutionary war 103–5, 110, 112–13, 125
Rhee, Syngman 76
Rhine River 49, 51, 62
Richthofen, Wolfram von 41
riots 132, 133, 134, 146
road networks 50, 72, 74, 147, 191
ROK Army (ROKA) 67, 76, 77, 80
  1st Infantry Regiment 71, 74
  17th Regiment 74, 79
Rokhlin, General 157, 158
Rokossovsky, General Konstantin 37
Roman Empire 20–1
Romanian Army 36–7, 39
Rouen, siege of (1417–19) 21
Royal Ulster Constabulary (RUC) 135, 138,
  139, 140, 141, 142, 143, 144, 146, 148
  B Specials 130, 132
Ruhr district 51
Rundstedt, Field Marshal Gerd von 52, 54
Russia 17, 28, 151, 152–3, 165–6, 167, 168,
  214
Russian Air Force 161
Russian Army 151, 155–6
  Motorized Rifles 157, 158, 159, 160–2
  Spetsnaz special forces 155, 161, 163
  see also Red Army
Russian Navy 163

safe havens 118, 119, 204
Saigon 98
Salan, General Raoul 109, 119
salients 35, 36
sandbags 200, 201
Sands, Bobby 140, 141
sappers 23, 83, 85
Sattar Eftikhan Abu Risha, Abdul 203–4,
  206–7
Saudi Arabia 190
search operations 114, 133–4, 149, 200
sectarian violence 133, 134, 135, 137, 139,
  145
Seoul 69, 71, 72, 73, 74, **75**, 76, 77, 78, 79,
  103, 212, 215
  lessons of 101
Sevastopol 32
Seven Years' War (1756–63) 17–18
sewer systems 61, 74, 162

Seydlitz, General Walther von 35
Sharia law 193
Shark Fin, battle of (2006) 204, 206–8
Sharon, Ariel 169
sheiks 192, 193, 202–3, 204, 206, 207, 209
Shlein, Brigadier General Eyal 177
shock groups 42
siege warfare 19, 20, 22–3, 24
Siegfried Line 49, 51, 52
Sinn Fein 141, 145, 149
small-unit leadership 101
Small Unit Riverine Craft (SURCs) 195–6, 198
snipers 42–4, 77, 87, 88, 134, 145, 156, 159, 160, 161, 165, 175, 176, 179–80, 187, 199, 201, 209
South Korea 67, 68, 69, 71, 73, 79, 215
South Vietnam 81, 82, 83, 100, 101, 105
Soviet Army see Red Army
Soviet Union 27, 28, 29, 30, 32, 37, 63, 67, 152
    collapse of 153, 155
    tactics of 39, 40–1, 42–4
    see also Russia
special forces 155, 172, 176, 177, 187, 209, 212
Stalin, Joseph 29–30, 36, 37
Stalingrad, battle for (1942) 25, 28, 29, 33–6, 37, 45, 50, 62, 103, 153, 211–12
    early planning of 32
    layout of 30, 40
    lessons of 27, 49, 64–5, 101
    tactics in 39–44
Staskov, General 157, 158
stealth tactics 100
Stolberg 52, 53, 55
Stormont government see Northern Ireland Stormont government
streets 63, 77, 86, 97, 176
strike action 114, 116–17, 169
suicide bombers 169, 172, 193, 202
Sunni nationalists 192–3, 193, 194
Sunzha River 152, 157, 163
supplies 49, 56, 82
surge offensives 198, 209–10
surprise tactics 18–19, 69, 76, 80, 83, 100
Syria 19, 172, 190, 192, 193, 214

Tal Afar 194, 195, 197, 198
Tameem 199, 202
Tamir, Colonel Moshe 181
tanks 32, 41–2, 44, 60, 63, 68, 71, 97, 101, 156, 159, 160, 162, 163, 166, 175–6, 181, 182
    M-1 Abrams 195, 206
    M-26 Pershing 73, 74, 77
    M-41 95, 98
    M-48 13, 87, 88, 89, 95
    Merkava 180

Panther 54
    Tiger 52, 54, 56, 57, 58, 59, 62
Task Force (TF) X-Ray 86–7, 88, 97
Tay Loc airfield 85, 86, 95, 96
technology 24, 25
Tegart Fort 174
terrorism 107, 109, 112, 122, 126, 169, 170, 212, 213
    Palestinian 169, 171, 172, 174, 188
Tet Offensive 81, 82–3, 86, 99, 101
Thatcher, Margaret 140, 141
Third Reich 25, 28, 50
Thompson, Major Robert H. 96
Three Block War 213
Thua Thien Province 81, 89, 93–4
Thung Front 99–100
Topeka AO 191, 194, 195, 208
torture 113, 120–2, 122, 136, 140
towers 20, 21, 85, 200
training 68, 92, 98, 104, 130, 157, 159, 178, 195, 213
trenches 23, 34
Tri Thien Hue Front 83
tribal factions 191–2, 193, 202–3, 204, 207
Trinquier, Major Roger 110, 113, 118, 119
"The Troubles" 126, 131
Truong, General Ngo Quang 85, 94–5, 96
Tulkkarm 171, 174
Tunisia 105
tunnels 20, 22, 107, 162
Tyre 20, 21

Ukraine 32, 155
Ulster 126, 129, 130, 144; see also Royal Ulster Constabulary (RUC)
United Kingdom 126, 127, 130, 135–6, 141, 145; see also Northern Ireland
United Nations 105, 106, 116, 125, 185
United Nations Relief and Works Agency (UNRWA) 171
United States of America 27, 59, 181
    invasion of Iraq 191, 193
    tactics 53, 59–60, 62–4
unmanned aerial operations 182, 187, 206, 207
urban areas see cities
urban warfare 23, 32, 62–4, 90, 150, 157–8
    future of 211, 213–15
    hybrid 212–13
    training 92, 142
    see also cities
US Air Force 68
US Army 15, 51, 67, 71, 77, 85
    1st Brigade Combat Team (BCT) 189, 191, 194, 195, 196–8, 199–202, 203, 204, 206–8, 209, 215
    1st Cavalry Division 86, 99, 100, 101
    1st Infantry Division 47, 49, 50, 51, 53,

55, 56, 57, 58, 59, 61, 62, 64
2nd Armored Division 54, 64
3rd Armored Division 47, 49, 50, 53, 55, 61, 197
3rd Cavalry Regiment 194
3rd Field Artillery 195
6th Infantry Division 195, 197, 198
7th Infantry Division 71, 74, 78
8th Infantry Division 68, 69, 76
9th Infantry Division 206, 207
12th Division 49, 50
16th Engineer Division 195
16th Infantry Regiment 55, 56
18th Infantry Regiment 55–6, 57
26th Infantry Division 53, 55, 59, 60, 61, 63, 64
28th Infantry Division 61, 194, 196
30th Infantry Division 53, 54, 55, 56, 57, 58, 59, 62, 64
32nd Infantry Regiment 78
35th Armor 195, 197, 198, 199
37th Armor 195, 199, 207, 208
75th Ranger Regiment 189–90
101st Airborne Division 194, 195
117th Infantry Regiment 56, 57
119th Infantry Regiment 57, 58
120th Infantry Regiment 53–4, 56–7
506th Infantry 194, 195, 198
1106th Combat Engineer Group 55, 61
VII Corps 53, 54, 59
X Corps 69, 71, 72, 73, 74, 76, 78, 79, 80, 215
XIX Corps 53, 58
US Marines 77, 86, 101, 102, 189, 196
  1st Amphibious Tractor Battalion 73
  1st Division 71, 72, 74, 76, 78, 86–7, 88, 89, 90, 92, 93, 195
  1st Marine Air Wing 78
  3rd Tank Battalion 87
  5th Regiment 72, 73, 74, 88–9, 90–1, 93, 96, 97, 98
  7th Regiment 74
  8th Division 194, 195, 197, 198–9
  Fox Company 89–90, 90–2, 93
  Gulf Company 89, 92–3
  Hotel Company 90, 92, 93
US Navy Sea, Air, and Land (SEAL) 195, 199–200, 201

Vasilevsky, General Aleksandr 36
Vatutin, General Nikolai 37
Vauban, Sebastien Le Prestre de 22–3
vehicle-borne improvised explosive devices (VBIEDs) 193, 199, 203
vehicles
  armored 15, 44, 74, 132, 138, 156, 159, 161, 162, 165, 180, 183

Bradley Fighting Vehicles 195, 206
  Landing Vehicles Tracked (LVTs) 73, 74
  mechanized fighting 25, 159
  personnel carriers 14, 73, 156, 158, 161, 176, 182
  trucks 49, 87, 88, 116, 200, 201, 206, 208
  see also tanks
Viet Cong 82, 83, 94, 98, 101–2
Viet Minh 110, 111
Vietnam War (1955–75) 26, 81, 101, 102, 103, 111, 125, 180; see also Hue
Vietnamese Marines (VNMC) 96, 98, 101
violence 25, 104, 107, 121, 127–8, 132, 133, 134, 135–6, 137, 138, 145, 149, 169
Volga River 28, 29, 30, 33, 34, 39, 45
Volgograd see Stalingrad
volunteer forces 85, 130, 156

Walker, General Walton 68
walled cities 22, 23, 24, 25
weaponry 67, 101
  bangalore torpedoes 55
  bazookas 60, 77, 90
  flamethrowers 55, 60, 63, 163, 166
  grenades 41, 42, 77, 92, 94, 156, 159, 160, 165, 201, 206
  Light Antitank Weapon (LAW) 90
  mortars 61, 63, 77, 90, 92, 162
  nuclear 125
  rockets 86, 90, 92, 98, 156, 160, 163, 191
  satchel charges 55, 77
Wehrmacht 41
Weichs, General Maximilian 29
Wellesley, Arthur, Duke of Wellington 23
West Bank 170–88
Western Front 47, 51, 52
Westmoreland, General William 82, 89
Wilck, Colonel Gerhardt 58–9, 61, 64
Wolfe, General James 18
women 109, 117
World War I (1914–18) 25, 34
World War II (1939–45) 15, 25–6, 37, 42–4, 47, 67, 68, 69, 76, 77, 78, 90, 103, 105, 110, 111, 125, 153, 211–12, 213, 216
  see also Aachen; Stalingrad
Wurm River 53, 54, 58, 62
Wurselen 54, 57, 58

Yacef, Saadi 107, 109, 111, 117, 118, 119–20
Yeltsin, Boris 152
Yeremenko, General Andrei 37
Yongdungpo 71, 72, 73, 76

Zaitsev, Private Vasily 44
al-Zarqawi, Abu Musab 193, 199
Zhukov, General Georgi 36, 37
Zilmer, Major General Richard 195